A Commentary on Selected
PSALMS

A Commentary on Selected PSALMS

David Pawson

Anchor Recordings

First published in Great Britain in 2019 by
Anchor Recordings Ltd
DPTT, Synegis House, 21 Crockhamwell Road,
Woodley, Reading RG5 3LE

For more of David Pawson's teaching,
including DVDs and CDs, go to
www.davidpawson.com

FOR FREE DOWNLOADS
www.davidpawson.org

For further information, email
info@davidpawsonministry.org

ISBN 978-1-911173-91-5

Printed by Ingram Spark

Contents

This book is based on a series of talks. Originating as it does from the spoken word, its style will be found by many readers to be somewhat different from my usual written style. It is hoped that this will not detract from the substance of the biblical teaching found here.

As always, I ask the reader to compare everything I say or write with what is written in the Bible and, if at any point a conflict is found, always to rely upon the clear teaching of scripture.

David Pawson

READ PSALM 1

I remember visiting a little South American country of which you may never have heard. It was formerly Dutch Guiana and there were some five hundred thousand people in that little land, almost half of whom live in the town of Paramaribo. Even though it is such a small country it has a total mixture of people. Walking through the main street it was pointed out to me that there was the main group of Creoles, who are descendants of slaves brought over from Africa, then the next largest group, the Hindustani, who have come all the way from India to make a living. Then I picked out Chinese people who tend to control the business and the money of the city. Then I saw Javanese and of course, there were Dutch and their descendants from colonial days. There was one poor British tourist walking around in my clothes, and people were looking at him and feeling he was the odd one out. Such a mixture, and looking around you could see people belonged to different groups and that these groups were not mixing even though they were rubbing shoulders in the streets, but they wore their own style of dress and maintained their own culture.

As we look out at a world packed with the human race we tend to "type" people. We put them into pigeonholes. We have a category for this man and that woman and we say, "Oh well, they're that type." Psychologically, we put people into two brackets: introvert and extrovert. We might label them as being of different temperaments. Some people divide others by colour. It is a great joy to visit a country where there is integration and acceptance. I saw that mutual acceptance in both Brazil and Trinidad too. It is against the tendency to "type" people and split them up into groups that there is protest today. Treat everybody as a human being – we are each unique. Every one of us should be respected as a person. We should put everybody in the same category *homo sapiens* – for we are all human beings.

Now the Bible adopts neither of these positions. It is very offensive to natural reason because the Bible splits the human race right down the middle and says there are only two sorts of people. The gulf between them is a very wide and deep one, which could only be crossed by supernatural power. Many people do not like the Bible – they say it paints too "black and white" a picture of human nature, that we are all shades of grey in between, and you cannot categorise people like this. But God's Word does categorise, and the reason why it is offensive to natural reason is that by our own understanding of people we cannot divide people into two groups. But God, with his understanding and with his penetrating insight – not looking at the outside of people, how they dress or the colour of their skin, but looking at their hearts – can see only two sorts of people in the world. Looking at a congregation, he can see only two sorts of people.

In Psalm 1:1–3 you see God's definition of the one sort – the saint, the righteous; and, on the other hand, in verses 4–6 God describes and defines the wicked, the sinner. That is God's way of looking at it. You are either a saint or a sinner, there is nothing in between. You are either righteous or wicked in God's sight. You belong either to the sheep or the goats, either the wheat or the tares, the wise or the foolish virgins, the good or the bad fish. Jesus was constantly dividing people up into two groups. Therefore it is not surprising to learn that there are only two ways of life.

On my travels in South America I was in some of the

richest homes and some of the poorest homes I have ever seen. Within two days I was in a ranch-style bungalow that must have cost a huge sum, with a five-acre garden, and each bedroom had its own marble bathroom and sitting room. It was the home of an ambassador. Within twenty-four hours I was in a thatched hut in the heart of the Brazilian jungle talking to an Indian believer with his family, and their families, and the pigs and the dogs, all in one little hovel, in utter squalor. Yet still there are only two ways of life. You either live the way of the righteous or you live the way of the wicked. There is a narrow way that leads to life and a broad way that leads to death and there is nothing in between.

Now this is a cause of offence—people don't want to be carved off from each other. People don't want to be divided this way, but it is the hard truth that we are walking one way or the other and v. 6 reminds us of those two ways. Now why does the book of Psalms begin with this great division of people? You would have thought the compiler of Psalms would want to have one at the beginning that would get everybody interested, and then introduce this at a later stage – but no. The book of Psalms is saying this: until you face up to Psalm 1, none of the other Psalms are any use to you. Until you have decided which side of the picture you are on, don't go into the later Psalms or you could draw false comfort from them.

You have to decide first: on which road am I travelling? Do I belong to the righteous in God's sight or the wicked? If I belong to the wicked, then frankly none of the other Psalms apply to me; they are not for me to use, they cannot comfort me. You might think of Psalm 23, "The Lord is my shepherd," but he is not your shepherd unless you belong to verses 1–3 of Psalm 1. Or Psalm 90, "Lord thou hast been our dwelling place in all generations" – but he is not our dwelling place unless we belong to the righteous. Psalm 139, which I always repeat to myself when I am flying across the oceans: "For if I take the wings of the morning and dwell in the uttermost parts of the sea, even then shall your hand lead me." You cannot claim that one unless you belong to the righteous. So Psalm 1 tells us to get first things first. Look at the two sorts of people, ask which you are, and then you can move forward into the rest of the Psalms.

Let us look first at verses 1–3 and then at verses 4–6. There is a beautiful parallelism between the two halves. Verse 1 speaks of the strength of the righteous. Verse 4 speaks of the weakness of the wicked. Verse 2 speaks of the delight of the righteous. Verse 5 speaks of the sorrow and sadness of the wicked. Verse 3 speaks of the life of the righteous. Verse 6 speaks of the death of the wicked.

How beautifully ordered is God's thinking, and therefore the inspired writing of scripture. It is logical, it is straightforward, it is simple. Indeed I don't think you really need me to take you through this Psalm. You could get the message just by reading it, but maybe the Lord will bring it home to you in a fresh way as I go through. Now it begins with a beatitude. Not only are there beatitudes in the New Testament, there are beatitudes in the Old, and here is one of them, "Blessed is the man", and the word "blessed" means congratulations. This is the life most worth living, this is the person who is best off. Now the world would not count this man blessed when we study what he does and what he is. But God is saying: this is the man who is really to be congratulated; this is the man who is really going to have a happy life; this is the man who has discovered the secret of real living.

So let us see what this man is. What is the secret of life that is worth living? We are in for a shock. For the first thing that is described is negative, full of "nots". The first secret of a righteous life and a blessed life is to learn to say no. It requires great strength of character to do so – to be alone, prepared to be different, prepared not to be a jellyfish swept along by the tide of social fashion, but to be someone who says, "Here I stand, I can do no other." We need to dare to be like Daniel and stand alone, prepared to say no to the society that rushes past us on the broad way that leads to destruction; also not doing certain things – and the Bible is negative as well as positive.

Three ways in which he says no. There is Hebrew poetry here, not made up of rhyme. It had rhythm in it but primarily Hebrew poetry was to give parallel thoughts and to give them in different words. So we have three parallel thoughts and yet there is a progression as to where this man does not step, where he does not stand, and where he does not sit. They are parallel thoughts and yet there is an ordered progression in them.

First of all, where he steps. This is concerned with advice and counsel. Every one of us gets to the point where we need advice and counsel. Praise God when we swallow our pride and go to someone for counsel. We are meant to help each other in this way and advise each other. So we go to someone and we say, "I've got this problem. I'm in this fix, I'm in a mess. What steps can I take to get out of it?" Now how very important it is that you go to the right person for advice. The world is full of advice and most of it is bad advice. I just jotted down some of the things the world might tell me. The world might say to me, "Do your best and leave the rest." The world might say to me, "Don't worry, it may never happen," but of course it is going to. The world might say, "A little won't do you any harm." Have you heard that advice? The world might say, "Don't let your conscience dictate to you." The world will say, "Don't be narrow-minded or old fashioned." The world will say, "Go on do it, everybody's doing it." The world will whisper,

"Nobody will know." This is the kind of advice that comes from the wrong people.

In Bunyan's *The Pilgrim's Progress*, when Pilgrim set out on his journey, the first man he met after Evangelist was Worldly Wiseman who tried to tell him what steps to take to ease his conscience. It was bad advice. Someone who is going to be blessed does not step according to the advice of worldly, godless and wicked people. He goes to a man of God for it. He goes to those who know the Lord and says, "What step should I take?"

Now the second thing is, "Nor stands in the way of sinners." This is something more than just stepping in their advice. It is hanging around with them, as the Living Bible puts it. That is the perfect translation of the Hebrew. You can tell a man by the company he keeps, "birds of a feather flock together." Who you hang around with may rob you of your blessedness. I have seen this happen to older people but I have seen it happen to many young people. I have seen young people catch a glimpse of life in Christ and see what they could be in him and sincerely resolve and desire to be that person. Then I have seen them in town and I have seen who they are hanging around with and my heart bleeds. I wonder how long can they hang around with that group and still keep walking in the way that God has called them to. Sooner or later you find that if they go on hanging around with sinners it is not long before they are infected with the same outlook. Who you hang around with is important.

The Hebrew word is a vivid word. It is of a bunch of men hanging around on a street corner – go to a betting shop and see the men hanging around in little groups—that is the perfect picture described here. Blessed is the man who has learned first of all not to take steps according to the advice of worldly wise men. Secondly, blessed is the man who doesn't hang around with those who don't know God. Thirdly, blessed is the man who doesn't sit in the seat of scoffers. Now this is even further into godless society. To walk their way is one thing, to hang around with them is another, but to sit down in the seat of scoffers is a third step of involvement with a godless society. Blessed is the man who does not do it. It means to sit down and joke with them, and have you noticed how often jokes centre on sacred things?

All the swear words I have ever heard have been connected with the two most sacred relationships a man can know: with a woman and with his God. You think of every swear word and they come from those two sacred relationships. You see it is inherent in human nature to scoff at sacred things. If you sit down in that seat, it won't be long before you are making jokes about sacred things. There are plenty of jokes about the furniture of heaven and the temperature of hell and people joke away these things, they laugh at the pearly gates. But those pearly gates are real and very precious and very sacred and holy to the Lord.

If you sit down there, it won't be long before you share the scoffing. There may even be a more subtle meaning to sitting in the seat. To sit in the seat is a technical Hebrew phrase for becoming a teacher, a scholar, a theologian. It is possible and I had to sit in lectures at Cambridge and listen to great intellects, scholars whose names are household words, whose books have been sold around the world, and yet I heard them in an intellectual way scoff at things like the second coming of our Lord Jesus Christ. Said Charles Haddon Spurgeon of this verse, "They may have graduated, but their D.D. is a doctrine of damnation." A blessed person has learned not to sit in that seat of scoffing. It may be an intellectual seat, it may be a professorial chair, but he learns not to use it to scoff at the things of God.

So there is the first verse. This man is a man who has strength of character to say, "No, I will not go where you go. I will not hang around where you hang around. I will not sit down and scoff at the things of God with you." He has learned to say no. Well now, this must cut him off from a lot of pleasure, surely? Yes, it does – a lot of worldly pleasure. It sometimes makes him feel miserable because he feels a social misfit because he cannot join in on the fun at the office party just as everybody else does. Where then does he get his delight, or does he become a miserable killjoy? No he doesn't, he gets his joy from elsewhere. There are new sources of pleasure and delight in the man of God, in the righteous. What are they?

Well here is one of them for a start: a book that the world does not enjoy reading, but of which the man of God says, "I get more out of this than out of any other book; than out of any magazine, any television programme. His delight is in the law of God.

Now when David wrote of "the law of the Lord", all he was referring to was the first five books of the Bible: Genesis, Exodus, Leviticus, Numbers, Deuteronomy. His delight is in Leviticus. Now then, that is a change, isn't it? That is where most people get stuck when they read the Bible right through. They get through Genesis reasonably well, then Exodus, then Leviticus – then they take a dive. Oh you are in the righteous if you can sit down in the book of Leviticus and delight in it. What a book it is! I know a Jehovah's Witness who was converted through studying the book of Leviticus, meditated in it and saw the light. That book is that person's sheer delight now. There was a time when the Bible was a dull book. It used to be produced, of course, in a pretty dull way. It was often given a black cover and set in columns, not laid out like a normal book. But whatever its layout, a righteous man is one who delights to read this. He just loves it, he breathes it; it shapes his thinking. You are biblical not if you can quote text but if you think the way the Bible does, if you are so steeped in it that you cannot help approaching problems through its maxims.

Charles Wesley was so steeped in this Bible that when he wrote six thousand hymns he didn't look up the Bible to write them, but in one verse in one hymn I counted sixteen references to scripture. He was steeped. John Bunyan in *Grace Abounding*, describing his first few months as a Christian says, "I was always in my Bible." Thomas à Kempis used to say, "I have no rest but in a nook with the book." The righteous person's delight is in the law of God. He loves his Bible. It is a great new source of pleasure, which he will never exhaust. Now it is extraordinary that a man likes to read the law, delights in it. Can you imagine a man saying, "You know I just love reading the traffic laws." Well, I tell you there was a time when I did. I remember as a boy of seventeen I took the Highway Code and I loved reading it. Why? –Because I wanted to drive and I loved reading that book. When you really want to do something, you love the laws connected with it. So when the righteous read the law of God, it ceases to be a dark thundercloud of threatened punishment hanging over him. It becomes a bright ideal of how he really wants to live. He delights in the laws of God because they are guides to the kind of life he wants to live. Fancy delighting in the law, loving to hear how you should live – not only does he regard this duty as his delight but look at how he reads it: "day and night". That does not mean, as it does in colloquial English, all the time. He had a job to do; as a shepherd he had sheep to look after. Day and night means simply this: twice every twenty-four hours, and that is the normal amount of meals that a shepherd of those days got. What he is saying is this: I feed my soul as often as I feed my body; I have two good meals a day for my body. I have two good meals a day for my soul. I meditate day and night – twice a day I get into this book. That is a challenge.

Do we feed our souls as much as we feed our bodies? Could we skip a physical meal as easily as we skip a spiritual meal? Meditating is a lost art. So much is it a lost art in this country that a musician held a concert in Wigmore Hall, sat at a piano and announced to the audience that music was made up of notes and of silence – the silence was as meaningful as the sounds, and therefore he might or might not play the piano. He sat for two hours in total silence and then the audience got up and went home. They paid pounds for tickets for that concert. They were going away raving and saying, "What a marvellous concert – great!"

It was not a case of the emperor's new clothes. They had not been fooled. It was this: some of those people had never sat quiet for two hours. It was a new and wonderful experience for them to sit and meditate. In our crazy, hectic Western world, how conscious we are of the clock and how we burn up every minute. I found that in Brazil they referred to our ways as "English time".

I turned up for a meeting – two o'clock it was scheduled for, to meet a group of ministers. We got started at a quarter past three. Now a quarter past three was "Brazilian" time; two o'clock was "English" time. We just rush from one thing to another. We are tied to our watches. The ministers came in for an hour and a quarter, sat and chatted. It was not wasting time, it was relating. They had time for each other, so they did not feel upset that it was an hour and a quarter late in starting. If I did that in England there would be nobody there next week. People would say, "What a waste of time."

Now the righteous have learned not only to make time for people but to make time for God, to learn to meditate. It is a striking thought that many people in our Western world are taking up yoga and transcendental meditation. Why? Because the East has something to teach us here and is saying, "We know how to sit still; we know how to be quiet;

we know how to meditate" – but the key to meditation is not just meditation. That doesn't do good of itself – tying your legs in knots and sitting still for half an hour does not do good of itself. The key to meditation is what you meditate upon. You can have a horrible silence that is empty and fruitless because there is nothing really in your mind.

The word for "meditate" in Hebrew literally means to talk to yourself. Do you do much of that? You can have a very good conversation if you do. It says, "In your law I chatter with myself day and night." I have learned how to talk through a passage of scripture. The Bible is not to be read as: "ten verses a day keeps the devil away – then that's done." Daily notes can be an awful crutch if you are not careful. The important thing is: can you take your Bible and can you sit and meditate on it? Can you talk with yourself about it? Can you say, "Now what on earth does that mean and does that verse link up with this and why is that word used there and what has this got to say to me?" Talk to yourself and go on talking until you get answers. Go on knocking till it opens – that is meditating. The righteous person has learned to do that.

The third thing we are told here about the righteous is his life. David as a shepherd, and of course most of his thinking was in country terms, in agricultural, horticultural metaphors, so he searches around in his mind for a picture of the righteous man. What is his life like? Then, down by the Jordan River, looking down the hills, he spots what was called the Jungle of the Jordan – lush growth by the stream, and the big trees which were not to be seen on the hills of Judea. Lot saw that lush growth and chose it in preference to the hills where Abraham lived. David could see that a righteous man is like a tree transplanted by the waterside. Nobody starts life by the waterside. You need transplanting to get near to the river of the water of life. A righteous man is like an abundant tree by the water's edge.

I saw the meaning of this in Brazil so clearly. I was in two parts of Brazil. First, Brasilia is on the plateau a few thousand feet up and it is poor sandy red soil, and its scrub land, a bit of grass, and the trees probably mostly no more than eight or ten feet high – stunted, twisted, and you know that in the season of dryness they really have a struggle to keep going. They are poor little trees. Then I flew in a little plane and we went down and waded through rivers and got through to the jungle. The lush growth there was so thick it was almost impenetrable. The lush trees grew straight and strong to their full height.

That is the picture here. A man who is not righteous is a man whose growth is stunted. He becomes crooked. He cannot be an upright man. He hasn't the strength of character. He hasn't the water; he hasn't the secret well springing up within him to eternal life. So he is stunted. But a righteous man is like a tree planted by the river – he produces fruit. We know what the fruit is. In Galatians 5 it is listed as love, joy, peace, patience, kindness, goodness, faithfulness, meekness, self-control, and these are nine lovely fruit of the Spirit, which a righteous man produces in season, which means the fruit is there when you need it.

In a situation where love is needed, the righteous man is loving. In a situation where patience is needed, the righteous man is patient. In a situation where self-control is needed, the righteous man controls himself. He is like a tree bringing forth fruit in its season. He is not only such a good tree producing fruit, he is a beautiful tree – lush green growth. Down in the Jordan Valley there was a bush which I don't think grows in that species anywhere else in the world. It grows near the water and is called the Oleander. It has the most gorgeous, dark green leaves, which never drop. An evergreen, it produces flowers a little like Rhododendrons

– a beautiful bush. I am sure that David is thinking of the Oleander when he talks about the beauty, the fruit being produced, the leaf not withering, the sheer beauty of this life by the water's edge – transplanted near the river, roots going down into perpetual moisture, and there in the Amazon Basin along all the rivers you see this lush, green growth so thick it seems to smother the river at times. Righteous people are like this. Their life is rich, full; they are evergreen fruit bearers. They are attractive, and in everything they do they prosper. That is not promising that they will have a big bank balance, nor promising they will be successful in business. It is making a promise more wonderful than that. I know many men who have reached their mid-fifties, who have made a lot of money and been successful in business, and who look back over their life and say, "What have I done that has really been of lasting value?"

When the Bible says, "Whatever he does shall prosper" it is not saying so much the man will prosper but what he does will be worthwhile – and he will have the satisfaction of reaching the end of his life and looking back and saying, "What I've done was of lasting value." What a reward – and when we get to the end of the road we need to be able to say: I finished my work. He is like a tree planted by the waters; everything he does prospers.

Now let us turn to the black side of the picture. I am glad that the Lord saw fit to give us the bright side first. "Blessed is the man...." Now the beginning of verse 4 is terribly negative. In fact the words "not so" are repeated twice in the Hebrew. Who are these wicked people? What does God mean by "wicked"? He means something different from the world's meaning. When we say "wicked" we think of a cannibal or a criminal or somebody who is terribly perverted. We say, "Oh, it's wicked," but we never say it of ourselves. I will tell you what God's definition of wicked is. The word in the Hebrew is a synonym for *ungodly* – a person who lives without God. It is all you need to do to be wicked – just ignore God. That is what God means by "wicked" – people who take the life he gave them that he might have their love, and they have never given him that love – that is wicked in God's sight; people who live as if there is no God in heaven who cares for them, that is wicked. "The ungodly are not so"; "not so the wicked".

First of all they are very weak. Again David searches his memories of his farming life for some picture of the wicked. The righteous man is like a gorgeous tree by the river. Look at such trees and say: "If I'm righteous in God's sight, I'm like those trees." But what are the unrighteous men like? Not trees but chaff. I wonder if that conveys to you what it conveys to me. It conveys to me a hot summer's day, threshing with an old-fashioned thresher with a tractor and a big belt to the big box on wheels we call the thresher. It conveys to me: dust everywhere getting into my eyes, my ears, everywhere. It conveys a wind blowing bits of useless stuff all over and you just wish you could get out of it.

It conveys a day on which we drank cold tea without milk and sugar, and there is no more refreshing drink when you are in the middle of threshing corn. It conveys the sight at the end of the day of bags of corn stacked up and bales of straw stacked up, and a whole field littered with little bits of chaff that are blown away because they are no longer of any use. It is the only part of the corn that you cannot use. The only thing to do with it is to burn it. It is the little husk, the skin around the grain of corn. The straw you can use again so you bale it and use it. The corn is the most precious part, that is the food that you did it all for. But the wicked are like the chaff – they may have fulfilled a very important function for a time. They may have been very useful in their time, but the wicked come to the point where God says, "That's the only bit I can't use." Chaff to blow away – a vivid picture.

You see, a person's life contains so much goodness, which God has put there. It is only because of God's Spirit moving on the chaos – not only of the waters but of human life – that there is goodness in unbelievers. Unbelievers should be told: the goodness that you think you have is God's work in you. If God withdrew his Spirit from you, if his Spirit was not influencing society generally, there would be no goodness. I don't think people realise that without God there is finally no goodness left. So a man's life who doesn't know God may have some goodness in it that God has put there but there comes a point where the goodness is withdrawn and there is just chaff left. There is nothing that can be used, the person has become useless and so he is blown away.

That is perhaps the greatest tragedy that the Bible speaks of. You see, the laws of God you either delight to read now or you will hear them read to you then. Everybody is going to read the laws of God some day. We either read them now as guidelines to our life, and delight in them, or one day God will say, "You have broken my law," and the wicked will not stand in the Day of Judgment.

There is coming a congregation in which there will not be one sinner. Now at the moment services of worship are public. We hold public services of worship and sinners are welcome to come in. If people think the church is full of sinners we just say that there is always room for one more – come and join. But sinners can come into the congregation of the righteous. Sinners can join the saints. They can sing hymns along with them. But the day is coming when sinners will not stand in the congregation of the righteous. The day is coming when the chaff will not be joined to the grain, when the useless parts will be taken away, and that is a day of separation. It is interesting, isn't it, that at the moment sinners seem to want saints to go along with them and to join with them and exert social pressure to go along with them. Some sinners come along to join the saints in public worship, but one day there is going to be a real separation; the harvest day separates chaff and grain. The grain is gathered and the chaff is blown. Have you ever seen a picture of traditional threshing in the Middle East? They did not have big machines such as we have. They would choose a flat hill top and wait for a windy day and then they would tip all the corn onto the top of the flat rock and then they would take two sticks joined by a thong of leather in the middle to make a hinge. They would beat the corn, or if they had an animal, an ox or an ass, it would walk around on the corn – beating. It is almost a lovely picture of the last days and the great tribulation that is to come, because tribulation means threshing sledge. If you can imagine beams joined together in a kind of lattice work, and from each joint a spike going down – that is a tribulum or a threshing sledge. The tribulation will sort out the wheat from the chaff and the tribulation will thresh the human race. Grain and chaff will be separated – it is a marvellous picture of God's harvest time. Then the wheat, having been through that threshing, comes out pure, usable for God and is taken into his barns, but the chaff blows away – it just goes.

This is the meaning of the word "perish". It does not mean to cease to exist. In the expensive home I visited, they pulled out for me a lovely plastic webbing, aluminium framed sun chair so that I could lie in the sun for half an hour in a beautiful garden with hummingbirds around me. Can you imagine it? But as soon as I sat on this chair, I went straight through it! Can you imagine my embarrassment in this house? There I was, sitting on the grass in the middle of this aluminium frame, it just gave way. It was nylon, woven plastic. It had seemed so strong. But the household said, "No don't worry. That's all right. We've left it out in the sun and the strength of the sun up here is such that it just rots this." Even the plastic had rotted. They used the very word, "it's perished." There is nothing else to do with it but to throw it away. The chair looked perfectly good until you sat in it. When God looks at human beings, the way of the wicked shall perish. It means that one day God will look at some people and say: I can't use that person any more; the goodness has gone out of them; they have perished; they are just chaff. There could be no greater tragedy than that.

So there are two ways. This is where the Sermon on the Mount finishes up. There are two ways: the way of the righteous and the way of the wicked. Notice what it says about the way of the righteous: that the Lord knows that way. How does he know it? The answer is he knows it because that is the way he walks. God the Father has only known that way. God has never known the way of the wicked. He knows it secondhand but he has never known it in his own experience, he has never walked it. When Jesus was on earth the way he walked was the way of the righteous. He did not know any other. The Lord knows the way and therefore when I know that way and when I walk in it I know the Lord and he knows me. If I walk the other way then it is a way the Lord does not know and therefore he does not know the people on it. He is not travelling that way. He doesn't get to know them. Therefore one day he will say to them, "I never knew you."

This is the choice that this Psalm presents to us all. One way the Lord knows and one way he does not. The tragedy is that all of us in church have known the way of the wicked. We have tasted just a little of how useless it is; of how it perishes your character; of how it perishes the good things that you want to keep; of how it perishes your relationships; of how it perishes your dreams and visions of what you could be. You know it is a way of perishing. You become harder and more useless to the Lord, but praise God for those who have known the way of becoming right with God through Jesus Christ our Lord.

This is a simple Psalm – really so simple that I am sure I have pointed out very little that you didn't know about it before. But one final thought hits me hard: in verses 1–3 the way of the righteous is described in terms of one person—the man. But in verses 4–6 the way of the wicked is described in terms of a crowd – sinners. Why this contrast? Here are two simple facts. First: that the righteous are in a minority – you may be the only one in your house, in your place of work, in your neighbourhood. You may have to stand alone, "Blessed is the man..." just one person who will walk the way of the Lord. He is with the Lord, and the Lord plus one is a majority. Blessed is that man. The way of the crowd is the broad way and many there be that find it.

If you want human company, then go the way of the wicked. If you want lots of friends, go the way of the wicked. Friendship of the world is enmity to God. Friendship of God will mean the world's enmity—there is no middle way. So you will be one in a crowd. The second fact this simple difference points up is that you walk the way of the righteous by a personal decision on your own. You cannot just join a group and say, "They're the righteous." The sinner cannot stand in the congregation of the righteous. He has got to take a fundamental step himself. He has got to turn to God's law. He has got to turn to the Lord.

Did you notice where Jesus was mentioned in this Psalm? Let me tell you where I found him. The Lord knows the *way*. Do you know that long before our religion was called Christianity it was called "The Way"? But do you know something else too? On the night before he died, Jesus said when Thomas did not know where the way was and how to walk it Jesus said, "I am the way." This is the way of the righteous. Nobody ever got to walk this way outside of Jesus Christ. When I take the step of stepping into him, I have started on the narrow road that leads to life; I have been transplanted beside the river, and the waters of life begin to flow. I have become a tree that grows the fruit of the Spirit. Not so the wicked for they know not Christ who is the way.

READ PSALM 22

What would you think if Queen Elizabeth composed an anthem for Westminster Abbey every Sunday? That was the privilege of the king of Israel and the choirmaster must have had quite a task keeping up. Psalm after Psalm poured out from his pen, from his lips, from his stringed instruments. He was a songwriter and his songs are still in the charts after three thousand years. But the choirmaster never got a greater shock than when Psalm 22 was given to him to sing the following sabbath. I believe that David himself got a terrible shock when he composed it.

You see, the feelings expressed in this Psalm are so real but the facts were not. It is in two halves and in the first half a man is sinking to the depths of human sadness. He is being hurt horribly; he is being physically tortured; he is being mentally humiliated; he is being socially outcast and he is being spiritually desolated. In the second half he is so happy that he wants to share with the whole world. It is the words of a dying man. How can a dying man achieve happiness under such circumstances? The feelings are so real and you must have a heart of granite if you do not see that. Yet David never went through this. There was no situation in his life corresponding to these facts and they are there in detail.

The thing which he described did not happen until one thousand years later when they happened to a descendant of David, someone still in his loins while he composed this song. How could he know the feelings and the facts that his descendant would go through? It is a miracle. There is no naturalistic explanation, no extra-sensory perception or telepathy. But there is a supernatural explanation and it is so extraordinary that if you are not a Christian you won't believe it.

It is not just a miraculous revelation from God who knows the future as well as the past, it is something even more remarkable than that. The fact is that David's descendant who was going to go through this one thousand years later was alive when David wrote the Psalm, for that descendant was later going to say: "Before Abraham was, I am."

The explanation of this Psalm lies in one verse in the first letter of Peter chapter one, where Peter, talking about prophets, writes: "The Spirit of Christ was telling the prophets what he would suffer and the glory that would follow" – and that is how it all happened. It is easy for us; it is as plain as daylight to us that this Psalm is not about David even though he was able to describe the feeling so intensely. This Psalm is about the Son of David and the Son of God and the Son of Man all in one. It is without doubt Jesus on his cross. In the last few moments before he died, Jesus cried out the first verse of this Psalm, and so deep an impression did it leave on those who heard, that it has been remembered in the original language to this day: "*Eloi, Eloi, lama sabachthani.*" "My God, my God, why have you deserted me?"

So we may approach this Psalm as a preparation for Easter to understand something of what it meant for the Holy One to bear away our sins. The poetess Gertrude Stein when she was dying said to the friend who was sitting by her bedside, "What is the answer?"

Her friend, confused, remained silent so Gertrude Stein said, "In that case, what is the question?"

I can answer that. The question is, "My God, my God, why have you forsaken me?" For death is not a normal biological, natural event. Death is an artificial event that was never intended for the human race. Death is a judicial event. Every person's death is a death sentence. Death is a separation not only from your family and your friends, it is essentially separation from God. That is why he said to Adam and Eve, "The day you touch that tree, that day you die. You say goodbye to me." That is what death is all about.

It is the one question that people should ask when they die. "Why are you leaving me?" Not just: why are you taking me from my family, my friends, my home, but why are you taking me away from you? For everyone there is a very simple answer to that question. The answer to Gertrude Stein is that you die for one reason and one only: God is good and he made the world good. You are not good and you are spoiling it and he is not going to let you go on spoiling it forever. That is why you die. That is the question and that is the answer. Why, then, do people not ask that question? The answer is that unbelievers do not consider the question. They have never been friendly with God. They are not fond of God so they do not think they will miss him. They do not know what it is to be forsaken by God because they have never been close to him.

Unbelievers never ask the right question. Saints ask it because once you have got to know God, one of the most dreadful experiences is to feel that he has let you go. Once you have tasted his love and had some friendship with him, to be forsaken by him is one of the most horrible and dreadful experiences you could have. Saints have called it the dark night of the soul. Every Christian has been through periods when they have felt that God's presence was not with them.

The saints feel being forsaken by God where unbelievers do not, because they have known what it is to be close to him. But that Jesus should ask this question – that is the mystery for there seems to be no answer to that one. Within minutes of dying, when he knew that he would be going to be with the Father: why, my God, why? We see the agony of the question and the pressures, spiritual, mental, physical, that were on him that made him ask the question. The Psalm gives the answer to the question, though not until the last verse.

It is a long Psalm and I want to go right through it because I want you to see it as a whole. I divide it into two halves. The first twenty-one verses I call "a prayer from suffering in the dark". Then vv. 22–31: Praise for salvation in the daylight, in the dawn. Let us look at the first half. It is a desperate prayer. Like many prayers it alternates between being conscious of self and being conscious of God. It alternates between me, my, and you, your. Three times Jesus thinks of himself then of his God his Father. The prayers about himself, the parts about himself get longer and longer. The sections about God remain the same length but they get deeper and deeper. There is a progression in this prayer which you will notice.

The three alternations between me and you are linked with the three pressures that he felt most at the end of his hours on the cross – the spiritual pressure, the mental pressure and the physical pressure. We take first the spiritual, and people have called this the problem of unanswered prayer. We have all known what it is like when the heavens seem as brass, when you feel you are talking into a telephone and there is no one at the other end. Jesus went through this.

For six hours he had been trying to get a reply and he did not get one. Now for us this is pretty bad – we feel it deeply. Unbelievers, of course, deal with the problem of unanswered prayer by taking refuge in atheism or agnosticism. Believers cannot do that. Above all, Jesus could not do that. So how did Jesus cope with this? Do you realise we will never understand what this meant to Jesus to have this unanswered prayer? Why? Because all of us have known what it is to be away from God and he had never known it.

To be out of direct communication with his Father was a strange new experience he had never had before. He knew it was going to be horrible in the Garden of Gethsemane; he shrank from this cup which he knew he had to drink but he had no idea it would be this horrible. Through all eternity he had been in instant touch with God the Father, and now for six hours he has been out of touch. So verses 1–2 describe his loneliness. I am using this language advisedly and theologically but to be forsaken by God is sheer hell, and he was going through that.

To Jesus the thing was incredible. There is a straight answer to the death of everybody else but not in his case. Everybody else was not good enough to go on living in God's good universe forever, but he was. Now let us get one thing clear: he had not lost his faith; he had lost his fellowship, and it is important to get the difference. When you are going through this problem of unanswered prayer, heaven's brass, a feeling of being left alone by God it is terribly important not to confuse faith and fellowship. Jesus never lost his faith. "My God, my God, my God" – three times he said it. He did not doubt the existence of God; it was the absence of God that was the problem. So his faith had not gone but his fellowship had.

Now when our fellowship goes, the devil whispers in our ear that our faith is gone and we get it confused, but that is not the situation. The problem was not God's existence but God's absence. He could not understand it that such a person as God the Father should leave such a person as his Son in such a plight. That is the problem. Where would you put the emphasis on this question? "*Why* have you forsaken me?" "Why have *you* forsaken me?" "Why have you forsaken *me*?" I put the emphasis on the last because I think that is what was troubling Jesus—me of all people, the one you should have never left. Here is the cry of a lost child who has lost everybody. His friends have gone; angels ministered to him both in the wilderness and Gethsemane, but the angels have gone. His mother has gone, taken away about noon by John. Now his Father has gone and he is alone. It is a desperate cry for help. God the Father is apparently not even listening to him, and Jesus is the one person who had every right to be listened to by him, and he is not getting any reply. It is so bewildering.

Having expressed the loneliness of Jesus, this Psalm turns to the thought of God's loyalty. What makes the frustration worse is the memory that down through the centuries people far less worthy and deserving than him have trusted God and God helped (see vv. 2ff.). God, it doesn't make sense. I don't understand it because you are holy. I can understand you deserting an unholy person but to desert a holy person when you are holy. Not only that, you are so utterly good that even our ancestors...." This reveals the humanity of Jesus (our ancestors – Jesus was a Jew, remember). Our ancestors when they relied on you, were rescued. Time and again it happened. They celebrated every year at the Passover. They trusted God and he got them out of trouble. They were surrounded—the mountains on the south, the desert on the west, the Egyptian army on the north, and the Red Sea on the east. They were trapped but they relied on him and he got them out. Jewish history is based on annual celebrations of occasions when their ancestors trusted God and he got them out of trouble. The word "trusted" comes three times in the Psalm. So that is the spiritual pressure that is on him. He can't believe that the fault is on God's side, "You are utterly holy. This nation praises your holiness, lifts you up on your throne in praise." Jesus had never disobeyed the Father. He had lived with him, loved him, never said anything the Father didn't want him to say.

The second phase of this prayer moves on to the mental

suffering, which came from men, not from God. Mental cruelty can hurt very deeply. Banter can hurt even more than blows. So the Psalm describes humiliation. We read the words "I am". That was a phrase that had been on Jesus' lips time and time again. It is the name of God, Yahweh – I am, and it is an incomplete name. You are? You are what?

Time and again in the Old Testament God completed his name, "I am your righteousness"; "I am your strength"; I am this, that, everything." When Jesus came he said, "I am," implicitly claiming to be God, but he always completed the name, "I am the bread of life"; "I am the light of the world"; "I am the good shepherd"; "I am the door of the sheep"; "I am the resurrection and the life"; "I am the way, the truth, and the life." But at his trial he didn't complete the name.

At his trial they said, "Are you the Son of God?" He said, "I am." They put him to death for it. But the last "I am" here is, "I am a worm...." I paraphrase that as: "They treat me like a worm." When gardening I have cut a worm in half with my spade, treading it under foot – just a worm. The psalmist is telling us how Jesus would be treated. When Jesus, the Son of God, became man he was made lower than the angels. Now in his death he is being made lower than the animals. He is being given no more consideration than a writhing, bleeding worm.

How were they doing that? Well they were doing it with mockery. They were hurting him at his most sensitive point. They were shouting at him the very question that his heart was shouting inside. He had to face the question from outside and inside which just added to his pain. They mocked him, saying to him: "You said the Lord would prove you right. Let's see him get you out of this. You say the Lord's fond of you; let's see him free you." Do you know it is an almost verbatim account of what they said to Jesus on the cross? It is satanic, it is diabolical, because Satan tells half-truths all the time. The first half of each sentence is true. "You said God would prove you right" – that is true. "Let him get you out of this" – that was not going to be true. "You said God delighted in you, was fond of you" – that was true. "Then let him free you" – that was not going to be true.

Satan loves to hurt saints with half-truths. They mocked Jesus at his most sensitive and tender point—his relationship with his Father. He claimed all through his three years in his public ministry to have total and immediate contact with his Father. "Every word I say," he said, "comes from my Father and I don't say anything but what he tells me", and now they taunt him with it. It is a terrible taunt; it must have gone right through him. You see they thought they knew the answer to his question. He had cried out, "My God, my God why have you forsaken me?" They thought: Simple, God is disgusted with his blasphemy in claiming to be his Son; God is disowning him, there's no problem. So they mocked because they thought they had the answer, but man's answer and God's answer were totally different, as we shall see. So from his own mental suffering under this cruel taunt, Jesus turned again to God and talked about God's help – my humiliation; your help. He did not reply to his enemies in their taunting.

The psalmist continues, in v. 9, and we are taken to the other big crisis in Jesus' life on earth—his birth. Now birth and death share this in common – at both occasions human life is so frail and so weak it can end quickly, especially in those days where the infant mortality rate was so high. Even more particularly in the case of Jesus—his pregnant mother had to travel seventy miles just before the birth, on the back of a donkey. He was born in the filth of an open courtyard among animals. He goes back to that. "God you brought me safely through childbirth and you kept me safe while my mother was still feeding me from her breasts." Yes, God had kept him safe. He had to take him down to Egypt to do so, but God had been looking after him through that other crisis, at the beginning of his life.

Birth and death are both times of extreme human frailty, just as with an aircraft the points of danger are take-off and landing. It seems to be that life is in peril at these two points. "You kept me safe." I have had to depend on you from my birth. You have been my very own God since my mother brought me into the world. Of who else is that true? His heavenly Father had looked after him as well as his earthly mother had looked after him. Now his mother had gone and the fruit of her womb was being torn and mangled on a cross.

We move to the third phase of the prayer – the physical suffering. The reality of his incarnation is so clear now – that the Son of God really did become the Son of Man, that he had a human body and that body could suffer and be tortured. This was no play-acting; this was real. As the psalmist begins to describe the pain he uses animals. In the title to the Psalm the animal mentioned is a hind. The Psalm is dedicated or called "The Hind of the Dawn". So we have a worm and a hind. Three more animals that are going to appear: bulls, lions and dogs. I have had direct experience of fear of two of those three latter categories. When I worked on a farm we had a bull of a breed with a reputation for ferocity. I tell you, there were times when those huge animals really put the wind up us. You discovered quickly that to your surprise you could clear a six-foot fence in one jump. Have you ever handled a mad bull? I remember one occasion when this huge beast tore the ring out of its nose. Its nose was torn and bleeding and it went berserk, smashing up its pen. Have you seen the notice, "Beware of the bull"? Dogs! This isn't talking about pet dogs but dogs in the Middle East. One day I went into a town in Arabia to take some photographs, and outside the town I noticed some interesting ruins which I thought would make a wonderful snapshot, so I walked over to them, not knowing that they were inhabited by a group of wild dogs. They came for me and I think I beat the four-minute mile, or even the three-minute mile, back to my car. For those wild scavenger dogs are savage. Have you ever seen a notice, "Beware of the dog"? Lions? We see them in zoos and we are not afraid of them. We drive through Longleat and see them, but they had to produce a film at Longleat, which they did with dummies sitting in cars with open windows, to show what a lion could do. They photographed a lion grabbing that dummy by the head, dragging it out of the car, and crunching it to pieces thinking it was a human being, to warn those who drove through Longleat. It is interesting that all these three animals were ones to beware of.

Such savagery – why are they included here? It is because man can behave like a beast. Indeed he can behave like a lot of beasts rolled into one. A pastor once said, "To say that man is descended from the apes is an insult to the apes." We can be so bestial to one another. We now have this miraculous prophecy given in such detail that we have a perfect description of what it is to die by crucifixion, even though crucifixion was not to be known until another eight hundred and fifty years after David wrote this Psalm. It is a literal description. Crucifixion is the worst form of death ever devised for human beings because it does not immediately affect any vital organ—you are nailed by hands and feet, a nail through your heart would finish you quickly – but hands and feet? No. No vital organ is immediately affected and so you just die slowly in agony. When we want to use an adjective to describe pain that we have had—shame on us we even use it after a visit to the dentist. When we want to say it was the worst pain you could feel we say, "It was excruciating," from the Latin *cruciatus*, crucified. It is the worst pain that can be endured.

The things that happen to a man who has been crucified are described here. His flesh drains away like water. Gradually his joints dislocate as if on a rack. His body is desiccated in the noonday heat and dries up. The first point at which he feels it is that his mouth goes dry – and dry until his tongue is stuck to the roof of his mouth. They tear hands and feet. It is all here, and that David should write this in 1000 BC is remarkable. It is a slow death and the description finishes with this cry, which is absolutely true to crucifixion. Your body is turning to dust and disintegrating before you die instead of after. The last cry is: "You're letting me disintegrate into dead dust," the thing that normally only happens after an execution.

So David got all the details right, even to something that did not normally happen at a crucifixion. The victim was always crucified stark naked and his clothes were shared out by the soldiers. In Jesus' case alone as far as we know his robe was too beautiful to do what they usually did – to tear it up into shares. They gambled for it and David even got that right. Who doubts the inspiration of Holy Scripture? Let him explain this Psalm.

So from his pain he turns to God's power. He still did not doubt that God could get him out of this, even at this late stage. He still believed God was the only one who could help. "You are my strength. Hurry back! Come!" he cried, and all this prayer was in midnight blackness. The sun had gone from noon and this prayer was a prayer in the dark. Now at this point I want to take you back to the original title of Psalm 22. It is a Psalm of David to the choirmaster and the title of the Psalm is "The Hind of the Dawn".

The Lord Jesus said, "I am a worm. I am surrounded by lions, bulls, dogs." But lions, bulls and dogs don't bother with worms. He was being treated like a worm but David, with that insight which God gave him, saw a hind encircled by a pack of hounds closing in for the kill – a hind who is not an aggressive creature, but why hind of the dawn? I will tell you why: because there is a total change at the end of v. 21.

The last phrase in the Hebrew of v. 21, which is often disguised in translations, is a cry of a very different kind, "You've given me the answer. You have answered me." If you have a Bible with alternative readings in the margin, you will see it there. "You've answered me. Deliver my precious life from the fangs of these dogs, from the jaws of these lions, from the horns of these bulls." After six hours there came a reply. It was a strange and unexpected reply.

From now on the answer has dawned on him. It has dawned in his mind why God has forsaken him. Here I must admit I am going to speculate a little and you can reject it if you feel it is not right, but I believe it not only dawned inside Jesus but it dawned outside Jesus. It says, "There was darkness on the face of the earth till about the third hour," and it was about the third hour that Jesus said, "My God, my God why have you forsaken me?" I had assumed that it stayed dark until Jesus died and then the light returned. I wonder now if in the last minute of his life it came back. The whole thing dawned.

There is a flood of light. You have changed darkness to dawn – the only day that dawn happened at three in the afternoon. The hind of the dawn lifted up its head. Prayer turned to praise, sadness turned to gladness. His God was back with him again. Now it is true that when you are sad you want to be alone, you feel alone, you want to be like that worm, burrow in the ground and hide. But when you are glad you want to share, you want to be together. Luke 15 is full of this. The woman who lost the coin was alone sadly looking for it, but when she found it she was glad and she called her neighbours in. The shepherd losing his sheep was sad and alone looking for it, but when he found it he called them together. Bad news you tend to keep to yourself; good news you want to share. The rest of the Psalm, Jesus rejoices, and it is as if a stone of praise drops into a pool and the ripples spread out.

The first circle he thinks of are his own Jewish people. Within that circle he thinks of his own brothers. Who did he mean? Not his physical brothers. If you read the end of Mark 3, Jesus said, "My family is composed of those who do the will of God. Who is my mother? Who is my brother? Who is my sister? He who does the will of God." Who were his brethren? Who did he mean when, immediately after he rose from the dead, he said, "Go and tell my brothers". That inner circle of Jews who were closest to him.

When you get good news the first people you share it with are your immediate brothers. So when they met together he was going to meet with them and share his testimony; he was going to tell them that God had lived up to his name. What name? Saviour; righteousness. That is precisely what Jesus did when he was raised from the dead. As soon as his brethren met together, he met them. He did not want to meet them separately. As soon as they were together, he met them and he was in their midst.

What did he do between his resurrection and ascension? In Luke 24:44 it tells you he showed them all the things concerning himself in the Psalms. I believe he gave them the Bible study concerning his sufferings and the glory that should follow, but he was not going to limit it just to his brothers. He thought now of his fellow countrymen and the next verse calls on every Jew to praise God not for things in the past, not for the Passover, not for the entry into Canaan, not for the return from Exile in Babylon, but for the biggest thing of all—Jesus, died and risen again. So let all who belong to Israel, let all who claimed descendance from Jacob, let every Jew, give the credit to God and hold him in high respect and praise his name.

So that is the first circle and he calls it "the great congregation". He first talks about his brothers meeting, then he talks about the great occasion, and that, in Jewish terms meant one of the three annual assemblies when the whole nation came together. That came true, for the very next great occasion when they came together was Pentecost. When they came together, the good news was shared there and the very first day three thousand praised God for what had happened. So the ripples have spread from his brothers to the great congregation. From congregations, whether small or large, he moves on. But those congregations are going to have thrilling experiences. There is a lovely little verse in there: "He who suffered will be satisfied; those who have been seekers will become singers," and this thrilling experience will last forever. The literal Hebrew is "eat and be satisfied". Well, he is the meal for you. Now the ripples spread out from congregations of Israel to nations of the world. Here we are reading Jesus' very last thoughts on the cross, and his outstretched arms embraced the Gentiles too, and reach out to the uttermost parts of the earth, and he can see the people in every corner of the world are going to think about God again. They are not going to forget him anymore. They are going to remember him. You see, mankind is not in a state of never having known God and trying to find him. Mankind is in a state of having known him and forgotten him – that is the real situation.

So they are going to be converted, and we are reminded of three simple things about conversion: remembrance, repentance, reverence. They shall think again about God. They will remember him. They will turn to God, which means turning away from anything or anyone else that comes between them and God; and they will worship him with awe; they will reverence him. That is true conversion.

This at last will produce a "united nations" – a thing that we have longed for which was tried after the First World War with the League of Nations and after the Second World War with the United Nations. Both have failed.

But God has his plan for united nations and all races and nations will worship him together. Isn't that exciting? But that is not the end of it. God is really in charge of international affairs—never forget that. When you read your papers, hear the news, remember God is on the throne. He is in charge. He gives man a lot of rope, but man will hang himself. God is in charge and he will one day bring the nations of the world, every kindred, tribe, tongue and people, and will unite them in worship.

But the ripples go out not only through space but down through time, and Jesus in his dying moments thought not only of all the nations, but of all the generations that would follow. There were congregations of Israel small and large; and the nations of the world of his day, and the devil had shown him all those nations and said, "You can have them", but Jesus was not having them on the enemy's terms, but he will have them.

Finally, there were subsequent generations and Jesus thought: even the top people will bow down because they are just mortal; they are heading for the grave and they cannot hold on to their life forever. Do you find it a little pathetic sometimes to see on television great people of a bygone day doddering across the screen? We are all marching to the grave. No one can stop it, however great you might be. Someone might have an expensive and impressive funeral. His medals may be laid on top of the coffin. But inside he is the same as every mortal man. Every knee shall bow including things under the earth and confess that Jesus is Lord. So the dying will bow down one day but, more than that, those whose lives had not even started yet, those not yet born, will hear of God's work, and God's Word will be passed on to them. They will serve him; they will hear about him.

God's work and God's Word will pass down through the generations. This generation will tell the children after them and on it will go. There is not one shadow of a doubt about this in Jesus' mind. He does not say he hopes it will happen. He says it will happen and it has happened. The church is growing faster today than it has ever grown. The gospel is being preached to more people today than it has ever been preached to before. One crusade alone in South America reached eighty million people with the gospel. So it is passed on. It will be, until history ends. Can't you feel the excitement of all this, the exuberance in Jesus' soul?

Do you realise that modern people are included here in this last verse? People yet unborn will hear. Jesus had you in mind when he died. But one of the most exciting discoveries I made was at the end of this Psalm. In the Hebrew the very last phrase is: "It is finished." What is finished? God's deliverance is finished. God's liberation is finished. Now we have the answer.

There is a double meaning to this answer; there is a double aspect to it. The last phrase I paraphrase freely: the coming generations will be told that God has worked it all out and it is finished or completed. What is that deliverance referred to? Two things: first, Jesus was rescued by God; Jesus was delivered by God right then. Nobody died after six hours on a cross – far too early. Pilate was astonished that he was already dead, but at three o'clock in the afternoon God replied and Jesus knew it was over, completed. God was back with him.

Do you notice the progression at the beginning of the Psalm? He says "God", and that is a very distant word. Halfway through the Psalm he says "Lord", and that is a little more intimate. But when God replied, Jesus said, "It's finished Father; Father I commit my spirit to you." He was rescued from the taunts and the cruelty and the suffering and taken right out of that situation. That is the first meaning: the deliverance came. But it leaves remaining one vital question: why then had God waited six whole hours to give that deliverance? That was the question. The other side of the deliverance is the glorious answer to it. It is that through that six hours of sheer hell, God has rescued us and delivered us; that Jesus was forsaken that we might not be when we die.

If the saints have cried, "My God, my God, why have you forsaken me," they rarely say it when they die. They say it while they are living, but when they die they are not forsaken. Jesus went through hell that we might never see the place. Jesus tasted death that we might live forever. That is the deliverance that will be passed on down through the generations: parents telling children, one generation telling another, and the word and work of God will go on. It is a finished work and yet he desires those to serve him by passing the news on, so the work goes on though it is finished.

I finish this study with two quotations from elsewhere in the Bible. One is from Isaiah 53: "... he shall see the fruit of the travail of his soul and be satisfied...." The other is from Hebrews 12: "... looking to Jesus the pioneer and perfecter of our faith, who for the joy that was set before him endured the cross, despising the shame...."

READ PSALM 23

David's songs have been in the charts for three thousand years now. Today, even three years for a song would be quite a long time; thirty years would be incredible. But for three thousand years these songs have gone around the world and they are still sung by more people than any other songs that have ever been written. Of these songs there is no doubt which has been at number one in the charts for a very long time. Psalm 23 is undoubtedly most people's favourite. I can understand why for sheer literary quality—its beauty, its simplicity, its clarity, its brevity. It comes across as a masterpiece of literature, but the reason is deeper than that. It deals with experiences that life is made up of. It speaks to life. Life is made up of fears and of quiet times. It speaks about life and it meets a very real response in the human heart. It has put more courage into human hearts than all the philosophers in the world put together.

It is a Psalm of tremendous consolation, of tremendous comfort and we are going to draw that comfort now. It has inspired poets like Byron and like Ruskin. Almost every century someone translates this Psalm into a hymn. In the sixteenth century it was translated into, "The Lord's my shepherd I'll not want". Then in the seventeenth century, "The God of love". In the eighteenth century, "Jesus the Good Shepherd is"; in the nineteenth century, "The King of love, my shepherd is". In the twentieth century, "A pilgrim was I and a-wandering". I am quite sure somebody will rewrite this Psalm and it will be sung again and it will go on being sung until history ends.

Like Psalm 22, it is full of animals – though this time it is just sheep. David saw a lot of human truth, and even divine truth, in animals. Why? Because God made the animals, and from the animals you can learn a great deal about yourself and about the Lord. That is why our Lord Jesus is called a Lion and a Lamb (and in Psalm 22 a hind and a worm are mentioned), but in this Psalm 23 you are called sheep, which is a title never given to our Lord Jesus. He is the shepherd. He was never a sheep, but you and I have been and are sheep.

If we live in a country with many sheep we understand something of all this, but I want to make quite clear at the beginning of this Psalm that however much you have seen of sheep, that will not help you a great deal when studying this Psalm. Looking after sheep in England and looking after them in Palestine is a totally different task. They are much the same animals, yes, but there are at least four major differences which I want to highlight.

First of all, a shepherd's life in Israel is much more difficult; they don't have fields full of grass into which they can turn the sheep. The fields are kept for corn or for vines. The sheep have to be taken miles, wandering over the hills looking for a bit of something to eat and something to drink. They travel up to fifteen miles a day and the shepherd has to walk with them all the way; that doesn't happen in England.

Secondly, a shepherd's life out there is much more demanding in the sense that it is a twenty-four hour job. He has to watch over his sheep not only by day but by night. He lives with them, eats with them and sleeps with them.

Thirdly, the shepherd is therefore much more devoted to the sheep than we are. I have been a shepherd, and we looked after sheep but we had something like six hundred and you don't get to know them too well. You know the eccentrics among them fairly quickly, but it takes a long time to know them.

Sometimes the Lord chooses leaders for his flock who have looked after animals because this is a preparation. An elder who had been a shepherd told me that it took him some weeks to begin to know his sheep as individuals; he was just getting to know them when they had to leave him. A shepherd in Israel knows them individually because they keep them not for meat but for wool. He stays with them a long time; he has a small flock, maybe just ten or fifteen. He calls them by name, he calls them Short Ears, Long Legs, Black Face. They know their name, and when he calls their name they come.

In other words, the relationship between a shepherd and a sheepdog in this country is much nearer the relationship between a shepherd and a sheep in the Middle East. If you have ever watched the national sheep dog trials on television and seen the relationship between a man and his dog: his control of the dog, the dog's response to him, the pat on the head at the end, you have got the relationship more clearly than if you simply watch a herd of sheep being pushed along a country lane and being chased by a lot of sheepdogs.

Finally, in the Middle East a shepherd's life is a good deal more dangerous than here. In fact, somebody who visited that land about a century ago came back and said when he met his first shepherds he was shocked; he thought he was looking at brigands. They had pistols, clubs, axes and I don't know what else. They look like brigands because they had to be fighters and they knew that they had to risk their lives for the sheep. To bring that flock safely home at the end of the day they would have to fight their way through. Now all of that is strange to a shepherd in England, yet there are other things, which are similar that will come out.

Like Psalm 22, the twenty-third Psalm is in the first person singular, but this time it is as real in fact as in feeling for the writer; because David had been a shepherd, he is drawing on past experience. In Psalm 22, we saw that he had this miraculous feeling without facts; he felt about things that had never happened to him. But now he is feeling about things that had happened. Only he had been on the giving end, not the receiving end, in his previous experience. He was a shepherd boy when God said: I want you as the king of this nation. I want you to shepherd these people.

So it is autobiographical and you might almost call it A Day in the Life of a Shepherd. As a king, David shepherded the nation; now he was writing as a sheep. The only true shepherds there can ever be for people are those who still admit that they also are sheep. As soon as those who are called to shepherd God's flock begin to think of themselves as having ceased to be sheep, then they will get into serious trouble. Even the pastors, elders, shepherds of God's flock on earth are still God's sheep, whereas the Good Shepherd never was one.

Now let us take a fresh look at the Psalm. At some points the Authorized Version is misleading in its wording and therefore in its application and your understanding. There are some words in the Authorized Version that are not in the original and should not have been put in. Alas, it has led many people off track in applying this to themselves. Nobody likes their illusion shattered, especially our cherished beliefs in religion. This provides us with our security, yet I believe that we gain rather than lose by facing the truth and reality. So I am going to tell it as it is even if I am afraid some cherished notions suffer; they will be replaced by some more beautiful thoughts for you.

Here are the first two things I want to say to clear up misunderstandings: Number one: this Psalm is not for death but for life. It is not for those who are dying, it is for those who are living. The second thing I want to say is this Psalm is for sheep and not for goats, an obvious thing but

I want to say it. Take the first point: it is not for death; it is for life. I know it is the favourite Psalm for funerals. I know that many people, including famous ones like Sir William Hamilton for example, died with the words of this Psalm on their lips: "Yea, though I walk through the valley of the shadow of death...." I know that St Augustine said, "This is the Psalm for Christian martyrs", but I believe that this Psalm is primarily for life, and not just the final crisis. It is of more help to you now than when you are on your deathbed if you understand it truly.

You see, one reason why we apply it to death is that in the Authorized Version the word "death" was put into the Psalm and it is not there. It is, "Yea, though I walk through valley of deep darkness I will fear no evil." You can walk through that valley tomorrow morning without dying. It is also due to the inclusion of the words at the end of the Psalm "forever", making it a reference to the future life. But in fact, if you have a Bible with marginal references, you will notice at the bottom it is Hebrew "as long as I live". Now Christians can read eternity into that, but David was talking about as long as he lived here. So this Psalm is to help you Monday, Tuesday, Wednesday, Thursday, Friday, Saturday, next week – however near your death or far from it you are. It is a Psalm for life and not for death.

Secondly, it is a Psalm for sheep and not for goats. I mean by that, far too many people sing this who have no right to. Again we have been mislead by the English translation, which has: "The LORD is my Shepherd." You will notice that "LORD" is usually in capital letters, indicating that there is something unusual about that word and that is not the word in the original. That word in capital letters in the Old Testament has been slipped in for an unpronounceable word, which is not a description or a title but a name. In English: "Yahweh". David is not saying "God is my shepherd". If that is what he said then everyone could claim the Psalm because everybody has one god – the god who made them. But the name indicates a particular God; the God who gave his name Yahweh, which means "I Am, I really exist." That God and that one only is referred to in this Psalm. He is the God of the Jews and there is no other god who exists. The name of every other god in the world is "I Am Not". So the first verse says, "Yahweh is my shepherd". I Am is my shepherd; the God who really exists is my shepherd; the God of the Jews is my shepherd. Until someone knows the God of the Jews, he cannot claim the rest of the Psalm. It is not a Psalm for general mankind. It is a Psalm for those who got to know a particular God with a particular name. If you have not got that first phrase, the rest of the Psalm is wasted on you. It is more than wasted; it will delude you into a false sense of security. The relationship in v. 1 is the condition for everything else and without that the whole thing falls to the ground – this particular God, of all the gods in the world. The god of the Muslims is Allah, his name is "I am not". All the gods of the Hindus in India, every one of them, their name is "I am not". There is only one God whose name is "I Am" and 'I Am" is my shepherd. Now that is where we begin. So it is for sheep and not for goats. Before we claim the promise we must be aware of the presence. Before we claim the benefits we must be aware of that blessing.

Now if you are going to be one of the sheep, then that is going to involve one of two things. First of all, that you would admit that you are a sheep – that is quite an admission. You know, human beings in the Bible are described in many terms. Some are called wolves in sheep's clothing – but still wolves. Jesus called Herod a fox. In Psalm 22 men were called bulls, lions, dogs. But who likes to call himself a sheep? Those others at least have some virility, some aggressiveness about them, some life in them but you say to someone, "You're sheepish," and see what their reaction is! It is not a compliment.

So the first step to claiming this Psalm is to say, "Lord I am a sheep and I need a shepherd." Do you know that is very hard for a mature man to say? It is easy for little children to say. That is why children's missions are fruitful. It is easier for elderly people to say, "I need a shepherd." It is easier for women than men to say, "I need someone to lead me." But for a mature man to say, "I am a sheep and I need a shepherd," is quite an admission. Until you have admitted it you cannot claim this Psalm.

David wrote this at the height of his maturity when he could have said as most men in this world say, "I can manage my own life. I don't need anyone else, I'll sort out my own problems," but he didn't. Even though he reached the top of his career if you like; even though he was the top man of his nation, the King of Israel, he was saying: I am a sheep and I need a shepherd. That is the first step.

What is sheepish about people? One very simple thing. Isaiah 53 says it: "All we like sheep have gone astray. We have turned every one to his own way." That is precisely what makes you a sheep – that you go your own way. That is precisely what gets you into trouble and why you need a shepherd. If you do your own thing you will need a shepherd very quickly. If you plan your life you need a shepherd. If you try to sort out your own problems you will need a shepherd. We go our own way and then we stray, just like sheep.

The fact is that we need provision or protection, whether we admit it or not. It is beyond a man to know when he needs to rest. I speak from bitter experience. It is beyond a man to keep his soul in good condition; he needs someone to restore it. It is beyond a man to get through the valley of the shadow without being overcome by evil. It is beyond a man to walk in the paths of righteousness. He needs a shepherd.

Until he admits it, he doesn't have one.

The second thing that is implied in this first part of the Psalm is not only that you admitted that you are a sheep, but that you are confessing that you have found the shepherd. Not that you are a seeker but that you have found. Psalm 22 said that seekers will become singers. Well this Psalm is not a Psalm for seekers, it is a Psalm for singers who found and who are able to say "The Lord is my shepherd". I am not hoping he is going to be; I am not hoping to try to find him. He *is* my shepherd. That is the present continuous text – right now, and that is where we begin.

I have used so many words on just the first five words and there is still more to say about them. You can use the five fingers on a hand now. Think of the word "The" in "The LORD". There is only one God; he is unique; he is "I Am". "LORD" – remember the *name*. Then *is* – the third and tallest finger is a reminder of the most important thing, in the sense that your *present* relationship is there. Then *my* – a personal finger. They used to believe that a nerve went from that finger up to the heart and so when we would put a wedding ring on, we would put the ring on that finger to surround a love. Finally, think of *Shepherd* for the smallest finger. Did you know that the shepherd was the lowest socially; disregarded by all other callings? If you wanted to insult somebody you called them a shepherd. A shepherd was the very bottom, the smallest in society. Think of the contradiction, "The Lord is my Shepherd." The great God came to the bottom of the social scale to look after me.

Many years ago two church ministers went for a holiday, hiking through the mountains of Wales. There in the mountains they came across a little Welsh boy who was looking after some sheep. They began to talk to him and discovered that he could neither read nor write. One of the ministers pulled out of his pocket a little New Testament with Psalms and read to him this Psalm because he thought he would be interested. The boy was captivated so they explained to this boy and they tried to help him to memorise the Psalm but he couldn't even memorise that, so they just taught him the first five words on his left hand, as I have just taught you.

Many years later those two ministers went hiking again in the very same area. It was a hot summer day and they were very thirsty. They went to a cottage, and knocked on the door. A woman answered and they said, "Would you make us a cup of tea? We are willing to pay for it but we are so thirsty."

She replied, "I'm not going to charge you, come on in," and took the two in.

They noticed on the mantelpiece a picture of the boy they had talked to, and they said, "We have met that boy before."

She said, "Yes he is dead. It was a great tragedy; there was a blizzard and the boy went out to see that his sheep were safe and he fell over a cliff, down a precipice and came to rest on a ledge still alive. But they didn't find him until too late and he was frozen to death. They said that when they found him that right hand was holding that finger so tight that they could not separate the hands, and they buried him like that."

"The Lord is *my* Shepherd." Until you have got that kind of tight hold on the only God who exists then don't you dare to claim anything else in this Psalm. But when you have got that tight hold, then everything else follows. Actually I said that you have to have found a Shepherd, but really every Christian will tell you: "It was the Shepherd who found me; he went looking for me." But it is the same thing – we found each other.

When I first read these words, "The Lord is my Shepherd," do you know what question flashed in my mind? The Lord is my Shepherd, who is yours? That was the question that came: Who is yours? Some people would say, "Myself; I am my own shepherd. I trust in my own money, my own skill, my own knowledge, I'll see me through." Some people say someone else, "My wife, my husband, my business partner, my friend. They'll see me through." Some people point to a corporate body and say, "The Trade Union will look after me and my family. The welfare of state will look after me." Some people talk about other gods. Some people even say, "The church is my shepherd," or "the pastor is my shepherd." None of those is what the psalmist says. "The Lord is my shepherd". Who is yours? You see, all those other shepherds will leave you; they have got to – that is life. There is only one Shepherd who can really see you right through.

So we begin with the true Shepherd. Verse one I have called his *decision* because behind it lies a decision as a mature man to trust this shepherd. That's the biggest decision a man will ever make. I would say that "The Lord is my shepherd" was David's creed, long before any other creeds were written. If you could ask him what he believed, he would have said "the Lord is my shepherd."

A true shepherd involves a trusting sheep that has pinned his hopes to one person – who puts his whole future into the hands of one person. That is what gives this strong sense of security: "I shall not want." Now there is a phrase that is out of date. Compare the ancient meaning and the modern meaning of "want", which are so different that you could misunderstand this verse. "I want" today means "I desire"; "I want this, I want that, I want the other." It doesn't say: the Lord is my shepherd, I can have everything I want. It does not promise affluence or luxury. The ancient meaning of the word, "want" was "need". Therefore, in paraphrasing, I expanded it to: "I'll never lack anything that I really need." This is the answer to covetousness. Covetousness and contentment are the two main attitudes in life. You will meet a lot of covetous people as you go through life, and you will meet some content people as you go through life. The most content people are those who say, "The Lord is my shepherd I shall not want", meaning: "I'll not need anything. He may not give me luxuries but I will never lack necessities." Or as one girl in Sunday school recited it to her teacher and got it rather wrong but got it right said: the Lord is my shepherd, that's all I want. That is real security.

Now let us move on to verse two, which I call "his dependence". It is a very tender verse: the needs of the sheep are the cares of the shepherd; also the skill of the shepherd – his thoughtfulness in planning ahead. The shepherd has to plan – that route to get them to green pastures and to still waters. He has got to know where they are. He has had to have explored first. He has got to be able to take them where he has been. That is the sheep's security – that the shepherd has already been there and knows the way ahead and has planned the route.

Now food and drink are not easily found out there, and that is why they travel up to fifteen miles a day, but sheep must not be rushed. That is why, if you have watched the sheepdog trials, you notice constantly the shepherd is telling the dog to slow up. To rush the sheep will get them into a bad condition, into a panic; they will do silly things. They must be gently walked on. I get excited about this but sheepdog trials are fascinating; you must go and watch some if you have never been to see them. In the North of England we used to control the dog so the sheep could just walk.

Now a good shepherd knows that he has got to keep the sheep's life in good balance. When a sheep loses its balance it is in serious trouble. When I preached on John 10, "The Good Shepherd," I got a letter from a shepherd afterwards. He said, "These are two thoughts really arising from two heavily in-lamb ewes. The first ewe was over on her back, helpless, partly held by the size of her abdomen. As I turned her over I held her steady before she ran off so she could re-orientate herself. Previously I've seen sheep stagger and fall down before regaining their balance. It helped me realise how we need to stop and get our balance right when Jesus sets us back on our feet."

The balance between eating and drinking, and the balance between resting and activity: how important it is for sheep to get the balance right. You notice how they are linked. Eating is linked with resting and activity is linked with drinking. If you are going to digest your meal properly, you should rest over it. The shepherd knows this balance and yet he has got to take those sheep fifteen miles. So the skill of a shepherd in the Middle East is to know when to make them lie down, when to move them on, where to take them – it is a highly skilled business.

So he makes them lie down in green pastures where they can both relax and be nourished; plenty of green grass for them. When does he do that? He does it at noon. If you read the Song of Solomon 1:7 you will find there that it says: "Where will my beloved lay down with his flock at noon?" You see, midday is when the heat is on. Many sheep would foolishly go on wandering in that heat, but the shepherd knows that is the time for them to relax and rest. I am going to be bold and point out that I think that is equivalent to middle age. To keep up the pace of your twenties when you are in your forties – you may not want that. He forces us to rest, he makes us lie down and get nourished. But then he doesn't want you to settle down in middle age for the rest of your life and do nothing more.

Then he moves us on, and he always leads us beside still waters. I don't know if you have ever studied a sheep but its nostrils are close to its mouth. A sheep cannot drink from running or tumbling water; it has to have a well or a trough or pool – still water. The shepherd knows exactly what kind of refreshment the sheep needs and where to find it. While he is moving you on, he will see that you get just the right kind of refreshment.

Isn't it lovely that each detail is so full of meaning? To the Christian, the word "pastures" inevitably brings scripture to mind, and "pool" brings the Holy Spirit to mind – a spring of living water. Somewhere between the "pasture" of the scripture and the "pool" of the Spirit, the Christian will be balanced by the Shepherd, and the shepherd is responsible for getting the sheep back into balance and holding it steady until it is on its feet again.

Verse 3 – development of the sheep. They must be kept healthy, they must grow, and they must mature. The result of the balance in v. 2 is not exhaustion but energy. So he "restores my soul". The word "soul" here is misleading because we think of the soul as the spiritual part of us. But animals are souls in the Bible. In Genesis 1 the animals are described as "living souls". In Genesis 2 God breathed into the dust and man too became a living soul. Here, "soul" means life, energy, and movement.

So "he restores my soul" doesn't mean that he makes me spiritual again, it means he puts life back into me; he gives me energy again. But energy without direction is harmful. I must not only have energy, I must know how to expend it. If it goes into the wrong channel it is harmful. So immediately he says, "He restores my soul, he puts new life into me"; he says also: "He directs me into the right channel and he leads me into the right tracks." The word is "track" and the track is so narrow. Have you seen a sheep track? It is not a road or a highway. The Good Shepherd will lead you in a narrow track because it leads to life. Sheep will inevitably go for the broad gap and not the narrow one—that is one of the problems. Have you seen the final triumphant conclusion of a sheepdog trial, getting them into that pen? Not just where they have got a gate to swing and a bit of rope and a crook that extends the barrier, as it were – about twenty feet – but when there is a narrow opening and they have to get them through, sheep will never take the narrow opening. That is one of the problems with sheep.

Jesus said, "Narrow is the way that leads to life and broad is the way that leads to destruction," and he will get me into that narrow track because it leads to life. Why? Because his reputation as a shepherd is at stake. In the sheepdog trials it is not the dog that gets the credit, it is the man. The dog gets some but it is the man whose name is at stake. That man puts everything he has got into that sheepdog trial because he knows perfectly well that if his dog makes a mess of it, he will get the blame. It is his reputation, his name, his honour that is at stake. Jesus the Good Shepherd will get us into those tracks anyway. He can, so that he keeps up his good name as a good Shepherd, as a righteous Shepherd, as a holy Shepherd. It is his responsibility and his reputation.

In v. 4, David talks about his defence. So far there have been reasonably pleasant circumstances but the Bible is honest. It is not all up on the hilltops; there are deep valleys to go through. A sheep has no insurance against hazards. Now a harsher note creeps in: enemies; evil. We live in a world with enemies, we live in an evil world and the sheep have to travel through it. You would understand this if you saw the country around Bethlehem. You will know that to get to the green pastures and the still waters the sheep have to be taken through deep gorges. There, in that place, in Bible days, there were lions, bears, hyenas, leopards, jackals; they lived down in the Jordan valley jungle. The wild beasts lived there, and they came up into the hills at night, looking for food. The shepherds were watching their flocks by night to prevent it. The critical times for the valley of the shadow were early mornings and late afternoon when the sun was dropping. The shadows were deep. So at either end of the night, in the early morning and late afternoon, the predators were lurking in the shadows. To get to the pastures the shepherd had to travel through those gorges and the sheep had to go through them too. The Bible never promises an easy passage; there will be crises. I am going to press this day in the life of the shepherd a bit further. The valley of the shadow could be early morning and late afternoon; it could be in your teens as you are setting out to look for life. It could be in your fifties and sixties as the afternoon twilight begins on your life. These are critical periods, as many will testify.

For the valley of deep darkness is not the valley of death. John Bunyan realised this. When he wrote *The Pilgrim's Progress* he put the valley of the shadow in the middle of Pilgrim's life – not at the end when he died and crossed the Jordan, but right in the middle. You can go through the valley of the shadow while you are riding on a tube train, when you are in the bank, when you are watching television you can go through the valley of the shadow. It is the valley where evil lurks in the shadows. The sheep has to go through it and fears evil – not death, evil. A rod and a staff are no use to a dying sheep. This is not death, this is life when the pressures are on. It is the place of moral darkness. It can happen anywhere, but there are those danger times I believe particularly setting off in the morning and coming home at night when Satan can be very real. Two things give the sheep courage: the presence of the shepherd and the protection of the shepherd. Like Nehemiah's workman, the shepherd had a tool in one hand and a weapon in the other: a cudgel, which was a piece of wood with a big knob at the end; and a crook – a long stick with a curve at the end.

A Roman Catholic Archbishop of Westminster, when he was enthroned, was given the most gorgeous crook with a beautiful, elaborate gold curve at the top. I found myself wishing one day that a bishop would get just a plain, ordinary, wooden shepherd's crook. It is just a piece of wood with a curve. Two bits of wood: one is a tool; one is a weapon. The tool is a deadly instrument. It is weighted at the end and it is used at close quarters. When a wild animal has grabbed a sheep, that is brought down on its skull so that it drops its victim. The crook is used to catch hold of the sheep by the neck and pull it back into line.

In the Lord's discipline is our security, and I am not afraid of the cudgel. If I am grabbed by the enemy, Jesus will knock him on the head. If I am just getting a bit too far away from the shepherd, his crook yanks me back in. It may hurt a little at the time but it is good for me to be got back into line, close to the shepherd. So the disease of fear is cured even in the valley of deep darkness.

Verse 5 – his delight. This short Psalm is a mixed metaphor and mixed metaphors are sometimes bad English. But the Bible is not afraid of mixed metaphors. Jesus says, "Be wise as serpents, harmless as doves" and there is another truth from the animal world for you – a mixed metaphor. David couldn't keep this metaphor up because he is dealing with human beings. While they are like sheep, they are not sheep. So the metaphor gets all mixed up here; the comparison between animals and humans breaks down because the Bible says we are only *like* sheep.

The picture turns from out of doors to indoors, from a sheep to a guest. In fact, from now on the sheep is treated like a shepherd. Have you ever heard of a sheep sitting at a table drinking from a cup inside a house? No, the metaphor has changed and David has had to burst out of it because he is a human being and he is more than a sheep. Yet it is still related to v. 4 because the enemies are still around. There is a continuity of theme even if the metaphor has changed.

But now his enemies are beaten, licking their wounds, looking on amazed, because he is not only now being treated like a shepherd; he is being treated by the shepherd. The shepherd is spreading a table, and those beaten enemies are looking on amazed. Quietly, the shepherd is spreading the table and it is a picture now of eastern hospitality, and you have got to understand eastern hospitality to appreciate this verse.

There are three things you do when you invite people over for an eastern meal. First, you get the best meal you can ready. Second, when the guest arrives you anoint his hair with oil to make it smooth, shiny, and smell nice. They did not do that themselves before they came, it was the host's job to spruce up his guest. We might say, "Would you like to go and wash your hands?" But then they said, "I'll anoint your head." The third thing you did was to give them a drink before the meal, which is still done today. But to show real hospitality, you went on pouring until it ran right over the top. It was a gesture saying, "I'll give you all I can."

Here is the sheep, sitting at the table with the wolves looking on, and the shepherd is laying a spread, smoothing his hair down, filling a cup to the brim. How does the sheep feel now? It is a lovely picture, isn't it? That is how you feel when you come out of the valley of the shadow. You come out of the gorge to gorge yourself. You come to a feast after the fight. That is why the metaphor changes; what a delight it is. In v. 1 he says, "I'll always have necessities"; in v. 5, luxuries – brimming over.

Finally v. 6 – his destiny. The final verse puts both metaphors together; the pictures get mixed up again. There is a fleeting glance back at the sheep and at the guest. In the first half of the last verse you have got a sheep and in the second half you have got a guest and he puts it all together in one glorious thought with Hebrew parallelism, which means that their poetic form was to repeat the same thought in other words.

So he looks forward to two things and there is a paradox here because he has mixed metaphors: he is outdoors and indoors at the same time; he is walking along the road, and he is sitting at the table at the same time.

These are two aspects of the Christian truth. You can never contain the whole of the Christian experience in one metaphor. So look at the first part: he looks forward to peaceful days – all the days of my life, not just some of them; the bright ones and the dark ones. What is going to happen? He is going to be chased. The sheep is not basically aggressive; the sheep's instinct is always to run. They are easily chased – anything can chase them and they instinctively run in panic.

Sheep are forever looking around and tense if there is something else around – ready to run. They expect to be chased. They have no real defence, no sharp fangs. A few rams are an exception but most sheep can't defend themselves. So they are always being chased. Literally, the Hebrew word is not "follow" but "chased". The word "surely" is not the word "surely" but the word "only". I am sorry to destroy all these illusions. But he is saying this: all the days of my life the only things that will ever chase me will be goodness and mercy.

A schoolboy once wrote for his R.E. lesson that the names for God's sheepdogs are Goodness and Mercy. I like that: chased by Goodness and Mercy. You don't run from those two things, you let them catch you – only goodness and mercy will chase me all the days of my life. The word "goodness", however, means generosity. It means someone near me who will just go on giving and giving. I am not going to run away from someone who is going to keep on giving to me, are you? Not on your life!

The word "mercy" is a lovely Hebrew word, *chesed*, which means loyalty, steady support, sticking to someone through thick and thin. It is the word that is used of marriage. It is the word that is used so often of God for his people. It is often translated "loving kindness" or "mercy", but I think "loyalty" conveys the heart of that word. Well, with generosity and loyalty chasing you, who is going to run? Not me!

That is the sheep; now the guest. "I'll be at home with this God as long as I live." The Hebrew words are not "forever" but "as long as I live". It is a parallel to the first part. He is talking about the rest of his life: all my days; as long as I live. He says: on the one hand goodness and mercy will chase me and I'll let them catch me; on the other hand, I will never be without a home; I'm going to live with God. David wrote this Psalm at the time which ended the period when David himself was hunted, when his own son tried to seize the throne and David went into hiding. He hid in the dark valleys of the shadow, down by En-Gedi by the Dead Sea. David had been hounded but one day he came back to Jerusalem to stay, and he knew he was there for the rest of his time, and he said, "I'm going to dwell in the house of the Lord; I'm going to live with God for the rest of my life." He was thinking of a particular building – the temple. He lived right next door to it; his palace was almost part of it, "I'm going to live there." For us there is no literal temple on earth we can go into and say, "That's where God lives." In the New Testament we are told, "You are the temple of God". So the Christian, even while he is travelling the road as a sheep, is dwelling in the house of the Lord at the same time. For he *is* the house of the Lord; he is at home with God.

You may not have a house, but you will never lack a home, for the Lord will be your dwelling place through all generations. So that is how he finishes. What a triumphant conclusion! As a sheep, he will only be chased by generosity and loyalty. As a guest, he has not only come to the house of the Lord and sat at his table, he has come to stay. Unbelievers only visit the Lord from time to time when they are in an emergency. Believers live with him and they stay with him for the rest of their lives.

In conclusion, did you notice there are three things missing from this Psalm? They are not here, they are somewhere else in the Bible, but I want to mention them. It is not surprising that in six verses you miss something out, is it? What are these three things? Number one: the relationship of the sheep with each other. That is a very important part. If you are going to follow this Shepherd you will be with other sheep. When Peter responded to Jesus' call "Follow me", his brother Andrew came along too and they were so different. When James responded to the Good Shepherd's call "Follow me", John came along too. They had to learn to live together. When sheep are in-fighting their danger is much greater.

Jesus the Good Shepherd, on the night before he died, said, "I want you to love one another". There must be peace among my flock, there must be harmony, there must not be back biting; you must follow me together. Some of the sheep he even entrusts with the task of helping him to care for the others. To Simon Peter he said, "Feed my sheep." Simon Peter later said to elders in a church, "Tend the flock of God." Our relationship to each other as sheep is not in this Psalm, which may be why people outside the church like it – because it doesn't challenge them about their relationship to the flock.

The second thing that is missing here is the responsibility of the sheep to the Shepherd. It is all: he leads me; he will look after me; he will keep me safe. It is all about the responsibility of the Shepherd, but there are responsibilities of the sheep and they are there implicitly if not explicitly. The responsibility of the sheep is to feed when he produces the green pasture; it is to follow when he leads; it is to feast when he lays the table. He doesn't do everything for us. A sheep must follow, a sheep must feed, a sheep must feast. He provides and he protects but he doesn't want you doing nothing. The responsibility of the sheep to the Shepherd is there implicitly. Above all, are you willing to walk in righteousness? We will look at that in Psalm 24.

The third and last thing that is missing from this Psalm is the readiness of the Shepherd to die for the sheep. To David, that would be the ultimate disaster for the sheep. They would be left without protection. They would be left without anyone to look after them. So David did not put into this Psalm what was true – that a shepherd in his day and until the 1930s could be killed for looking after a sheep properly.

As late as 1930, H.B. Morton in *In the Steps of the Master* describes how they found a shepherd dead, battered, bleeding, by his wandering sheep. Why didn't David include that? Well, because to say the shepherd would die would be to take the Shepherd from the sheep. He did not know what we know now, so he could not put it in.

Jesus said, "I am the good Shepherd." The one thing a good shepherd does is to value the life of the sheep more than his own and he is willing to lay down his life for the sheep. He said he would do that and he did. He told them he had many sheep to die for. He told his Jewish disciples he had other sheep which were not of this fold, referring to us Gentiles. We have got to learn to get on together, Jew and Gentile in the flock. But he said: For other sheep, for you as well, I lay down my life and I take it up again. So Jesus could include it, and he did.

God saw it all and knew it all from the beginning to the end, before he inspired David to write this Psalm, edited

David's psalms, and when he edited them he put Psalm 23 right after Psalm 22. So God put it in if David didn't. The fact is that you cannot come to Psalm 23 until you have been through Psalm 22. You can't have a shepherd until you have got a Saviour. You cannot come under the crook until you have been under the cross. You cannot be served by this Saviour until you have been saved by him.

READ PSALM 24

Psalms 22, 23, and 24 are a sandwich in much the same way as 1 Corinthians 12, 13, and 14 are a sandwich. In both cases, most people lick the jam out of the middle because it is sweet. Whereas many people know Psalm 23 and could probably recite it backwards, Psalm 24 is not so well known and certainly not so popular. Its theme is not so sweet, and so we lick the jam out and we leave the two pieces of bread on either side. I return briefly to Psalm 23, to the sheep and their shepherd, I quoted a shepherd who gave me two illustrations from his work for my work.

The second was this: he talked about a ewe that was blind because for some reason she had not been eating enough of the right food. On top of this, the lamb she was carrying was growing so rapidly during the last month of pregnancy, she had to convert her own body resources to provide energy for herself and the lamb. Because she is not getting enough carbohydrates, the fat breakdown is incomplete and poisonous toxins are built up. One of the early symptoms is blindness, which in turn affects further feeding and accelerates the problem. Now that is what happens when you don't get enough carbohydrates, and if you lick the jam out of Psalm 23 and don't take the carbohydrates of Psalm 22 and Psalm 24, then you will be blind to further truths. So we are going to eat the whole sandwich. You see, the general theme of Psalm 22 is pain, and that is mentally disturbing—we don't like to think about pain. The general theme of Psalm 23 is an atmosphere of peace and green pastures and still waters. Ah now, that is a little more congenial; we like that. The theme of Psalm 24 is purity, and that is morally disturbing.

So we are mentally disturbed by Psalm 22, we are morally disturbed by Psalm 24, but Psalm 23, "Oh, that's nice; that's comforting," as long as we just switch off slightly when we talk about the "valley of the shadow" and the "paths of righteousness." But Psalm 24 comes in to complete the sandwich, and that puts the whole thing in context, as we shall see. These three related psalms are a balanced diet for the sheep, if you like. They have the sweetness but they have the carbohydrates, so let us look at the way they relate.

The theme of Psalm 22 was a judicial execution, a cross. The theme of Psalm 23 was a pastoral occupation, the crook. The theme of Psalm 24 is a ceremonial coronation, a crown. These are the three dimensions that give us a beautiful, deep view of Jesus Christ—the cross, the crook, and the crown, and they are in the right order, too. You come to the cross first, you have his crook laid upon you second, and one day you will share his glory and wear his crown – third. So that relates the theme and we are first going to look again at our Lord as Saviour, then again as Shepherd, and now as sovereign—who is this King of glory?

At first sight, Psalm 24 is a bit of a hotch potch. Did you get that impression? In fact, the psalmist himself realised that and he split it into a number of songs, and he said, "Selah," in the middle. Did you ever know what that meant? Nobody actually knows. Scholars have just guessed at it; I have even seen one who thought it was what David said when he broke a guitar string. I'm quite sure that is not the right one, but I think the meaning that certainly clicks with me is the meaning that scholars say is: "Pause, stop; think about that; just give a little time to let that sink in because we are going to move on to something else, and if you rush on too quickly without thinking about it, then you could lose the challenge of what you have just read. This particularly applies where the word "Selah" comes in twice here. There is a very deep challenge to every one of us in the middle of the Psalm, and then it says, "Selah". Before you rush on, stop, pause, wait a moment, think about it. Then it moves onto a totally different vision of the Lord in all his glory. When you get to the end of that, it says, "Now don't rush onto the next item of worship; stop – think about that too and let it sink in." So it is not a hotch potch, but it is a variety. We have moved from the worm's eye view in Psalm 22 to a bird's eye view in Psalm 24, and we are now looking at the whole world, at the whole human race. It has become less personal; there is no "I", no "me" in this Psalm. We are now looking out at our world, out at the human race, and up to God. It is more objective, and it is good to be taken out of yourself.

Many people have been touched at points of personal need when studying Psalm 23. Some have told me they have been through a valley of deep shadow and the Shepherd saw them through. But in Psalm 24 we are not preoccupied with ourselves except insofar as we shall do a bit of self-examination. We are going to finish up looking at the Lord and the King of glory, and that is a very healthy thing for us to do.

A zoom lens is a very familiar object to us now. I haven't got one; I wish I had. They are great things for photographers. It is as if the psalmist had a zoom lens and he zooms in from a wide picture which includes the whole earth, a shared place for all people to live in, and then he zooms in on one hill, a holy hill, which is a special place where some people can go. Then he zooms right in to one place: the glorious gates of a citadel; the supreme place for one man to live in. So there is a kind of zooming in, and that gives you the thread between the three parts of the Psalm, which otherwise might not hang together in your mind. We are starting with a broad landscape; we are zooming in to a hill, and then we are focusing on one set of doors on that hill, which opens up a very special place for just one man.

I have often taught people to look for a key word. Did you notice one in this Psalm? The one which will unlock the whole Psalm and its meaning for you is "who". Now of the three sections in the Psalm, the question is not asked of the broad landscape because it does not need to be asked. He doesn't begin, "Who shall live in the earth and the fullness thereof?" because we know perfectly well who lives there: billions of people. But when you zoom into that special hill, you have to ask the question: who is going to go there? When you zoom further in on those special gates, you have to ask: and who is going to go through those gates? You have to answer these questions. In the second part, you have to ask whether you will be among the "who" of that second section. In the third, we have to ask: and who will ultimately be the King in this world of ours? Who will ultimately reign? Well, you know the answer to that one already.

Let us look at verses 1–2, which I call *the established earth; a shared place for all.* We all live in it. The big question here is: who owns it? The answer comes very emphatically. In the Hebrew language, when you want to emphasise a word you don't underline it, you put the word at the beginning of the sentence. In Hebrew, it doesn't say, "The earth is the Lord's and the fullness thereof," because that would make the earth most important. In the Hebrew it says: Lord's is the earth. The God of the Jews owns this planet. He is the owner, but he is not fully the occupier.

Now the implications of these first few words are staggering. When I began to write down the sheer implications of those words I realised I could preach a whole series of sermons on the implications and still never exhaust them. The first one that hit me hard was their religious implication. We are now in a day when it is assumed that there should be tolerance between all religions and that the religion that fits that culture is best for those people. So there is now the general idea that "Allah" is the best god for the Arabs, and Hindu gods are the best gods for the Indians, and so on; that we should be tolerant of one another and not interfere with one another's culture – "stay with your own religion; don't spread it".

Don't be fooled; other religions are not taking that attitude. Behind a three-month exhibition of the world of Islam in London (which was happening when I was teaching on Psalms) is a direct evangelistic desire to make Britain Muslim. It is not a cultural thing; behind it is a direct attempt to introduce another religion to British people in this country and not just to Pakistani immigrants. The Queen opened it, and the then bishop of Guildford wrote a very controversial report saying we should be favourable to Islam, but there is just one, simple answer to all that: "The earth is the Lord's."

The earth is the Lord's; he owns the whole planet, and that is why Christianity is both universal and exclusive. It has got to be taken everywhere and it can never be mixed with another religion, and it can never be tolerant of another religion. There is only one God, the I AM. In fact, the Hebrew here says: "I AM owns this planet". It is all his, and God is no more the exclusive property of the English or the Americans than he is of the Chinese or the African or the South American.

Woe betide us if we overlook the implication for religion. People are shopping around now; they will try anything –meditation from the East, yoga from the East, and so on. But the earth is the Lord's, and the God of the Jews is the only God who exists.

Therefore, not only is he the only God for us, he is the only God for everybody else. We have just got to take this message to the whole earth. If it simply said he was the God of the Holy Land, that would be a different matter. Every land is his land already. England is his land. He is not foreign anywhere.

There are other implications as well. The political one comes next. Think of the political implications of the first sentence "The earth is the Lord's." As I look at the daily news, in every place where there is serious trouble it is over one question: who the land belongs to. It is because one group is saying, "It's ours; it's mine," and another group is saying, "It isn't; we got here first." The atheists and the agnostics think that the earth is up for grabs, but it isn't. It already belongs to someone.

There is no such thing as freehold, and even if your solicitor tells you that you have got freehold, you haven't. The Lord could take it from you tonight. "You fool, tonight your soul will be required of you" – and you will leave it behind. You have only got it leasehold; you are not the landlord. You are the tenant. Nobody owns this world; the earth is the Lord's. There was a time in Britain when this influenced our political outlook and decisions. That time has long since gone, alas.

In 1851 they opened the Great Exhibition in London. It was an exhibition of what we were able to produce and what we had done, an exhibition of our culture. Now it is the Islamic culture that is exhibited in London, but then it was British. We had something we could exhibit. Do you know what the motto for that exhibition was? It was on the notepaper and above the exhibition: "The earth is the Lord's and the fullness thereof." When they built the Royal Exchange in the City of London, there it is written on the Royal Exchange.

How many of them look up and read it before they go into the office? The earth is the Lord's – and whatever part of it you handle, it is his you are handling, not yours, whether it be shares, property or whatever – the earth is the Lord's. The political implications – if only you could get warring factions just to sit down and agree on one thing, that each country is the Lord's, and start there. Then ask *him* how much of it he wants them each to have.

Can you imagine the transformation there would be on the world's scene if we could do that? If Jew and Arab could sit down and say, "It's the Lord's – which part does he want us to have?" Because I am sure the Lord wants the Arabs to have a home, as well as the Jews. In Acts 17 Paul in Athens said, "God has allotted the boundaries of habitations of the nations." God has planned it all out; he has drawn the atlas up. It is because we don't listen to him and we grab, grab, grab. We forget that it is his to begin with.

In the long run, all the land we will get will be what God allows us. If we try to get more than what he allows us, we will finish up with less than what he started with. It is not just Hitler who learned that, Britain has learned it too. The earth is the Lord's.

Then two little codicils are added. First, everything it produces and all its people. Now again, think of the implications of that. This earth, says the Psalm, is fullness. It is full, and if you have ever seen pictures of the moon or of Mars, have you noticed how empty they are? This is the only planet in the entire universe, as far as we know, that can support life, because it is full. It is teeming with minerals, vegetables, animals. It is full, and because it is full, billions of people can live on this tiny little speck of interstellar dust – and all that belongs to God.

Can you imagine what would happen if we felt the North Sea oil and gas was not ours but his? Or if the Arabs thought of all the black gold underneath their desert sands – oil as his, not ours? The world would be a very different place. You see, God didn't put minerals evenly through the world. He put gold and platinum in South Africa, not to make South Africa rich, not to enable them to hold out militarily against others, not to make them better than any other country, but to give them something to share with the whole world.

You see, God gives you something to share with other people. The biggest difference that comes when you grasp this first verse is that you don't talk about your rights any more, you talk about your responsibilities. You don't think about what you can grab; you think about what you can share with those who have not got that in their land. Those with valuable minerals on their property will say, "Now those people over there don't have that, so we must share. They have something that we don't have so they share." Do you see?

The world was meant to be operated as one economic unit with one owner, and the problem is that it is not; it is operated by hundreds of owners, each thinking that what they have managed to grab is theirs as a bargaining point. The earth is the Lord's. All its produce and all its people, whether they be rich or poor, clever or simple, black or white, whatever they be. They all belong to him in one sense. There is another in which they don't, but there is a sense in which they do, which means simply that every person is at God's disposal.

My life is not my own to do with what I want; it never has been. If I do that, I will pay the bill. My life belongs to him, and as soon as I find what he planned for it, then I will find the fulfilment for which I seek. Because I belong to him, and he planned a life for me which would be for him. My main object in being on earth is for him, not me. I belong to him and my ultimate destiny is in his hands, and he will do with me what he decides. All the people in it belong to him.

This would be a revolution if we didn't study any other verse but took this and worked through its spiritual implications, its political implications, its social implications, its economic implications. Why, I could produce a manifesto for the next election just on this one verse. It wouldn't get many votes: it all belongs to him. Why? What reason has he to claim such rights and give me only responsibilities? What right have you, Lord, to say this? Why does it all belong to you? Why do I belong to you? Why do all the minerals belong to you?

God would say two reasons, and I think they are good enough and beyond dispute. One: I made it; two, I manage it." Is that good enough? There would be no land to live on unless he had literally, as it says here in Psalm 24, "raised up dry land from the bed of the ocean". Now remember this is a pre-scientific era in which this was stated, and remember that at the top of the Swiss Alps you can find the fossils of sea urchins, and you get something of the marvellous inspiration of scripture. He pushed up the dry land from the bed of the ocean and gave us somewhere to live. But if he had stopped there and just sort of pushed it up and said, "There you are, there's a dry land to live on," we would be dead because we can't live on a dry land.

Flying over the Sahara Desert, I looked down. Nobody lived there. It is dry land; it is pushed up from the ocean bed, but you cannot live there because dry land needs water again for life. So God, in his amazing mercy, lifts millions of tons of water from the sea, purifies it, and drops it gently enough not to hurt us on the dry land. He manages it. It doesn't do it like clockwork; it doesn't do it by itself. If God was not awake, the sun would not have risen this morning and so he made it and he manages it, and that gives him the right to own it. I can think of no better reason.

Our Maker and Manager says: "All the produce and all the people on this planet are mine – cattle on a thousand hills, all the silver and the gold is mine", and, "If I were hungry I would not tell you". It is all his.

We move on to the second section. It is interesting, by the way, that the Jews sang Psalm 24 every Sunday morning. Did you know that? The Jews sing a different Psalm every morning, and on Sunday morning they sing this one. But remember for Jews that is not the day of worship, it is the first day of work in the week. Psalm 24 is for those who are going to work. So as you go to work, just say to yourself: "The earth is the Lord's, everything and everyone in it, those people sitting around me – they belong to the Lord. Those fields I can see out there—they belong to the Lord. Those factories, every bit of raw material going into those factories, belongs to the Lord." It is exciting; it transforms the world for you.

Now when God made all this planet and its produce and its people, he looked down from heaven and said, "That's very good." Not even a man would say that today, much less God. He looks down at the way we have grabbed it and squabbled over it and fought over it and killed each other by the million for its produce and for its land. Think of thirty million dead in World War II, and many more killed since then. You consider it. God looks down and he says, "That's not so good. In fact, that's very bad." Even men are saying, "I don't know what the world's coming to. It's a dreadful place, a dreadful situation."

So God looked down and he said, "Out of all that world which has gone so bad, I'm going to keep one little place good, as it was originally." He chose a little hilly land. He chose, out of all the land in the world, a little patch the size of Wales, where three continents meet – Europe, Asia, and Africa, and of this little land he said: now that's going to be my land; all the land is mine, but this is going to be a holy land.

The word "holy" means healthy. That is why he chose a hilly land and not a swamp or a low-lying river delta, which is where human civilisation invariably grows. In fact, I've told you that if God allowed the polar ice caps to melt, the oceans would rise by two hundred feet and almost every major city in the world would go under, but Jerusalem would be safe. He chose it up in the hills, much healthier than the low-lying delta and swamp where civilisation began at the Tigris, the Euphrates and the Nile. This was to be his healthy, holy land.

The people in that land were exactly the same as everybody anywhere else, indeed worse because they had had more blessing and a better chance. So out of that land he kept one hill, less than a mile long, one ridge, and he said: "That's my holy hill and that's the place I'm going to meet you. I'll only meet you in a holy place." So there was a holy hill, and on it stood the holy place. Inside the holy place was the holy of holies, just one hill out of the whole planet that God was trying to keep right – a very precious place to every Jew and to every Gentile too.

Now comes the question: who could possibly step on that hill? He that has clean hands and a pure heart. That rules me out for a start. I think it rules every one of you out. That is the problem. How is God going to keep that hill clean? How is he going to keep it as it was meant to be? It is like an operating theatre. Can you imagine somebody going into his garden and spreading it with muck and then digging hard and weeding, and then marching off to his friend who is a surgeon in an operating theatre and rubbing his hands and going in saying,: "How are you getting on? I've had a good day." Can you imagine it? You wouldn't go into an operating theatre with dirty hands; you watch the surgeon scrub even his nails out; slightest bit of bacteria could be death. If you were invited to Buckingham Palace, would you go with grubby hands to shake the hand of the Queen? If you are going to meet the King of kings, the first thing is clean hands. The hands are a symbol of what we have done, our work, our leisure, what we have done underhandedly. That is an interesting term, isn't it: "underhand".

The Queen would only be bothered about your clean hands if she got her white gloves dirty through shaking hands with you. But God goes further still. He doesn't look at clean hands; he looks inside as well. Notice that he does look at the outside. I have heard some preachers say he is not bothered about the outside, but he is. He is bothered about hands, and cleanliness is next to godliness. But he is also bothered about hearts. He is not impressed with appearances where they are not matched with something inside: he that has clean hands and a pure heart. The man who wrote this Psalm had neither.

Who will ever get into that holy hill? Who will ever be able to meet God? Who will ever be able to climb that hill? If we had been alive in David's day, we would have thought twice. We would have been frightened stiff about going on that hill. You would be safer walking into an asbestos factory full of dust than going into the presence of a holy God as a sinner. Who can ascend that hill? Who can scale those heights? If you manage to reach them – and it is uphill work to make yourself good – even if you managed it, who could stay there? Who could stand in his presence? Who could climb that high anyway? But even if you could, could you keep it up? Could you stand there? Never.

Purity in heart is here defined in terms of two more things: one, those who have not based their life on things that don't ring true. In the Authorized Version, he has not lifted up his soul to vanity. The word "soul" doesn't mean the spiritual side of us, it means "life". The word "vanity" means "hollow". This means somebody who has not based his life on such hollow things that he has become an unreal person – one of the plastic people of today who has based their life on such toys, such baubles, such idols, that ultimately he finishes up a hollow, unreal person; a person who is only on the outside. Do you know what I mean? A person whose heart isn't in what he says or what he does, a person who is doing it for sake of appearance, for the sake of the neighbours. He who has not lifted his soul up to vanity, not based his life on things that don't ring true.

Because what you build *on* you build *in*, and if you build your life on hollow things, you become a hollow person. If you live in a plastic world, you become a plastic person. The other definition of "pure in heart" given here is a "man of his word", someone whose word is as good as his bond, who if he makes a promise keeps it – because God is a God of truth. To be pure in heart is to say what you mean and let your "yes" be "yes" and your "no" be "no."

Here is the question: who? There is not a single person among us who could have walked up that hill in the days of King David. By a special concession, only one man, once per year, was allowed in, and it wasn't King David, and it was only a concession; he had no right to be there. Oh, who will do it? The admission is pretty high, but if you could do it, if you could be holy as he was holy, if you could be perfect as he was perfect, then you would receive God's approval which would mean two things: he would succour you, and he would support you. He would succour you by blessing your family, your work, your relationships – everything. You would receive blessing from God. More than that, he would vindicate you because we are in a world where people attack you, where they criticise, libel, slander, try to attack you, and he would protect you and prove you to be in the right. If you could only reach that height, he would defend you against anyone – that is what it says here. The Lord would save us from our critics. He would do all that for us, and that is why we need to go and find him because we need succour; there are situations which need his blessing, which are beyond us.

Life is too much to cope with. There are situations in which we need his support, when we feel that others are against us and we need somebody to stand for us. He will do both provided we have got clean hands and a pure heart – there is the dilemma.

"Such," says the psalmist, "is the generation that seek God, that go looking for God." This is the real generation gap, you know. There are only two generations: the generation that seeks God and the generation that doesn't. The biggest gap is between those generations and they are not age gaps. Such is the generation that goes looking for God because frankly, unless you are in this condition, who is going to go looking for God? You would keep right away from a holy hill if you could. You need his succour; you need his support. You may be asking for that but you wouldn't seek him. You would seek his blessing and you would say, and unbelievers say, "Well, God bless." Comedians say it at the end of their act, "Good night and God bless you." Everybody says that; they want the blessing but such is the generation of those who seek God because until you are fit for God's company, the last person you want to spend time with is God. It is too uncomfortable; too disturbing.

That is what Jacob did, he met God face-to-face and that is why he is mentioned here. He had an immediate encounter with a holy God, and do you know what happened? He limped for the rest of his life. He was lamed; his leg was pulled out of joint as he struggled and wrestled with God, and for the rest of his life you could always tell Jacob, limping along. He limped away from that encounter and he came off worse. Those who want to seek God know that they will wrestle and that God will have to defeat them and break them in. So the only generation that seeks God are those who really want to climb that hill and want to be fit for his company. The rest don't bother.

We may well ask the question then: who? Do you know my answer? If I were living in David's day my answer would be, very simply: nobody! That is why the Old Testament is not the gospel. That is why the Old Testament is not good news. If the Old Testament tells me I have got to have clean hands, which means my conduct has got to be faultless; if the Old Testament tells me I have got to have a pure heart, that my character must be flawless before I can dare to climb that hill, much less stand in his presence, before I can have his blessing, before he can vindicate me, before I can see him face-to-face and have a personal relationship with him; if that is so, that is bad news because nobody can climb that hill.

But this is where the New Testament comes in. It reverses the Old Testament. The New Testament would read Psalm 24 in this order: verses six, five, four, three. When you read it in that order it says: "Those who seek the Lord will be saved by him, vindicated, justified, blessed, and given clean hands and a pure heart" – and that is good news. It is just putting it the other way around. That is why preaching the Old Testament alone is bad news. For the Old Testament says that when you are good enough, you can go up to God; the New Testament says: God came down to you and accepted you as you are and is going to lift you there. Not because he has lowered his standards but because he is going to lift you to them – that is grace.

Law came by Moses, and law bangs you down. Law says: Don't you dare come near God like that. Law says: Get away until you're holy. But grace and truth came through Jesus Christ, and grace says "Come", and sinners start climbing that hill. That was the very hill on which Abraham offered up Isaac and nearly killed Isaac. It was the very hill where that happened. When Abraham was about to kill his own son, God said: "Stop!" The angel held his hand, and when he turned around he saw a sheep with its head in thorns, and he offered the sheep up instead. Two thousand years later, on the same hill, the Lamb of God, with his head caught in a ring of thorns, was offered up. God had provided. This is the holy hill referred to here. Sinners now climb it, not to offer themselves or their sons, but they climb it to see God offer his Son. It is the same hill. They climb it not to go to the holy of holies; they climb it to go to the cross, and they start as they are and then God begins to lift them.

We move on now to the third and last section of the Psalm, vv. 7–10. The holy hill is a special place for some – in the Old Testament none; but in the New Testament all who will come. Now let us look at the supreme place for one man. There is a change of tone. You feel like pausing there for a few moments of silence. We now look at the glorious gates that are going to open for one person. You almost have to shout these verses or certainly to sing them: fling wide the gates! There is a change from the serious to the joyful; from what could be disturbing and depressing to something that is exciting and stimulating.

First of all, our invitation – it is a call to all people to open up. Who is there? Who is outside waiting to come in? It is the king – open up. Now there are two things described to be open, I believe. I don't think it's just parallelism referring to the same entrance. I believe the gates belong to the city and the doors belong to the citadel within the city. Old gates had to be lifted up. Indeed, many large doors had to be. They were counter-balanced; they were in grooves, and they were pulled up with ropes, like a portcullis, for defence. They were not easily opened and they were only able to be opened from the inside. "Fling wide the city gates! Open up! Be lifted up! Be lifted up, O gates," and it would be the people inside who would have to lift them up.

But the citadel doors have to be opened up from the outside, and I get a strong impression as I read these verses,

I can see very clearly an ancient city with a very thick, stark wall, and a gate in it that had to be hauled up with ropes, and right in the heart of the city, an empty palace—a prince has been away for years at the wars, and now he is on his way back, victorious. The shout goes up: "The king is coming; up with the gate! Open up those ancient doors!" That word "ancient" gave me that impression. Why "ancient" there, as if they had not been used in a long time – as if the palace had been lying empty and the king had been away and now he is coming back victorious? That is the impression I get distinctly. I think that fits.

But if we then ask the fundamental question as to who this king is, we can answer it by asking when this came true. Here I have seven answers and I don't mind which one you take. I know which I take, and I will probably hint at that. Who is this king of glory? The Lord. Now the word "LORD" in the Old Testament in capital letters means "Yahweh"; "I AM"; it is a name.

If we take it solely to mean "God; Yahweh; the God of the Jews", then there are two possible occasions, one of which to my mind is just nonsense. But it came from no less a person than the blind poet Milton in *Paradise Lost*. He thought this Psalm referred to the day when God went back to heaven having created the earth in six days. If you read Milton's *Paradise Lost*, it is there imagined that the angel shall fling wide the gates. God has been so busy on Earth, making Earth, and now he is coming back to heaven. I just don't think that is what is referred to at all. But it is a possible, and you can take it if you wish.

Much more meaningful to me is this: there is a place called Kiriath Jearim. It is where the ark of the covenant rested when David had defeated the Philistines, rescued the ark of the covenant – which was the symbol of God's presence – and was bringing it back to Jerusalem. A man called Uzzah dared to touch this holy thing and died of a heart attack immediately. Everybody was a bit scared, so they decided to leave the ark at Kiriath Jearim for a bit.

A short while later they brought it in triumph to Jerusalem. It was as if God was coming, having defeated the Philistines, having been mighty in battle, having been undefeated, having enabled David to come through victorious – and now the ark, the presence of God, is being brought back into Jerusalem. "Fling wide the gates, open up the doors of the holy place inside! The Lord of Hosts is coming in." David was so excited that day that he danced before the Lord. His wife did not approve of dancing in religion but I am sure the Lord did. They brought the ark in with tremendous joy and I think that would be the original setting of this Psalm—would you not? Open up.

David coming with the ark towards the holy hill has two feelings. One is a feeling of hesitation, "I don't have clean hands or a pure heart. I shouldn't be climbing that hill." Yet then there is the triumph, "Oh, but the king can go in, so open up the gates. We'll bring the ark in." I think that is when it was written, but I am not going to limit the meaning of this phrase there. The answer to the question, "Who can be brought in?"—If it isn't Yahweh alone, who else could it be? Well there is one other and his name is Jesus. For Jesus of Nazareth is the Lord of Hosts. The titles that are given to Yahweh in the Old Testament are given to Jesus in the New Testament – that is why we call him "the Lord".

When you look at Jesus' life on Earth there are five possible occasions when this Psalm is appropriate. There is first the occasion on Palm Sunday when he rode into Jerusalem, down from the Mount of Olives, up the other side of the Kidron Valley, in at the golden gate, the Eastern Gate, to the temple area and came right in triumphant.

"Who is this?"

"It's Jesus of Nazareth" – but it was the King of glory. That is one possible meaning.

Another possible one you find in what is called the "golden legend" in southwest France. It is a legend: that for the three days Jesus spent in Hades after his death, the angels kept shouting "Fling wide the gates", and the gates of hell on the third day gave way. He rose from the dead and came back to Earth. That does not convince me, partly because it is legend, but it is a possibility.

Yet another possibility, and the one which the Christian Church has made most of, is that this refers to the ascension. Psalm 24 is sung in Anglican churches on Ascension Day, when he went up, no longer feeling like a worm on the cross, but like an eagle soaring through the clouds: fling wide the gates! He led captivity captive. All authority in heaven and earth is now given to him. The King of glory is coming back; open up the doors of the citadel. Well, it is appropriate then, but I still do not think we have exhausted it.

What about the day when he comes back, when his feet stand on the Mount of Olives again? The King has been absent, and he has been absent because he has been by the right hand of God until all his enemies are under his feet, even death. When all his enemies are under his feet, he is coming back, and he will come back across the Kidron Valley. He will come back and it says: he will suddenly return to his temple.

Here is the most striking thing: of all the gates and the city walls of Jerusalem, there is just one that is bricked up. You can walk through every one of the others. But the one that is bricked up is that golden gate, the east gate of the temple. Nobody really quite knows why it is bricked up. There are some explanations but I will give you the best one. Ezekiel said this, five hundred years or more before. "Then he brought me back"– in vision that is – "to the outer gate of the temple which faces east, and it was shut. And he said to me, 'this gate shall remain shut. It shall not be opened, and no one shall enter by it. For the Lord, the God of Israel has entered by it; therefore, it shall remain shut.'" Only the prince may come into it.

Is that not striking? "Fling wide the gates" – how appropriate it is when he comes back and comes to that very gate to enter his own temple on that holy hill. He has been away for so long. "Open up the old doors; let him in".

But I still don't think we have exhausted it. Why is it repeated at the end of Psalm 24? Twice it says, "Fling wide the gates, who's coming? Fling wide the gates, who's coming?" Why twice?

Well, I believe there are two ascensions of Jesus. There is the one that happened two thousand years ago when heaven welcomed the returned victor, but he went by himself. There is another ascension coming when he will enter heaven with all his saints, and the gates will be flung open for the King of glory, the Lord of Hosts. There will be hosts; there will be at least a thousand million with him, even if he came this week. The Lord of Hosts is coming. We will sing Psalm 24 again on that day.

This has been an impersonal Psalm: looking at the universe; looking at mankind; looking at the world we live in. Now I want to look at you and to look at myself, and I want to look at three personal levels and give you a paradox, an apparent contradiction, at each level. I want to challenge you at the material level, I want to challenge you at the moral level, and I want to challenge you at the mystical level.

Here then are three simple paradoxes. Paradox number one: everything is ours and nothing is ours. The material challenge at the personal level of Psalm 24:1-2 is this: you are not the owner of anything you posses. The only person who can be robbed, in the strictest sense, is God himself because everything belongs to him. Therefore, my challenge is to sit loose to your possessions, to let material things be second in your life, or even lower down, and to realise that everything you have is his – not mine, not even ours, but *his*.

If you do not think that way, and if you start thinking, "Look what I've got," the Lord may say to you, "You fool, tonight you lose it." But if nothing is ours, everything is ours. The Lord Jesus made the world. Without him was not anything made. The Lord Jesus manages the world; he upholds all things by the word of his power. If the earth is the Lord's, and I am the Lord's, then all things are mine in Christ, and I shall inherit the earth. Isn't that a lovely paradox? Nothing is mine and everything is mine in Jesus Christ. That is the material challenge: to regard nothing as yours and to rejoice that everything is yours.

The paradox at the moral level is this: none of us is fit to be accepted by God, but he accepts us as we are. I want to underline that very deeply. God's standards are far too strict for human nature as it is. We might just manage to get the outside clean, which is what we usually get more concerned about. We will certainly not get the inside clean, so none of us is fit to stand in heaven before God. That is what makes us a little hesitant about going there too soon. But he accepts us as we are and he imputes Christ's righteousness to us and then he imparts it to us if we are hungry and thirsty for it. So that when we get to heaven we shall be holy, we shall be like him, for we shall see him as he is. After all, if I went to heaven as I am, I would spoil it for everybody else – most of all, for God. Yet he is willing to accept me and start there.

The third paradox is at the mystical level. This Lord is almighty; he has never been defeated in battle. He has overcome strongholds. He can batter his way into any city, yet he waits for the gates to be opened from the inside. The citadel in the heart of your life has been closed for a long time. Open it up. Even though this is the Lord who commands all the forces of the universe, who is strong and mighty in battle, the Lord of Hosts, he still waits for the person inside to open up. Remarkable! But as soon as I open the door of my heart, he flings wide the gates of heaven.

These are the three challenges to you. If you haven't flung wide those gates before the gates of Hades close on you, the gates of heaven remain barred from the inside to you forever. Fling wide the gates; open up those ancient doors, and let the King of glory come in.

READ PSALMS 42–43

We often hear of great tragedies, and many people are disturbed and perturbed and find themselves asking very big questions when they occur. It does not help if Christians are unreal in such situations and do not admit that we have problems for our peace of mind. There is, of course, a general problem: why does God allow any suffering at all in this world?

The oldest philosophical argument against belief in the God of the Bible is this: how can you believe in a God who is all loving and all-powerful and explain the world as it is? Proponents of that position might say: if God were all loving, but not all powerful, then we could understand why things happen as they do; God sympathises, but could not do anything about it. Like us, he would be trapped into the laws of cause and effect, which make these things happen. And likewise they may say: if God is all-powerful, but not all loving, then it might seem that he is using his power in an arbitrary and even cruel way, choosing some for blessing and some for evil. But if you believe that God is all-powerful and all loving, then you have a problem, for he could have stepped in to stop it. The question is facing us squarely in the face, "Why did he not do so?" We must be honest and face that question.

It comes to us all the more poignantly and powerfully when the tragedy has come to God's own people. If it is a mystery that anyone should suffer in this world, it is an even greater mystery when those who belong to God suffer as much, if not more, than those who don't. The cynic has a right to ask the question: "Why does God not look after his own people?" That is the question that has been raised by the history of the last two thousand years of the Jewish people. The more I read of their history and their sufferings, not just in our century, but down through the last two thousand years – with pogroms, genocide, concentration camps – I find myself saying, "Lord, why?" There is no slick answer to that question. "These are your people, yet they have suffered as much and more than any other people on earth." The most sobering experience you can have is to go through the Yad Vashem Memorial in Jerusalem, the memorial erected to the six million who were burnt in the crematoria of the concentration camps of Europe. "Why? God, if you are all powerful and all loving, why should your people, above all, have to go through this?" But Jews are not the only ones who have suffered through belonging to God. Christians also have a very stark record of profound suffering. I was reading Fox's Book of Martyrs. Its first chapter is entitled: Containing a History of the First Ten Persecutions of the Primitive Church from the Year of Our Lord Sixty-Four and the Reign of Nero until the Time of Constantine the Great".

I read this story with a mixture of horror and amazing admiration for a Saint Laurentius who, as he lay on the gridiron being fried to death, could tell the crowd he was done on one side and it was time to turn him over. I read here of a slave girl, again fried to death rather than betray her Lord; of a mother separated from her baby, allowed to hear the baby crying for the milk and being told, "You can suckle your baby if you deny Jesus." Why? Saint Teresa of Avila once said, "Lord, do you treat all your friends this way?" when she was going through a time of deep suffering. The Lord said, "Yes." With daring and bold faith she said, "Then Lord, I'm not surprised your friends are so few."

Honesty is needed in two areas before I declare anything

to help bring some peace of mind. First of all, I believe that when Christians are confronted with such tragedy, there is demanded an honesty about the presence of questions. Secondly, an honesty is demanded about the absence of answers. Here are two aspects of a basic honesty, which help us to be real. Let us face up with the fact that such tragedies raise questions in our mind. They are there, and however we pray and however outwardly we show a stiff upper lip, inside there are questions – why? But I want to say that the question of the unbeliever is quite different from the question of the believer.

I read the book of a film called *Voyage of the Damned*, about the voyage of a ship, The Saint Louis, which left Hamburg in May 1939 with 937 Jewish men, women and children on board. They set off in the hope of landing in Cuba and finding refuge on the other side of the Atlantic. But when they got there, Cuba refused entrance. They sailed for America, but America refused them entrance. They saw the dazzling lights of Miami from ten miles out, but they were not allowed in. They were shunted backwards and forwards while the nations decided where they should go. Each nation suggested somewhere else. America suggested Madagascar; Russia suggested central Africa, and each nation suggested somewhere else. Many of these people had already been in Dachau concentration camp and this book is based on the diaries and first-hand memories of those who were on that ship. They were finally shunted back to Europe, where some were accepted in Britain, some in Belgium, some in Holland, some in France, which meant that over two-thirds of them finished back up in the concentration camps from which they had escaped. On board the ship, one of the members of the German crew was making friends with one of the Jews. The Jew was called Aaron Pozner and he described Dachau, described the memory of the day when a guard had offered a prisoner a cigarette. When the prisoner accepted it, the cigarette was smashed into his face by a savage blow from the guard's riot stick. The Jew finished his description with, "That is what it is like to be a Jew in Germany."

The German crew member said, "But have you never lost your faith?" It was the first time anybody had asked Aaron such a question and it left him momentarily speechless. He later realised it would have been easier to say he was a Jew through an accident of birth, but he knew that would have been less than the truth – that, for him, being a Jew was far more than merely observing the ritual of his faith—that it reached deep into every aspect of his life. He had decided to say none of these things. Instead, he rose to his feet and simply said, "No; I have not lost my faith, but only a Jew would understand why."

For the Christian believer too, the question is different from the question of the unbeliever. The unbeliever throws in our face, "Where is your God?" In Psalm 42, the psalmist, going through intense suffering and opposition from other people, says in his prayer, "Lord, one of the worst things is that my enemies keep crying out, 'Where is your God in this situation? What is he doing about your suffering? Where is he? Where is your God?'"

Now the psalmist did not ask that question because he believed in God; he belonged to God. His question was not, "Where?" but "Why?" and he was honest enough to express it. He didn't say, "Where are you?" He said, "Why, God, are you doing this?" This is the difference between a man who believes in God and a man who doesn't, when he hears of the tragedy. The unbeliever says, "Where is God?" The believer says, "God, why?" That starts you from a different place.

There is a two-fold question, or it is in my mind and you may not identify with these, but you may. When I heard of some Christian workers killed, one after another, my first question was, "Why, Lord, are you wasting your resources? You could have stopped that, why did you not? Here are people you desperately need. Here is a situation which needs those missionaries. Lord, you seem to be throwing away your resources. You seem to be wasting lives. Why?"

Then, behind that, there was another question. It was again a question "Why?" It was not, "Where are you, Lord?" but, "Why are you hurting so many families, especially when they have made so much sacrifice for you? Men and women who have left their homes and their comforts and their culture, and they have done it for you, Lord; and parents and grandparents who have made the sacrifice of family life and let them go – why have you done this to them?"

So the first honesty that we must have is the honesty of admitting the presence of questions. The second honesty that I want to admit openly and freely is the honesty of the absence of answers. Years ago, I saw the film, *The Hiding Place*, the story of Corrie ten Boom. I met dear Corrie and she listened regularly to tapes from our fellowship.

Corrie went through Ravensbruck concentration camp. She went through as a Gentile, but she went there because she and her family had harboured and hidden Jews in Holland. It is one of the most moving films I ever saw. There is another film behind *The Hiding Place* about Corrie herself, and her reactions to seeing the film made, and some of her inner feelings.

I sat through the first film and I don't mind telling you, I wept through it. But there was one scene in which the women in their rags and their hunger, and their lice-ridden hut, turned on Corrie and Betsy as the two people in there who openly belonged to God. They said, "Why? How can you believe in a God who allows this to happen? How can you believe God is a God of love and a God of power when he doesn't do anything about this situation?" They were asking, "Where is your God?" I praise God for the honesty of Corrie in her reply, which was: "We do not know the answer to your question; we only know that we can face this situation with our faith and we could not face it without our faith." But she was honest enough to say, "We do not know the answer." There is an element of mystery in suffering and I remember someone saying to me when I was a young man, "David, if you understood everything about God then you would be God." Think that one through.

Consider Job's comforters: Eliphaz, Bildad, and Zophar. Their main problem was that they gave a cliché – an oversimplified answer to the question. Oversimplified answers are out of place when confronted with the mystery of suffering; glib clichés are cruel. They said to Job, "The answer's very simple: people who sin suffer. So you must have sinned, so you better get alone somewhere and look into your heart and find out what's gone wrong."

We, in the Christian Church down through these two thousand years, have given too glib an answer to the suffering of God's ancient people, the Jews. We have given the glib equation: your people killed Jesus two thousand years ago; no wonder you go to Dachau. That is too simple; that is to be a "Job's comforter". I do not believe it is the answer to the question. The question is much deeper than that and a Jew has the right to resent such a glib cliché. So let us be honest and say: "There are real questions and there are no answers."

Having said that, I now want to pick up the threads of something that was said quoting Dr Martin Lloyd Jones. When the doctor was approached by someone who had a real question of this kind on their minds, the doctor replied to the question: "Don't let the things you don't know spoil the things you do know." Now I want to pick that thread up and mention very briefly three things that we do know which we may apply to a tragic situation and which will help us to peace of mind, though it will not give the answer. I cannot give you the answer. If I could, I would be God. If you came to me and asked, "Why did God allow men and women who were serving him, who had given so much to him, to lose their lives suddenly and tragically?" Then I would have to say, "I cannot answer; I am not God", but I could talk about three things that have held me in my thinking and of which I am sure. Number one, the sovereignty of God in the present holds me; number two, the suffering of God in the past holds me; number three, the salvation of God in the future holds me.

Let me spell them out very simply. First of all: the sovereignty of God in the present. If people say, "Where is your God?" My answer is, "He is on the throne of the universe." There is no one above him and he is in complete control. I have to say that by faith, but I believe it. "Where is your God?" He is in control; that is where he is. He is at the controls of the universe. Therefore, I must follow that up by saying two things, which are hard truths to accept, but which I must accept if I am going to face reality.

Truth number one is: God is finally responsible. I cannot be fobbed off with the distinction between God's ordained will and God's permissive will. I mean by that: those who draw a distinction between what God decides and what he allows. The distinction is helpful as far as it goes, but it still means that God has allowed something.

I cannot believe that God *caused* something terrible; I cannot believe that God is malicious, cruel to his children, but if you say it is his permissive will, that does not remove the problem. God is still responsible for what has happened; the very fact that he did not intervene, and did not step in and allowed those certain tragic things to happen means that he is responsible. But having said that, I must go on to declare the second thing, which balances it up: if God is responsible for tragic events, he is not responsible to us. Now I want you to grasp this very important truth: God is responsible for these events, but he is not responsible to man. Let me tell you what I mean. When I study the book of Job, I find there that Job appears to be trying to justify himself again and again. He appears to be saying, "I don't deserve these tragedies; I don't deserve this suffering." But when I read between the lines, I find that Job is saying to God: you justify yourself to me; you have got to satisfy my intellect that you have a good reason for allowing these things to occur. You must answer to me before I can go on trusting you.

At the end of that magnificent book, which you ought to read when you are facing this kind of question, God says: "Job, have you forgotten who you're talking to? It's I who ask the questions, not you. Where were you when I laid the foundation of the earth? Where were you when I called forth the winds and the snow and the rain? Job, have you forgotten who you are and have you forgotten who I am?" Finally, Job comes to the point where he acknowledges that God is responsible, but he is not responsible to Job.

Now here is an important truth. God is responsible, in the last analysis, for everything that happens on planet earth and throughout the universe because he is on the throne and because he is in complete sovereignty and because there is no power above God, and everything is under the Lord's control. Therefore, he is responsible even for what he allows. But what he is not responsible for is to give me an explanation as to why he is doing anything. It is profoundly unfitting for the creature to say to the creator, "Explain yourself to me or I can't believe in you."

The right response to this first truth of God's sovereignty in the present is the response of submission. A tragedy is an opportunity to submit to the sovereignty of God and to say, "Your will be done." Now that is not popular talk; it is not an easy attitude for human beings to take. There are three levels of submission that I want to mention, each of them deeper than the previous one. There is, first of all, the submission to God because he is powerful. In other words, "God, you're bigger than I am so I have got to submit." There is a kind of submission that just says, "God is big and I'm small, so I have to submit." That is not true submission.

Then there is the second level of submission, which is to submit to God because he is holy and I am sinful. Here is not so much a physical degree of submission, but a moral degree of submission. I began to think about this. If I object to evil coming into my life, if I object to being hurt, if I object to tragedy invading the peace of my existence, then behind that objection lies the assumption that I do not deserve it. But when I realise that he is a holy God and I am a sinful man, the real truth is that I deserve everything that comes to me and there is a moral reason for submitting to God.

The fact is, I do not deserve health. The real problem to my mind should not be about what goes wrong, but that anything goes right. If I really were humbled before my Maker I would say, "God, if you kill me tonight as I drive home, that would be no more than I deserve." There is a submission that is due to fear as there is a submission that is due to a fatalism, but there is a deeper submission yet, and it is the submission of faith. Fatalism says: "God is all powerful; I must submit." Fear says, "God is all holy; I deserve what I get, and must accept it." That interprets all tragedy as a punishment from God – that he is doing it because we have been bad.

I think that is a doubtful form of submission. There is a deeper one still, and it is the submission of faith that says: "God, I believe you are in control. I believe you are sovereign. I believe you are responsible for this, but I believe you know what you are doing and that if I did know what you were doing, I would know you had a very good reason for doing it." That is a deeper form of submission.

A minister prepared me for church membership, and I remember those membership classes very well because we began with fifteen of us and the class finished with one. I stuck it out to the end and the minister and I had the last two or three classes on our own. I remember him saying to me once, "David, look at my face. Do you see anything unusual in my face?"

I looked, and said no. It was a kindly face, an ordinary sort of face, a little Churchillian in looks.

Then he said, "Do you know what my earliest memory in life is? I remember my mother tying my hands and my feet with rope. I remember submitting to my mother; I didn't fight, I didn't struggle. She tied my hands and my feet with rope and then tied all four together with the same rope. I submitted. For years, I never understood what she was doing. Later in life I asked her, 'Why did you tie me up as a little boy?' and she said, 'You had smallpox. I tied your hands to your feet so that you would not scrape the pox and leave your face marked for life.'" She then stroked his face and scars, and the pockmarks, with a feather dipped in olive oil. "I didn't struggle," he said, "I submitted."

Submission does not say, "Lord, you had better explain what you are doing or I won't submit to you." Submission says: "Lord, I'm not submitting to you because you're bigger than I am and I'm not submitting to you because I think you're punishing me. I'm submitting to you because I believe that you have a good reason for what you're doing and I trust your love and I submit." Many who cannot understand what has happened to them, many who have not been able to answer the question "Where is your God? Why has he done this?" have nevertheless found one element of peace of mind in submitting to the sovereignty of God.

There are some lovely examples in scripture of this kind

of submission. One in the Old Testament comes readily to mind: Shadrach, Meshach, and Abednego. Do you remember them? Thrown into the fiery furnace for their faith. Yes, an anti-Semitic move was on and they were thrown in there because they would not break their own religion. Their last words as they were thrown into the fiery furnace, I remember so vividly: "But if not...." Remember those words. Our God is able to get us out of this trouble; we have a God who could put these flames out like that; we have a God who can bring us out of the impossible situation in which you have placed us; we have a God who can keep us safe. But if not – that is the kind of acceptance of the sovereignty of God that God wants.

I turn to the pages of the New Testament and I see a man in such agony that a well-known medical state occurs and there are drops of blood oozing from the pores of his brow. He is in such mental stress and he prays desperately that the crisis he is facing may be averted. Then he says, "Nevertheless, not my will, but yours...." You have it all in those two phrases from the Old and the New Testament: "But if not," and, "Nevertheless." It is a recognition of the sovereignty of God in the present. I have to say, "God, you have allowed these things to happen. You are not responsible to us. You do not have to explain to us why, but we submit to your sovereignty. We accept that this is your will."

I remember asking an undertaker what difference he noticed between Christian funerals and other funerals. I notice the difference when I take them; I can pick out almost straightaway those present who are Christians and those who are not. It is not by those who are crying and those who are not. Christians can cry. It seems as if death confronts us with the realities of life in a way that nothing else does. That undertaker said: "I have found sorrow in Christian homes and non-Christian homes, but I will tell you this: I have never once, in all my days as an undertaker, gone into a Christian home and found bitterness or resentment." That is a remarkable tribute.

When Job heard of the loss of his entire family in one disaster, he said: "The Lord gave and the Lord has taken away; bless the name of the Lord." Submission to God's sovereignty is a very wonderful thing. It is the first step towards dealing with tragedy.

The second step I can speak of even more simply. It is the thought of God's suffering in the past. I wonder if you know this little statement. It's called, "God Leads a Pretty Sheltered Life." At the end of time, billions of people were scattered on a great plain before God's throne. Some of the groups in the front were talking heatedly, not with cringing shame, but with belligerence. "How can God judge us? How can he know about suffering?" snapped a joking lady. She jerked back her sleeve to reveal a tattooed number from a Nazi concentration camp. "We endured terror, beating, torture, death." In another group, a black man lowered his shirt collar. "What about this?" he demanded, showing an ugly rope burn – lynched for no crime, but being black. "We've suffocated in slave ships, been wrenched from loved ones, toiled until only death gave release." Far out across the plain, were hundreds of such groups and each one had a complaint against God for the evil and suffering he permitted in this world. How lucky God was to live in heaven where all was sweetness and light, where there was no weeping, no fear and no hatred. Indeed, what did God know about what man had been forced to endure in this world? "After all," they said, "God lead a pretty sheltered life." So each group sent out a leader, chosen because he had suffered the most. There was a Jew, a black person, an untouchable from India, an illegitimate person, a person from Hiroshima, and someone from a Siberian slave camp. In the centre of the plain they consulted with each other.

At last, they were ready to present their case. It was quite simple. Before God would be qualified to be their judge, he must endure what they had endured. Their decision was this: that God should be sentenced to live on earth as a man. But because he was God, they set certain safeguards to be sure he could not use his divine powers to help himself. "Let him be born a Jew. Let the legitimacy of his birth be doubted so that none will know who is really his father. Let him champion a cause so just but so radical that it brings down upon him such hate, condemnation and the eliminating efforts of every major traditional and established religious authority. Let him try to describe what no man has ever seen, tasted, heard or smelled. Let him try and communicate God to man. Let him be betrayed by his dearest friends. Let him be indicted on false charges, tried before a prejudiced jury and convicted by a cowardly judge. Let him see what it is to be terribly alone and completely abandoned by every living thing. Let him be tortured and let him die. Let him die the most humiliating death with common criminals."

As each leader announced his portion of the sentence, loud murmurs of approval went up from the throng of people. When the last had finished pronouncing the sentence, there was a long silence. No one uttered another word; no one moved. Suddenly, everyone knew that God had already served his sentence. That statement captures my second point. We do not worship a God who stays in a sweetened, light heaven and is detached from our suffering. As Isaiah said to his own people, "In all their affliction, he was afflicted." If people say, "Where is your God?" my answer is, "There he is on a cross." Our God suffers.

I lived in Arabia where their religion was Islam, and Islam means "submission." "Muslim" means "a surrendered one". The heart of that religion is submission to the sovereignty of God. They teach that submission; they teach it almost to the point of fatalism. But I am now telling you something that Islam cannot tell you. I am telling you not only that God is sovereign; I tell you that God suffers. This is something new in the Christian faith that you do not find in fatalistic faiths like Islam. Not only is God sovereign and one to be submitted to, he is a God who suffers.

The right response to this truth is to be willing to share in his suffering. I don't know where we got the idea that Christianity is a way out of suffering. I am so glad when what is the truth is said: come to Jesus and you are into trouble. Jesus himself said it. We are in a hostile environment; so was he. God did not suffer until he entered into that environment fully and then did he suffer. Because we are in the same environment, Christ did not promise us a cushion but a cross. He didn't say: take up your cushion and follow me; that will protect you from the buffetings of life. He said, "Take up your cross and follow me."

I find that in the light of a God who suffers and who calls for a response to share in that suffering, tragedy becomes not a problem but a privilege. I say that very lightly because tragedy has not struck my life very deeply. There have been some things that others might call tragedy in it, but I have not had to suffer too deeply for my faith. Others have had to suffer more. But when I turn the pages of the New Testament, I don't find them saying: what a problem this suffering is; why should God let this happen? Surely because we're serving him, he has promised us safety....

I remember that the devil tried that line with Jesus at the very beginning of his ministry. One of the three temptations was: why don't you grasp Psalm 91 and make it a visible insurance policy for the world to see? It says there that if you make God your defender, your protector, he will guard you. A thousand may fall beside you, but nothing will touch you. You needn't fear death; you needn't fear disease. He will send his angels to catch you, lest you dash your foot against a stone. The devil was saying: make your faith in God an insurance policy for safety.

Jesus knew that he was to suffer, not to be safe. He rejected that call from Satan to regard it as God's obligation to keep his servants safe. God never promised me, in this life, safety. He promises me salvation, eternal life. He does not promise safety. Therefore, the second thought that comes to me as I think about tragedies is this: God is a God who's not only sovereign, to whom I submit; he is a God who suffers and who calls me to share in that.

The next dimension of my answer to this deep question is this: the salvation of God in the future. When Israel was trapped at the Red Sea, with the Egyptian army on one side, the desert on another, the mountains on a third, and the Red Sea on the fourth, their temptation was to panic and run. Moses' command to them was "Stand still", or as the Good News Bible has it: "Hold your ground. Stay where you are; hold on and see what God will do to save you." Then Moses said, "Now move forward," and God saved them. Our temptation, when tragedy comes, is to panic, to run, to shrink. The Word of God says: stand still; hold on and see what God will do to save.

This word, "salvation" is so much a part of religious jargon that I want to put a lot more letters in it to make it of real meaning. God is committed to a salvage operation. When people say, "Where is your God?" my answer is, "He is in the future. He is the God who inhabits eternity." From that future perspective of a total salvage operation, I can look back and I can see present tragedies in an altogether different light.

Paul's writings record how he suffered stoning, whipping, flogging, being shipwrecked, travelling dangerous roads, weary, every part of his body showing the scars of his ill-treatment. Yet, when you read Paul's writings about suffering, he always looks at them from the perspective of God's future salvation. He steps out of the present into the future and he looks back. He looks at all the pain and he says, "It is a momentary, light affliction which works an exceeding weight of glory". It is so small; anything that is far away looks small.

When you are in the present and you are in the suffering and you are in the tragedy, the future salvation seems small and far away. The New Testament is saying that in faith, which is the evidence of things hoped for and the substance of things not seen, step out into that future and look back at your suffering, look back at the tragedy, and you will see a momentary, light affliction and something which worked an exceeding weight of glory. In other words, not only has God allowed this suffering, not only has he experienced it, but he is also incorporating it into his salvage operation. Pain may be suffered if it is doing something worthwhile.

If I could feel that a tragedy was going to do something worthwhile, I could cope with it. God can work all things together for good. God is so committed to salvage the world that, one day, everything will be put right in it. If I did not believe it, I could not cope with present tragedy. I can bring my tragedy and say, "God, take that into your salvage operation, take it into your whole purpose. Let me look at it from the point of view of your salvation in the future and see that it was part of your plan to put the whole world right." That, I think, is the third answer.

The response that the Bible calls for to the salvation of God in the future is to sing; to suffer in song. I have known many who have suffered in silence. There is a dumb dignity about suffering in silence, of not complaining, of not saying anything, but there are those who suffer in song. In Psalm 42: "The waves of sorrow have just been rolling over me like billows. They've just got me under and so I will seek to put my hope in you and I'll sing to you. I'll get my harp out. I want to go to bed tonight with a song. So show me your constant love during the day so that I may have a song tonight."

In summary, here are three dimensions which I want to share with you: the sovereignty of God in the present to which my true response is to submit; the salvation of God in the future to which my true response is to sing; and the suffering of God in the past, to which my true response is to share. Such is the path along which those who have faced real tragedy find hope and find an answer.

I received a letter dated December the 27th, 1974, from a man in Jerusalem, Dr Bob Lindsey, a remarkable Christian. He saved a child from no-man's land when Jerusalem was a divided city, but in doing so he stepped on the land mine and lost a leg. In December 1974, he came to stay in our home and I took him a cup of tea in the morning and went into the room and tripped over his artificial leg, which was on the floor. He wrote me this letter a short time later:

> We've had a delightful Christmas, though the stern realities of life and death have been impressed upon us in the injury of a girl called Jeanie, whose right leg was amputated, after a tourist group suffered an attack by some person throwing a hand grenade at the tomb of Lazarus. The little lady is just sixteen and has been a brave, sweet one. It is one of the times when I feel I have been glad I could say I had also gone through such an experience.

James says, "Don't be surprised if you go through many trials."

Two men were thrown into prison because they were Christians. They were put in the worst part of the prison—

rats running around the floor, no light. They were flogged to within an inch of their life. They were bleeding. They were in the stocks; they were padlocked in. One of them turned to the other and said, "What hymn shall we sing?" At midnight, Paul and Silas suffered in song. You can't beat people who suffer in song. They may not be able to tell you why and they will have to say to you, "Unless you're a believer, you wouldn't understand," but they have come to terms with tragedy.

READ PSALM 50

I don't know if you ever read the little phrases at the top of the Psalms. They are all part of the Psalm and they are terribly important, and they give us the key that unlocks the Psalm. Who was Asaph? We only know two things about him but when you know those two things the whole Psalm unfolds – full of meaning and purpose. First of all, he was the choirmaster in the tabernacle, a man with an important position, responsible for all the music and worship. He had a choir of two hundred and fifty singers. He had an orchestra of over a hundred instruments. Asaph blended the orchestra and the choir together in praise every Sabbath.

Not only that but the congregations were good in those days. Israel was going through a time of peace and prosperity and they were thankful to God for it; the tabernacle was packed. The crowds came every Sabbath. Many sacrifices were offered. The whole act of worship was something of which everyone was proud. The choirmaster had many helpful composers who aided him in his music. For example, he had a group of singers within the choir called "the sons of Korah" and this little group, a kind of folk group within the choir, composed songs to be sung. If you look at Psalms 49, 48, 47, 46, 45, 44, 43, 42, they were written by this folk group and they produced music for him.

The king himself was a good musician. He could play a number of instruments well and he liked composing music and songs. King David was supplying music for the choir all the time. The worship was wonderful. There was only one thing that they lacked and they were doing something about this. They met in a very old building. So already the king had started a building fund and planned a new building and they were beginning to draw up the brief for the architect and they were looking forward to their new building. So everything was perfect: good music, crowded congregations, big collections, a new building on the way; they had everything.

Not only was Asaph a choirmaster, he was also a seer. Now that was a man who dreamed dreams and saw visions, a man who had the gift of seeing things that other people do not see, a man who had special revelations from God in picture form. Sometimes a prophet received a message in words, but a seer received messages in dreams and visions. He saw something like a movie film in his mind, and this was from God.

Now one night this man went to bed and had a dream. He had a vision and he saw in this dream so vividly something that shocked and startled him. He saw the worship on the Sabbath as God saw it. It was so different from the way he had seen it and everybody else had seen it. To every man taking part in the services they were wonderful; to God they were terrible. In this vision he saw a gigantic courtroom, a huge assize, and that is what the Psalm is all about. He put it down into a song after he had seen the vision. But he clearly saw this gigantic courtroom. He saw all the details of it and he listened to the case and that is now put down and recorded in this Psalm.

The Psalm divides into three parts according to the personal pronouns. In vv. 1–6 it is all about "he"; in vv. 7–15 "I"; and vv. 16–23 "you". This gives us the division into three parts. We would have guessed that by the word "selah" anyway at the end of v. 6. So we have got one special section, vv. 1–6, and then the rest of the Psalm divides into two. I will explain why soon.

Now in the vv. 1–6 we have seven things described which happened in a great court. The first thing is that there is a summons, and when a court case is held, summonses go out to many people. Not just to the defendant, summonses go out to the counsel, to the jury, to the clerk, to the court, to the men who stand at the doors of the court, to the recorders, the shorthand reporters, everything. A summons goes out and that is the beginning of a case. In his dream Asaph saw a summons from heaven going out to all of time and all of space, the whole of the earth and the heavens. God was summoning everyone to come. The summons comes from no less a person than God himself, who is given three titles: he is God, he is Almighty God, he is Almighty God the Redeemer. God who created, God who redeems, is the God who says, "Come, I summon you to my court." It comes by word of mouth, not in written form. He speaks and summons. It is sent from the east to the west.

The second thing we are told is something about the judge. Now they are usually resplendent in robes. They are given the highest seat; they are surrounded with glory, and here in v. 2 this judge shines forth. But I have noticed in many cases that one of the most common phrases used in a court case is: "Something came to light." Have you heard that phrase? "This came to light." "Evidence came to light." That phrase is very interesting because sooner or later everything that we have ever done must come to light because God is light and he exposes with his light everything that we have done.

So: "Out of Zion, the perfection of beauty, God shines." He is light and he summons everything to come to light. That is a disturbing thought. There isn't one of us who would be really happy about everything in our life coming to light, but that is what happens when we come to God. Whether or not we have the misfortune to stand in an earthly court, every man and woman will one day come to light. God is light.

Now the third thing that begins a great case is a procession. Maybe you have seen in an assize town the procession. Here they come: there are the police first, then come the mace bearers, the officials of the court, the judge in his wig and robes and his attendants. It is an impressive procession surrounded by all the pomp and pageantry of historic tradition and by the emblems of his authority and power. What is the procession here? "Our God comes," and the emblems of his power are a devouring fire in front of him, not a mace, and round about him not robes but a mighty tempest. These are fitting symbols of the judge of all the earth. Fire is carried in front and girded with a tempest. Fire and wind, the two symbols that came down on the day of Pentecost. These are symbols of power and authority; this is the judge of all the earth. Power before him, tempest around him, our God comes; here comes the judge.

Now the scene switches to the public gallery, and the gallery is already filling up for justice must be public and must be seen to be just. Who is coming in? The judge invites the entire universe to come and witness the case. He calls on the heavens above and he calls on the earth below and says, "Come, come and watch. Come and be present at this great assize." So the heavens above and the earth beneath fill the public gallery. Now this is not a vision of the final judgment. It is not a vision of the day of the Lord. It has nothing to do with that. It is a particular case that God is trying now in this day, and finally all eyes are on the dock. There comes a point where everyone turns to see who is being brought in. Into the dock come the congregation that had worshipped God last Sabbath in the tabernacle. This is the shock which Asaph gets. So the word goes down the corridors of the nation: "Call my people, call my saints, call my faithful ones," and they are brought in to be tried.

Now this is the shock because Israel was frequently in

the frame of mind of thinking that everyone else would be judged and not them. Here is the choirmaster and he sees the choir coming into the dock, he sees the congregation coming in, he sees the priests crowding in, and there in the middle he sees himself standing with the choir. The whole of God's people are in the dock. He must almost have woken up from the dream in shock when that happened – something he had never seen before. What is going to happen? What is their crime? They are called: "Gather to me my faithful ones who made a covenant with me by sacrifice." Now that is the relationship that the people of God have had with God in the Old and the New Testaments. You make a covenant with God by sacrifice.

Let me tell you how they did it first. At the foot of the towering Mount Sinai there is a plain of sand. There the whole of Israel gathered after they had been rescued from Egypt, and God said, "I am going to make a covenant with you by sacrifice. Repeat these words after me. 'Thou shalt have no other gods before me. Thou shalt not make any graven image. Thou shalt not take my name in vain. Remember the Sabbath day to keep it holy. Honour your father and mother. Do not kill. Do not steal. Do not commit adultery. Do not make false witness against your neighbour. Do not covet what is your neighbour's.' Repeat these words after me," and two and a half million people shouted the Ten Commandments. Then God said, "Now kill some animals. Take the blood, sprinkle it on yourself and sprinkle it on my mountain. This covenant, the words that you have said, sealed in blood, have become the basis of your faith in me." That was how they made a covenant with sacrifice.

We don't need to bring the blood of animals because we have the blood of Jesus. In the service of the Lord's Supper I say something like: "This is my blood of the new covenant shed for you and for many for the remission of sins." But I also say, before that: "Ye that do truly and earnestly repent of your sins and are in love and charity with your neighbours, and intend to lead a new life following the commandments of God." You see, once again covenant with sacrifice, taking the words of God upon your lips, sealing it in the blood of a sacrifice – that is our religion. It was people with that religion who were now called into the dock.

Now the scene changes—look at the jury. Well, they are not there. There is no jury, there is no counsel for the prosecution, there is no counsel for the defence, and there are no witnesses. Why not? Because in God's court they are not needed. God himself knows everything. Therefore, he does not need counsel. He does not need a jury. He does not need a single witness. So at this point the judge himself becomes jury, counsel and witness. Now is everybody happy about such an arrangement? Well the heavens are, but the earth is silent. The reason for that is this: everybody in heaven knows God is fair; everybody in heaven knows God is just, and therefore they declare his righteousness. God himself is judge, you don't need a jury; God is judge you don't need witnesses; God is judge, you don't need counsel, but earth does not say that. It is characteristic of men on earth to say God is not just; God is not fair; God does not do what is right. Why does he do this? Why does he allow that? The heavens declare his righteousness; earth remains silent.

At this point "Selah". Now I don't know if you know what that means; I don't know if I do either. I have read so many commentators and scholars and they all disagree. There are many reverent and irreverent suggestions about what this means, but as far as I can make out it means "pause". It means a musical direction to the choir to stop singing for a moment. It is so appropriate at precisely this point. Why? Because when the judge has come, when the gallery is filled, when those who are to be tried are in the dock, what is said? "Silence in court." In writing this song after seeing the dream, the choirmaster put in this little note "Selah". Pause. Silence in court. The scene is set, the trial is to begin; let us have a moment of silence before we hear the charge.

Do you see how vivid this is? It is a dream. It is a picture and we are already sitting there waiting for something to happen. The first words in the case are the most shocking and most horrifying of all. The judge looks at the dock and says, "O my people...." It is almost as if a boy got into trouble, was arrested, and was brought into court and realised with a shock that his own father was on duty as the judge that morning. It is as if the father, looking down at his boy, says, "My son, I never thought I would see you there. My boy, that I should have to judge you, but I will have to do it because you've done wrong." I don't know what would happen in English law in a case like this, if a judge's own son was on trial before him, whether they would choose someone else. I think they would, but since God is judge there is no one else to choose. So God is saying: O my people, I have to try you; I must judge my own kith and kin, my people, and I have got to testify against you.

There are two charges: one is made in connection with their sacrifices and one in connection with their covenants. Now what was wrong with these two things? Every week they recited the commandments, the covenant; every week they offered sacrifices. What is wrong? Well, we shall see in a moment. In each case God tells them what is wrong and tells them what would have been right until they can see why he has had to deal with them in court. Take first the sacrifices. What is wrong? Every Sabbath they brought their goats and their bulls, they slaughtered them and they sprinkled blood. They brought the best animals they could. What is wrong?

The answer is: why they did it. God looked into their hearts and he saw motives in worship that spoiled it for him.

The singing was wonderful; the sacrifices were costly; the congregation was crowded, and yet in their hearts they had entirely the wrong attitude. What was wrong? Well, they had got the notion that they were doing God a favour by bringing him sacrifices. That was all that was wrong. They were coming in a patronising spirit with the attitude: God, I'm doing you a favour. Here is a sacrifice for you. Isn't that nice of me.

I remember talking to a wonderful Christian, a Pakistani, Bishop Chandu Ray. He told us that as a little boy his mother used to take him around the Hindu shrines, long before he had heard of Jesus, and they used to take little precious gifts of butter, and butter for them was the most luxurious food they ever had. They were poor people. They used to take this butter and give it to the gods, and the mother said, "The gods like butter and we give them this butter." Years later he discovered that the priests ate it themselves, and it disillusioned him. But all those years as a little boy he thought that gods liked butter and he took butter for the gods and he thought that he was doing them a favour, and that the gods would be grateful and look after him as a little boy. That is a thoroughly pagan notion of religion and it can get into the church. It got into Israel here; it can get into our lives. The idea that when we come and give to God, God needed that and is pleased with it and grateful for it, and will show his gratitude to us – that is totally out of place in Christian worship. It is to come in a spirit of patronage, of largesse, as if you are coming to support God. That is altogether wrong, however nice the worship may be. The keyword in verses 10–12 is "mine". There is nothing you give to God that is not his already. He doesn't need it anyway. God does not need a penny of your money; he doesn't need an hour of your time, or even a minute. God doesn't need anything from any one of us. He doesn't need what you brought him. If we ever drop into the trap of thinking that he needs something from us then we have fallen into the trap of offering him patronising worship that is saying, "O God, I've come this morning to do you a favour."

Look what he says. He puts the truth in most vivid language. In vv. 10–11 he is saying: Every animal and every bird is mine before you bring it; you may bring a bull or a calf to worship me but the cattle on a thousand hills are mine; you cannot give me anything. Then he comes in v. 12 to a wonderful phrase that I have mentioned at a harvest festival. God says, "If I were hungry I would not tell you. If I needed a thing I wouldn't tell you. I would just go to my larder. I would just go and help myself to what is mine already."

When the Queen's birthday is coming up, do you ask yourself "Have I got her anything?" Supposing you were going to get her a present, you would have a job wouldn't you? I think you'd say, "Well, she's got everything. What could I possibly get that she hasn't got?" I wouldn't think there's a thing you could get her that she hasn't got. Why would someone give presents to the Queen? Why do people bring gifts? For the privilege of giving the gift and to honour her, that is why. Not because she needs it; she doesn't need a thing. The King of kings and the Lord of lords does not need a thing.

I don't like the hymn, "Rise Up, O Men of God" and I rarely if ever chose it. It says: "Rise up, O men of God, the Church for you doth wait. Her strength unequal to her task; rise up and make her great." You find me one bit in the Bible that talks like that! In the Bible, Jesus says, "I will build my church." It is our holy privilege to be invited to take part in that. His kingdom will come, whether David Pawson helps or not. God is capable of doing all he wills without me and without you.

If we give anything to God, it is not because he needs the

gift, it is because we need to give. It is because the need is on our side not his. He does not need our time, he does not need our money; he does not need anything to do what he wills. It is God Almighty the Creator and the Redeemer who summons you and would ask: why did you think I needed you? Why did you bring gifts as if I needed something from you? I don't need a thing. The cattle on a thousand hills are mine. If I were hungry I wouldn't tell you about it. I would go and help myself.

But he is not hungry because he does not eat flesh like a man.

How then shall we come to worship? How should we bring a sacrifice of praise? Well, there are four things said here. First, we come from a sense of debt. You owe God more than you will ever repay. You owe him your life, you owe him your money, you owe him your talents. You owe him everything you have got. It is a debt; it is not a favour to make him grateful; it is a debt because you are grateful. It is a debt that you pay. When you put something in the collection today it is not doing God a favour, tipping him, it is paying a debt that you owe.

Second, the judge says, "Come with a spirit of dedication to pay the vows that you owe." The early name for an oath or a promise was, in Latin, "sacramentum", and when a Roman soldier joined the legions he stood with his hand upraised before Augustus Caesar or the Roman flag, saluted the flag and said, "I swear to live and die for Caesar," and the oath was called the *sacramentum*, and that word became linked with the Lord's Supper because there you take a vow. You dedicate yourself again, and when you come into God's presence from a sense of debt there is born a sense of dedication: "Lord, here I am."

Third thing: a sense of dependence when you leave worship that you will go on praying to God and calling upon him in the day of trouble. It is one thing to call upon him in church; it is another to call upon him during the week. If we really worship there is *debt*, there is *dedication*, and afterwards there is *dependence*: calling on him through the week. Fourthly, we shall enjoy his *deliverance*. That will bring us back the next week, full of praise and thanksgiving. Do you see the cycle of true worship? You don't come to give God a favour. You don't come to make him grateful. You come because you are grateful. You come because you owe him everything. You come to dedicate yourself. You come that you might be able to call upon him in the day of trouble, and come back next Sunday and say, "Lord, you delivered me. Here I am again to thank you."

Now that was what was wrong with their worship. They did not feel they owed God anything. They felt that God owed them something for coming. They did not feel ready to dedicate themselves. They came because they felt God ought to dedicate himself to them. They did not come because they depended on God. They were peaceful, prosperous, they had everything they wanted, and so they did not bother to call upon him. Therefore they did not come praising him for their deliverance. You cannot give a single thing to God that is not his before he gave it. He could have taken it from you any time he wished.

Now the other thing that they are accused of in worship is connected with the covenant. Their sacrifices were all wrong because they were doing it as a favour. Their covenant was all wrong because what they said on the Sabbath was not kept during the week in their life. It was words. Now I remember one of the most honest men I ever met. I noticed that in certain verses of certain hymns he shut his mouth tight and hummed. I asked him about this and he said, "Well, I like the music but I can't honestly sing the words." In particular the hymn, "Take my life and let it be," there was one verse he would always refuse to sing, "Take my silver and my gold not a mite would I withhold." You see, he was quite comfortably off. He was chief accountant for a very large nationalised concern. There he was and he would not sing that hymn. I admired him for that because it meant he was honest. He was offering God honest worship, and he wasn't prepared to keep that during the week so he did not sing it on Sunday, until there came a day when he did sing it. I would be betraying confidences if I told you what he did with his bank balance and what he did with his property as soon as he sang it. His whole life was transformed. He is not even living in his own house now. He doesn't have his own house to live in. Not now, because he has said it and he meant it.

They were repeating the Ten Commandments every Sunday. They recited the covenant, "Thou shalt have no other gods. Thou shalt not make any graven image," and then they went right out of the Sabbath into the next day and they forgot all about it. A Scotsman, a businessman, who had a lot of money, had a dream ambition of visiting the Middle East. He told his minister, "I have it all booked up. I'm going out to Israel and Jordan. I'm going to visit the Middle East, I'm even going down to Mount Sinai."

He said, "It's my ambition to climb to the top of Mount Sinai and shout the Ten Commandments at the top of my voice."

The minister wisely said, "Ah, you would do far better to be at home and keep them." He knew that businessman well. Jesus' teaching was: if you listen to my words and do nothing about them you are building on sand and in the crisis you will collapse. But if you listen to my words and do them.... Blessed are those who are doers as well as hearers.

Now the judge says to these people: There are three things about you that I do not like even though you recite my commandments. First of all, you dislike discipline. You do not like being told what not to do. You resent the words, "Thou shalt not", even though you recite them. Inside you say, "who is he telling me what to do?" As soon as they were out of worship, therefore, they forgot about them. "You cast my words behind you; you hate discipline; you hate being told 'You mustn't do this.'"

The second thing he said was: even if you don't break the laws yourself you enjoy the company of those who do. Now, that is a serious charge. Just let it sink in. God not only charges a man with breaking his commandments, but even if he does not break them he says you like the company of those who do. You don't rebuke those who break my laws. You don't keep out of their company when they are doing this. Put in simple language: you laugh when a dirty story is being told in the office, when your companions are getting a bit beyond the line in their behaviour you either join in with them or you just hang around and enjoy it even though you don't join in. Now that's as bad as breaking it.

The third thing he says about them is that lips that have said lovely words in worship have gossiped outside. Now the Bible makes a great deal of sins of speech; they are serious— exaggeration, hypercriticism, gossip, saying things about others. Pascal the philosopher, remember his saying? "If everyone knew what each said about the other there wouldn't be four friends left in the world." George MacDonald once said: "Gossip is a beast of prey that does not wait for the death of the creature it devours."

So God says here: "You give your mouth free rein for evil". Do we sing beautifully on Sunday, and on Monday gossip about the next door neighbour? Somebody said to me in Czechoslovakia that the favourite American Sunday lunch is "fried preacher". Now, I understand that remark and I have been guilty of it when I have sat in a pew. It can be fried anyone for lunch.

These were the three things he said about their covenants. What is the point of repeating my commandments in church if you dislike being told what not to do and forget them as soon as you get out, if you enjoy the company of those who break them, and if having said holy things in worship you then go out and say horrible things about your brother outside? The charge is of inconsistency. It is a very important thing that, when we come and speak to God, we speak with clean lips.

"Holy, holy, holy Lord God of hosts, woe is me for I am a man of unclean lips and I dwell in a people of unclean lips," so spoke Isaiah. How can we worship God with dirty lips? "Then flew one of the seraphim from the altar having a live coal, which he had taken with the tongs from off the altar, and with it he touched my lips and said, 'Lo, your iniquity is cleansed. You've got clean lips.'" We all need the coal when we come to sing, to burn out of our lips what we have said about each other and about other people. None of these things we tend to consider as terribly serious but God considers them serious enough to bring them into his court.

Let me tell you about Origen of Alexandria. Origen was a saint who lived in the year 185 AD. Origen, as a boy of seventeen, saw his father burned at the stake for being a Christian and it left an indelible scar in his mind. Years later he became a Christian himself and was arrested. He was tortured and he denied Christ even though his own father had not. Origen was set free because he swore and blasphemed against Jesus even though he was a Christian.

A few years later he was invited to preach in a church in Jerusalem and he got up to preach and the Psalm for the day was Psalm 50. He read it through and he got to these words: "You have given your mouth to evil," and he thought back those years to the day when he blasphemed against Jesus, and he collapsed. He fell in the pulpit and he could not go on preaching. He said, "How can I preach with these lips? I blasphemed Christ." That's how we should feel if we have gossiped, or been overcritical of someone else, or said hurtful things deliberately, maliciously, when we come to church. This was what was wrong.

What is the heart of this kind of behaviour? The answer is very simple; v. 22 tells us. If this is the kind of thing we do, then we have forgotten God. Every time I am gossiping I have literally forgotten God because I have forgotten that he is listening. When I was in church singing hymns I thought, "God's listening to this, that's wonderful," and then I got out of church and I gossiped and I forgot that God was listening still. Oh, you who forget God, mark this. I suppose that most of the sins of God's people are due to forgetting God, just forgetting that he is listening, that he is watching, that he is in the room; that he is with you everywhere.

So we have a lovely promise: that if we order our way aright, if we offer true worship, if we do what we should, not as a patronising favour but as a debt of gratitude, not with lips that are going to say one thing on Sunday and another thing on Monday, but with lips that are clean and pure all the week; if we order our way aright, he will show the salvation of God to us and we shall be able to sing and speak his praise properly. Asaph woke up and it was all a dream. This never really happened. This is not history, it is not fact, it never happened.

You know how you wake up after a bad dream? Sometimes occasionally as a preacher I have a bad dream about a service. I get to the service late; I have left my notes at home; I can't find the hymnbook – it is a typical dream of a preacher and some of you preachers have this dream. You wake up in a cold sweat and think: Oh, it's just a dream and I thought I was in a service." Well Asaph woke up like that and he was probably perspiring, "Oh, I thought I was in the dock. I thought the choir was in the dock. I thought the congregation was in the dock, and it was all a dream." Asaph took out a piece of papyrus and he took his pen, and he said, "I'm going to share this dream; God has given me this dream for a purpose." He wrote a song, and he wrote Psalm 50 and he set it to music.

READ PSALM 51

There are two amazing miracles in Psalm 51. I will mention the first now, and the second I will mention right at the end of this chapter. The first miracle in Psalm 51 is this: that a man in mature years, at the height of his career, a man that knows power and popularity, was prepared to admit that he was a sinner. I have never known that happen except by a miraculous touch of God on a man's heart. For men as they grow older often get proud and independent – as they get on in life and gain their ambitions, becoming more and more difficult in this matter of facing up to their need of a Saviour.

When a man of forty or fifty, at the peak of his career, with everything that this world can offer him, falls down before God and says, "Have mercy on me," that is a miracle – and would to God we saw more of that kind of miracle. It is easier for a young man who is still struggling with initial temptations to see his need of a Saviour.

Now the title indicates that there are three people responsible for this Psalm, and without those three it would never have been written. The first is of course the writer himself: David. This would not have been written if he had not sinned. Described in the Bible as a man after God's own heart, he was the best king that Israel ever had – so much so that forever afterwards they prayed for another king like David.

This man at the height of his career, having brought peace and prosperity to his nation, sinned. The story is in 2 Samuel 11 and I hardly need to remind you of it. The army was away at war, the palace rather empty, the men of Jerusalem away fighting, and David, walking on the veranda of the palace, looks down into a private house and sees a woman undressing. With royal power he takes her, lies with her, gives her a child, and then wonders how on earth he can cover it up before it is discovered since her man was away at the war – that was the situation.

This is all too common, and indeed a situation that would have been quite normal for an oriental ruler. If you read the likes of the sheikhs and the despots in the Middle East, what David did was what any king would have done under the circumstances. Every king did it and filled his harem with any girl he took a fancy to, and any husband in the Middle East had to give up his girl to the king. So, humanly speaking, no one would have blamed him for this. Humanly speaking – but that is not how we speak. It was David's sin that lay behind this. He added to the sin of adultery the sin of murder because he arranged for Bathsheba's husband, Uriah, to be put in the very place in the battle where he would be most likely to be killed; and he was, and then David took her to be his wife. Now that was the sin.

Why did David ever tell anyone else about it? The answer is because of the second man mentioned in the title: Nathan the Prophet. The preacher in Israel came into the palace, striding in, and said, "King David, I have a story to tell you. A rich man with flocks and herds took a little poor man's ewe lamb and killed it for a feast he was giving. He had plenty of sheep but the poor man only had one ewe lamb," and it says, "David's anger was greatly kindled," and he said, "Where is this man? Bring him to me, we'll punish this man." Nathan said, "You are the man. You have got a palace; you have got women; you have got wealth, and you saw Bathsheba and you took her and that was all that Uriah had. You are the man." David was smitten because he realised that God had been watching, and that God said it was wrong.

You see, there are many things that other people will say are all right. But when God says it is wrong you can say no more. It does not really matter what society judges to be right or wrong, it is what God says is right or wrong that matters. David was stricken in his conscience. But why did he make it public? Why did he write a Psalm about it? The answer is the third person in the title "To the choirmaster Asaph". We have already looked at a Psalm by the choirmaster, which was a song about a dream he had, and he saw all the people in the dock of God's courtroom accused of a worship that was offensive to God. The charge was that people came to worship, recited the commandments, and went away and broke them.

When King David heard that Psalm he realised that God was speaking to him not only through the preacher Nathan but through the choirmaster Asaph. So he sat down and in his broken, humbled state he realised that there were others in the congregation who were doing what he had done, saying things to God and then denying them in life during the week. He realised that he needed to make confession and they did, and so he wrote a Psalm and he dedicated it to the choirmaster.

The amazing sequel to Psalm 50 is Psalm 51. The king himself said: Asaph, the sentence is just. I stand in the dock guilty and I write a Psalm for the next Sabbath which we can all sing and confess our sins. Isn't that an interesting sequel? I have met very few Christians who know Psalm 50 as well as Psalm 51, or have ever even seen the connection between the two, but you see how real life makes sense of the Bible.

Psalm 51 divides into two parts: vv. 1–12 where he confesses his sin, and vv. 13–19 where he describes what will happen if he is forgiven. This Psalm reminds me of a little story Jesus told of two men who went to pray. One stood up at the front and said: "O God, I'm a good chap I am. I thank you that I am better than some of the others who are sitting in the pews at the back there; I give a tenth of all my money to you. Oh, I've done so much for you Lord." Then there was a poor man at the back of the church and he beat his breast and said, "O God, be merciful to me a sinner." Jesus said that only one of those two went back to his house a better man than he came. It was the man who said, "God, be merciful to me a sinner."

He appeals to two things in God. He appeals to God's love and his mercy. If God was not love and not mercy there would be no point in appealing to him. If God was only just and good then you could not appeal to him at all. You would have to take your punishment, but God is a God of steadfast love and abundant mercy. So he comes back and his attitude is: God, I believe you still love me; I appeal to your steadfast love; you loved me before; I don't believe you have stopped loving me; I appeal to that love. Secondly: I appeal to your abundant mercy.

Mercy is to give a person what they do not deserve and God loves to do that. God would have mercy on every man and woman in the entire world if they would only ask him for it. He cannot give mercy until someone says, "God be merciful", and someone does not say that until they are broken and feel that they are a sinner. But when they say, "God be merciful", the gates of heaven fling wide to a person like that. Beggars get into the kingdom of heaven far more quickly than anybody else. They just have to knock and beg and the gates fling wide open. "Have mercy upon me according to your steadfast love and your abundant mercy."

He now appeals for three different things. I used to think that those three phrases, "Blot out my transgressions, wash me thoroughly from my iniquity, and cleanse me from my sin," were simply heaping up words. David had just got hold of the dictionary and was exhausting his oratory to express himself in different ways. Well, when you are really pleading for mercy you do not try oratory on God. Words do not get you anywhere. David is asking for three different things. The first word comes from the world of the library; the second from the world of the laundry; the third from the world of leprosy. David has realised that he needs three separate operations of God upon him.

Some people never realise that sin is more than one thing. They think that one operation of God will deal with sin, but it needs three. David realised that sin was an illegal deed; he had broken the law – that sin was also inherent dirt inside that needed washing. He realised also that it is an infectious disease that will go on spreading unless it is arrested. Here are three ever-deepening understandings of sin. Look first at "blotted transgressions". The word "blotted" means to erase writing. In the ancient days they wrote on papyrus, and when they had written with a brush and ink and they wanted to rub it out, they took a penknife and they scraped off the ink until it was clean and then they could write on it again.

The word for that scraping was "blot out". David knew that every wrong thing we do goes down in a book. It is kept in a written record of God. He is saying: "O God, take your penknife and scrape that off so that something new can be written on the page of my life. That is the first thing we need when we have done wrong: to get the record straight and to get it blotted out. But the second thing we need is to get the dirt out of our heart. Sin is not what we have done outwardly, it is what we are inwardly. Some time ago a security firm in England decided to try to invent a thief-proof briefcase so that people carrying important papers could avoid them being stolen. This briefcase, as soon as somebody grabbed it did two things. It set off a big alarm that aroused everybody nearby and gave warning, and secondly, it shot out purple dye in the direction of the man holding it – a dye that cannot be erased, so the poor chap on the run, covered with purple, would be noticed by everybody. The colour of his deed would be on him and everybody would see it, and he would be trapped sooner or later unless he managed to stay permanently in hiding. I don't think it was ever a successful product nor did it sell, but it was an intriguing idea. David realises that it is the colour that this deed leaves behind it, deep within, the dirt that gets ingrained in the fabric of our character. You see, once you have done wrong, even if you get it blotted out, it is what has happened to you that is the important thing. You have become a dirty person. So, he says, "Wash me thoroughly."

The third thing is something even more. He realises that sin is a kind of spiritual cancer that, once it gets a hold, spreads. It is like leprosy. As leprosy separates you from man, sin separates you from God. As leprosy eats away your flesh, sin eats away your spirit. Even if you manage to arrest the disease and stop it spreading, you need a creating act to restore what has been wasted. You will notice that note comes in the Psalm: "Create in me a clean heart". The old heart has been wasted. Even though the disease is arrested I need a new creation. I need a new spirit as a leper needs new flesh if he is going to be restored. So he prays, and the first part of the Psalm goes through these three aspects of sin.

Take vv. 3–4: he neither denies, nor can he forget, his sin. He knows perfectly well he did wrong. "I know my transgressions." Thank God David doesn't say, "Well, everybody's doing it Lord." Thank God that David doesn't say, "Well, I was ignorant that this was wrong," or, "I was under pressure. I was tired at the time." He does not excuse himself. He is saying: Lord, I know it and I cannot get away from it.

Martin Luther wrote in his diary these words when he was

seeking God: "My sin plagues me. It gives me no rest, no peace. Whether I eat or drink, sleep or wake, I am always in terror of God's wrath and judgment." You need to be brought to that point before you can be lifted up again, when your sin is ever before you. You dream about it; your first thought in the morning is: "Will somebody find out about it today?" "My sin is ever before me. I know it." David is acknowledging: God, it is in your sight that I did evil; you were watching and in your sight it was wrong whatever anybody else thought. They were all off at the war. I thought it was between me and Bathsheba, but you saw it. Against thee, thee only have I sinned.

Now, of course, human judgment cannot understand this. Human judgement would say, "David, you sinned against Bathsheba," but he says, "Against thee have I sinned." Do you realise that anything we do to our fellow human beings we have done to God because we did it to a creature made in his image? Against thee have I sinned. Have you been unkind to someone? You were unkind to God in so doing. David, unlike so many of us, in fact all of us, did not justify himself.

Christopher Mayhew did a series of studies on the lives of criminals. He visited prison after prison and he talked to the men. Nearly all of them used this phrase, "I saw, I wanted, I took." He noticed this phrase again and again and he wrote it down in the article. That is almost a verbatim account of Genesis 3. Eve saw, she desired, she took. That is what sin is: you see something, you want something, you take it – whatever it is.

Christopher Mayhew said: "Hardly any of the criminals I talked to would admit to responsibility for what they had done. They all tried to justify themselves. They all tried to blame someone or something else." But David says, "God, you are justified if you punish. I do not justify myself, I justify you." Thinking back to Psalm 50, he saw himself in the dock, and the choirmaster's dream was true about him and he pleaded guilty and said, "Oh God, you are justified. You are blameless in your sentence. I am not blameless, you are."

But sin is more than what we do; it is what we are. It is this inherent dirt. Now v. 5 is a verse that many people misunderstand and I want to deal with it. It does not mean that David was born out of wedlock. It has nothing to do with that. It does not mean that sexual intercourse is sin. Many people have made this verse mean that and it does not. God made people male and female. It does not mean that David is blaming some hereditary perversion, and saying, "Well, it was my father and grandfather responsible." What it does mean is this: the colour of my nature is not the effect of what I have done, it is the cause of what I have done. In other words, I haven't become a sinner because I have committed sins; I have committed sins because I always was a sinner. That is the difference. To be convicted of sin is to realise not that I am a basically good person who has done something bad, but I am a basically bad man who has done something bad. That is the Bible's diagnosis. You do bad things because you are bad. You were bad before you did bad things. Our three children are not born innocent, they are not born pure.

David realises it is not just one deed but his whole nature, his whole life. God, I shall never get clean even if you blot out this transgression that I have done; I am not clean as a result of that. The book is clean but I am not; therefore, I pray that you will get deep down. I am almost using the advertisements for soap powder now, but that is what he does. "Purge me with hyssop" – the ingrained dirt in the fabric of my nature you will have to get right down and get me whiter than snow. He is using laundry language here.

Wash me; you want me to be clean inside; you desire truth in the inward parts, not just that I should speak honestly but that I should be honest; not just that I should do clean things but that I should be clean. Therefore, get deep down into my nature. Get me clean Lord. It is a plea for an inward purging of his nature. Now you see this is going deeper. Plenty of people when they are discovered in a wrong thing want that wrong thing to be blotted out, but they do not ask to be clean, to be washed. They just want the record straight so they won't be punished. But this man is saying: God, I want to get clean right down, whiter than snow, pure inside, in my secret heart wisdom to know what is right – I feel like a man whose every bone is fractured. Let the bones that are broken rejoice.

Now he moves on to a third thing. Leprosy is a terrible disease, separating us from others, wasting our flesh. We don't know what leprosy is in this country. I used to visit a leprosy hospital in Newcastle. It was built for lepers but there wasn't one left there. He now sees sin as a disease that even when it is arrested has wasted his spirit. Now he is saying: "O God, I need something even more than washing. I need a re-creation. I need restoring. Create in me a clean heart O God, and renew, put a new and right spirit within me."

Now that is a miracle of regeneration. No psychologist, no social worker, no reformer can do that for a person. The reformer might be able to get things blotted out but the reformer cannot wash the inside of a person, and the social worker certainly cannot give them a new heart. They can only help to get the record straight, and that is not enough. So he prays for a clean heart: God, I can never do this on my own; so the one thing I beg you is, don't leave me; I realise my sin should separate me from you, but I beg you take not your presence from me, take not your Holy Spirit away, because only your Holy Spirit can give me a clean heart, born again of the Spirit, renewed, made perfect. He pleads with God to hold on to him.

He said: Even when you've given me a clean heart uphold me, hang on to me with a willing Spirit. Here is a man who does not go into the future cocksure. This is not a man who says, "Well that's dealt with that, now I can manage on my own." Here is a man who says: "God, unless you hang on to me from now on I'll not make it," and he pleads with God to hang on to him.

Once again he admits that he is miserable, and anyone is who has realised that they have transgressed. He says: "Restore to me the joy. I'm miserable. I've not been happy since this happened." If people are really honest when they have done a wrong thing – seen, desired, taken – it does not make them happy. They thought it would and they are miserable. Restore to me the joy of knowing that I am clean, the joy of knowing I am with you, the joy of being holy.

Now of course, again the world cannot see this. The world says that the quickest way to be miserable is to be holy, and the quickest way to be happy is to do wrong. Unfortunately again, it is a proof of our perverted nature from our earliest years that we get a greater kick out of something that is forbidden than out of something that we are told to do. But he now knows that if you want real joy and gladness then you get it by being clean. Just as when you have got out of a bath physically, you are feeling fit and sparkling and fresh and clean. It is a lovely feeling, so to get out of a spiritual bath is to have joy of your salvation.

Now before we leave vv. 1–12 I want you to notice that he makes sixteen requests in those few verses – sixteen things he has that he wants God to do for him. Do you realise that this list of David's is completely different from the kind of shopping list we bring in prayer unless we are growing in grace? We ask for health, strength, safety and happiness. Look what David asks for. He asks for cleansing, for washing, for restoration, for filling; these are the kinds of things he asks for. This is his list for God, and I will say that God loves to respond to this kind of request. To ask for a clean heart – this is something God loves to give.

Now we turn to the second half of the Psalm more briefly. This is not a series of promises as to what he will do then; it is a statement of consequences. Then certain things will happen. The first thing that will happen is that he will be able to give others an attractive witness. Now it is possible to give an unattractive witness – very easy so to testify to your Christian faith that you offend people and put them off – but if you want to give an attractive witness you will do it if you have been broken and cleansed. It is offensive unless it springs from this.

Now again, the world would say: "If you have made a mess of your life, if you have been in moral trouble, keep quiet about it. Don't you dare teach anybody else how to behave." But God would say: when you have been cleansed, go and tell someone; share it, tell the whole world about your sins because your sins are gone. The world doesn't talk like this. If an unbeliever gets into trouble they don't want to talk about it. They wouldn't, but have you noticed how effective Christian testimony becomes when a man says, "I did this, and I've been forgiven."

Do you know what happens when that kind of testimony is given? Sinners are converted to God. Why? Because the testimony is coming not from some holy Pharisee who says, "I thank thee that I am not as this man I'm witnessing to," but from a sinner like themselves who has found hope. This is the kind of testimony that says, "I have done what you have done – I have played the fool, but Christ saved me." That is the kind of testimony that brings sinners. Not, "I am pure and clean and I always have been, and you ought to learn to be too." That doesn't bring sinners to Christ, but the humble testimony of someone who has learned through forgiveness the grace of God. He will give this testimony in two ways: speech and song. "I will teach transgressors your ways" – he now has the moral authority to teach others because of forgiveness, not because he is good. You see, if we could only teach others the ways of God because we have been utterly good, then I could not be a preacher and a congregation could not be witnesses. But it is forgiveness that gives us the authority to teach transgressors his ways. It will come not only in instructive speech but in inspiring song.

He now mentions mouth, lips and tongue. "God, if you will deliver me I will sing aloud." These are the two grand channels of testimony: speech and song. Speaking to people; singing to them. Testimony in speech and song comes together wonderfully.

But you notice the psalmist won't be able to sing unless the Lord is in it: "Open my lips and my mouth shall show forth your praise." You cannot sing the praise of God just by opening your mouth. God has to open it. He has to do a work in your heart that will fling wide your lips and let it come out, and then you will sing forth his praise. That is the kind of singing God loves to hear – when he opened the lips by forgiveness; by delivering from blood guiltiness. The other thing that will happen when you know forgiveness for sin is acceptable worship because it is then real.

Let me tell you about a man who had been bad and who had found forgiveness through Christ. He went back to his (Church of England) church the next week. They went through the service that he had been through Sunday after Sunday, week after week, month after month, year after year, using the same words. But he came to me afterwards and said, "You know, that service was wonderful. I never knew it was as wonderful as that and I had been saying it for years." Now what had changed? The worship? Not a thing; something had changed in his heart.

That is the secret of true worship: it depends how you come. Forms of service have undergone many changes, but what makes for acceptable worship is a broken spirit. When did you last bring a broken heart to a service of worship? It is the one thing God wanted from you. Not a heart broken by suffering, but a heart broken by sin. A heart that has been shattered by the discovery of how evil one's nature really is. To come with a broken and a contrite heart – God never despises that. Other people do, they despise someone who is broken. If you bring that kind of offering in worship, you will love the service. Samuel Chadwick used to love to say, "God can do wonders with a broken heart if you'll give him all the pieces." He was referring to a heart broken by sin.

The last two verses of the Psalm tell us two very important things. They are added by way of parenthesis. The truth in v. 18 is this: nobody can sin privately. What you do is bound to affect the place where you live, the family where you live, the city where you live, the nation where you live, the world in which you live. No man lives to himself.

Therefore David now realises that he as king of Jerusalem may have put Jerusalem in jeopardy; he prays that God will do good to Zion, that God will not take it out on the city in which he lives. It is a very important thing to remember that even though your sin was privately done it will have public effects, whether you know it or not. The holiness of the church, any church, will be the sum holiness of the individual members. One member's sin can pull a church down and hold it back like the sin of Achan holding back the Israelites when they were conquering the Promised Land. So he prays that the public effects of his sin will be neutralised.

Verse 19 tells us the other important thing. Even though true worship is an inward thing of the heart, that does not mean that it should not be expressed in outward act. "Then you can bring the burnt offerings, then you can bring the sacrifices". Then you can go through the ritual and you can bring all the outward things; then God will have them. When the inside is right, the outside is acceptable. I mention this because there is a false idea that provided you have got the inward right you do not need the outward. Somebody, for example, will say to me, "Well, I'm right with Christ, I don't need to be baptized." Other Christians have said, "I'm right with God, I don't need the Lord's Supper." Others have said, "Well, I belong to the Body of Christ; I don't need to join a local church." This is a false inwardness.

Now it is true that being baptized, coming to the Lord's Supper, and joining a local church is of no value to God if there isn't the inward contrite spirit forgiven behind it. But, once there is that, then these things take their place, then baptism is right, then the Lord's Supper is right, then the outward committal of one's life to the local church fellowship is right. Then the "burnt offering". It is as if David is saying: I won't hold anything back. I'll give the lot then. Then all my time, then all my money, then everything, the whole burnt offering, will be given to God and he will accept it. David acknowledges to the choirmaster: I've been one of those who didn't offer true worship, but I'm doing so now, and here is a Psalm for us to sing next Sabbath as we confess.

I finish with two quotations. One is from P.T. Forsyth: "Our churches are full of the nicest, kindest people who have never known the despair of guilt or the breathless wonder of forgiveness." The other is from a Baptist minister writing in a magazine for Baptist ministers. He said that he found in a group of ministers that when he confessed his sin and found it forgiven, "It is a very blessed business, brethren, to know yourself truly forgiven."

READ PSALM 73

Psalm 73 is a Psalm of Asaph and I don't know much about him but I know this much: he was an honest man. Indeed, those who wrote the Bible were utterly honest. He has expressed in this Psalm the kind of feelings that you have had, those problems that you have struggled with. The basic problem to all thinking people who belong to God is this: there is such a stark contradiction between one's faith and the facts of life. Sooner or later every one of us must cope with this contradiction and come to terms with it. We believe one thing and we see another. We are quite sure that God is good, and yet we look at a world and we say, "Well, where is there any evidence of it?" It is this contradiction between what we believe and what we see in the world, between faith and facts, which lies behind this Psalm.

Now his faith is expressed in v. 1, that if God is good then he must be good to good people; that if a person lives a straight and upright life in a world made by a good God, then surely God must be good to that person. If they have sought to live as they ought to live, if they have sought not only to be good in their outward behaviour, but pure in their heart too, so that they have tried to get out of their hearts wrong motives, wrong desires, wrong affections, and have sought to live to God alone, surely God must be good to that kind of a person if he is a good God, but the facts are against this.

Sometimes it is those people who seem to be the best people who suffer most. On the other hand, there are wicked people who seem to play the fool and they don't have to pay the bill, they get away with it. There may have been times when you looked at some of your neighbours who never darkened the door of a church, never bother about God. They might put something in Christian Aid envelopes if you knocked at their door, but they never seek to live as God would have them live and they don't have half the troubles you have. They live happy, easy, comfortable lives apparently, with everything that you would like to have and don't have.

Have you ever felt: if God is good why does he allow this kind of contradiction? Why do the wicked prosper and the innocent suffer? Why do those who really try to live as God would have them live have so many burdens to carry, when their next-door neighbour who doesn't even try has so few? Now this is the problem that Asaph had, and he was honest about it. He is saying that he was on the verge of slipping right out of his faith because of it. He was honest about it. Not only was it an intellectual problem in his mind, it was a moral problem. The temptation was to say, "What's the use? Why try to be good? It doesn't pay. Why try to live as God would have you live when it just doesn't work out?" He was on the verge of saying that.

Now he describes his innermost thoughts, and this Psalm is made up of two parts. First of all, vv. 2–16. He makes a comparison between himself and his neighbours, which leads him to envy. He admits quite honestly: "I was envious". Sometimes people have said to me, "You know, I've looked at people who are not Christians and sometimes I envy them. Life is so much simpler for them and apparently much easier." From one point of view it is. Now let me say straight away that envy is one of the worst sins in the book. It was responsible for the first murder in history. Why did Cain kill Abel? For envy.

It was responsible for the worst murder in history. Pilate saw that the Jews wanted to kill Jesus out of envy. This sin which was responsible for the first and the worst murders of history is something that can find its way right into a Christian's heart. You may know the old legend of a saint in North Africa who lived such a holy life that finally Satan and his demons held a conference as to what to do about him, because his life was influencing so many people for good.

He sent the demons, so the legend goes, to tempt this man. They tried and came back and reported failure. So the devil said, "Oh, you're no good at this. I'll have to go myself." He went and he was back in five minutes. He said, "It's alright, he's sinned."

The demons said to the devil, "How on earth did you do it?"

"Well," he said, "I just whispered in his ear, 'Have you heard that your brother has been made Bishop of Alexandria?' and immediately envy smote his heart."

Envy can get right into a man of God. This man Asaph was envious, and he tells us how it happened. He had slipped in his thought. He nearly slipped in his words, and he was on the verge of slipping in his deeds. Once the wrong thought has got into your mind, the wrong words are likely to come out, and then the wrong behaviour follows. Thought, word and deed is the order in which we sin. Now look what happened. He studied the life of wicked people. He studied the life of those who did not worship God, did not try to read God's Word, did not do anything about God at all. On the contrary, they just looked after themselves.

This is what he found, and every verse describes a fact about their life. Verses 4–12, first of all he says: they do not suffer physically and they die peacefully; there are no pangs when they pass; they seem to get right to the end of the road with bodies that are sleek and sound; they don't suffer; many of them have jolly good health and they just don't have to go through sickness. This is true, some don't. He is not describing individuals, he is describing the group. Verse 5, he says they have a peace and a freedom from trouble and worry that the man of God does not have. They are not in trouble as other men are; they are not stricken like other men.

Verse 6, they are proud and this is a humble man speaking, but he says, "They are proud, they wear pride round their neck like a necklace. In fact, in the Bible the part of the body that most shows pride is your neck. I know we tend to say it is the nose. If somebody's nose is carried fairly high we reckon that is the part of the body where pride shows. But the Bible says it shows in the neck – as to how you carry your neck. They carry pride as a necklace, looking down at other people. They are proud, and they look at these poor men of God struggling along, and they say, "Look at you. What a mess your life is in, what troubles you have. We don't have those troubles," and they re proud of it. They have pride as their necklace and violence covers them as a garment. They do not care how they get what they get, as long as they do.

Verse 7, they are filled with pleasures. The word used here is "follies", which is an intriguing word, but it says their eyes swell out with fatness; their hearts overflow with follies. They enjoy life to the full, they have their pleasures, and they have plenty of them. Verse 8 describes their position. They reach the top. How do they reach it? I heard it said of a businessman some time ago that he had reached the top of the ladder by stepping on those below him and by licking the boots of those above him. That is how he got up the ladder and this is what verse 8 is saying in biblical language. They get on, they get up the ladder. How do they get up? By threatening violence and oppression, by speaking with malice, by scoffing, by setting themselves up. Verse 9 describes their profanity: "They speak against heaven, and their tongue struts through the earth." They do not care what they say about God. They are the self-made men. They are those who do not need God, and they will speak against heaven and nothing happens, nothing at all.

Verse 10 describes their popularity. Such people are envied and admired by the world. They have got on; it doesn't matter how they got on. They made it. They got there, and however they got there they have got it, and I wish I had got it too. They are popular. People turn and praise them and don't find fault with them. They find fault with men of God, but not with this kind of person. The world excuses its own but finds fault with those better than itself. Verse eleven describes their presumption. They say, "How can God know? He doesn't know about my life. Where is he? Let him strike me down if I'm doing wrong." They say, "Is their knowledge in the Most High? God doesn't care about individuals. God doesn't know what I'm doing. I'm keeping it to myself." They mock in their profanity and presumption.

Finally, v. 12, they make a profit at it. Things come easily to them. A man said recently, "The first ten thousand is the hardest to get. After that there is no limit. Once you have got there you re away, and the thing just multiplies itself." I do not think that is quite true, but things come easily to these people. They just seem to touch a thing and it turns to gold. They are in the right thing at the right time, and off they go. This poor man of God, Asaph, looks at this and says, "How can such a thing be if God is good? If God is a good God surely he wouldn't let people get away with this." Now that is part of his problem. The other part comes out in vv. 13–16; he is having a rough time.

Now there are four things that he finds very difficult. First of all in v. 13, the innocence of his conduct. He has tried to live right. He has tried to keep his hands clean in business and in other ways. He has tried to live an upright life, and it has all been in vain apparently. It is not worth it; it does not pay. I know that people have said that honesty is the best policy, I do not think that is true – the Bible doesn't say it anyway. If honesty is only a policy it is not honesty. The real test of whether it is honesty is whether you are still honest when it is a bad policy and does not profit you. He is saying: all in vain have I kept my heart clean and washed my hands in innocence; it has not brought me any benefit; it is my next-door neighbours who have got all the blessings in life. Oh, there are times when I say it is not worth it. It is too much trouble to try and live right; much easier not to try.

The second thing that troubles him, in v. 14, is the injustice of his life. Every morning he wakes and faces trouble. He is chastened every morning. He finds that life punishes him. Someone asked me once, "How is life treating you? Or are you having to pay?" He is having to pay in this verse: "All the day long I have been stricken." When he gets up in the morning it is not to a lovely morning full of blessing; he knows he is going to have trouble that day. The third thing, in v. 15, is the inhibition of his tongue. He must not speak about this.

Now here is a thorough man of God who is really going through all this trouble, and he knows that if he speaks about his envy, and if he speaks about his problem, he is going to discourage other people. What help is it if we have a testimony of someone who gets up and says, "It's just not worth trying to live right"? It would discourage others, causing other believers to slip and stumble. When we are going through it like this we must not give testimony – we have to keep it to ourselves lest we discourage someone weaker in the faith.

Then v. 17, "Until I went to the sanctuary of God." When you are going through it and you cannot understand why, then get to church. Go to the sanctuary and worship with God's people even if you do not feel like it. Even if you feel it is the last place you want to be, it is the very best place for you to be. When you feel it is just not worth it and that it is no good trying to keep on as a Christian, then get to the sanctuary of God and you will begin to see things in a different way. Why do you come to church? Well, you come to worship but among many other things, you come to get the right perspective on life, to begin to see things rightly, to get balance, and to begin to understand.

When I began my ministry in the Shetland Islands, when things got me down and I began to feel that things were wrong and that God was not blessing as he should, I used to go and climb the wonderful hills. Not a tree up there – you can see for miles, vistas of islands and sea. I used to get right up on top of the hill, look out and look down at the little crofts in the town where I worked. I saw my problems were much smaller than I thought. I got a new perspective; I got a big view of God. When you get a big view of God you get a smaller view of yourself and your problems and your questions.

But even better than going up into the hills from which your help can come is to go to the hill of God, to go to the sanctuary of God, to go to worship and begin to look at things rather differently. When you do, you begin to make quite a different comparison between yourself and that neighbour. You begin to see them in a different light; you begin to see yourself in a different light, and you begin to reverse the conclusion to which you had come. Asaph was really depressed, really down; it just did not seem worth it to go on trying to live as God would have him live – until he went to the sanctuary and could then see it all.

Now the interesting thing is this: in the first comparison two-thirds of the verses are about his neighbours, and only a third about himself, but now after he has been to worship in the second comparison, a third is about his neighbours and two-thirds about himself. He begins to see that he has got far more than they have. Now look at what he sees. He had looked at their prosperity in this world. When he went to worship God he saw their prospect in the next, and that gave him a different outlook. If you could see the future awaiting some of these prosperous, godless people you would not envy them, you would do something quite different.

So he looked at their prospect and he saw three things. First, he saw that they were to be destroyed. He had nearly slipped because he was envious of them. Now he sees that they are at the top of a glacier and that they are in the slippery place; they are in the danger, not him. Now the word "destroy" does not mean necessarily to cease to be. It means: to waste, to become ruined and useless for the purpose for which God made you. He can see that they are ruining themselves, that they will be perished one day. He does not envy them now. Do you envy someone who has a good time in this life if that is what it is going to lead to?

The second thing is that they are to be desolated and that means they are to be robbed of everything. They will have to leave their follies behind; they will have to leave their pleasures behind. There isn't a single thing that they can keep, not one—that is the hell of it. I remember hearing a joke about a golfer who went to hell and there was a lovely golf course. He thought, "This is going to be marvellous" – but there were no balls," said the joke. That joke was picking up a very real biblical truth. The opportunity and capacity to enjoy the things that have been enjoyed here will not be there in hell."They shall be desolated," says the psalmist.

Some are having a great time now; they have all the good things that life can offer – but when you die you cannot take that with you.

"How much did he leave?" said a lady of a wealthy man who died. The person she asked replied, "Everything." A shroud has no pocket. There are things that you can take with you when you die. There are things you can send on ahead. "Lay up for yourselves treasure in heaven where neither rot, moth, nor rust consume, and thieves do not break in and steal" (and a switch of fortunes in the stock exchange does not affect your balance).

The third thing he now sees is that one day they will be despised. People look up to them now and say, "My, I wish I could have been as clever as he has been. I wish I could have got the things he's got." But one day, instead of looking up, people will look down and say, "Poor thing, poor thing."

Someone who comes to faith begins to look at his own life a bit more. He realises for the first time that he has some wonderful things that his neighbour has not got. He begins to change his ideas about his own balance. But first he makes an apology to God: "O God, I have been beastly to you. I've behaved like an animal. When my mind was bitter and twisted like this I was no better than an animal." Why? Because an animal must live for this world and for no other. We talk about "creature" comforts – have you noticed that phrase? It is very significant. The kind of things that an animal would want: plenty to eat and a warm place to sleep. But now he can say: Lord, I've been talking as if I'm just an animal, as if when I die that is the end; I have been talking as if I am just a creature; why was I so bitter and so envious?

Now, from his beastliness, he begins to consider his blessedness. He lists four wonderful blessings that every man and woman of God has. The first is this: the presence of God. I was talking to a lady living alone. I asked, "How do you find it, living on your own?" She replied, "I'm never alone." What a blessing. The ungodly don't have that blessing. They are often alone and there is desperate loneliness. But the man or woman of God is never alone. That is a blessing. Your neighbour may have plenty of friends and be very popular, but there will be times when they will be desperately alone, and you are never alone. The psalmist says: "I am continually with you. You hold my right hand; you don't let me go." Other people may despise me. Other people may chasten me and persecute me and forget me, but you have got a firm grip of my hand. We don't have to hold on to God, he holds on to us. He has a way of pulling us back however far we get—your presence.

Blessing number two: your purpose for my life, which will go right through to eternity. "You will guide me with your counsel and afterward receive me to glory," and the ungodly cannot say that. They must sort out their decisions themselves. They must struggle with their own perplexities. The godly person says: you guide me with your counsel; you show me the way to go; you tell me what to do; even at the end of the road I am just beginning, because afterwards you will receive me into glory. God's purpose goes through all eternity.

Thirdly, he mentions how precious God is to him. He says, "There's nobody on earth I want more than you, and there's nobody in heaven I look forward to meeting more than you". That is a blessing. When God means more to you than your nearest and dearest, you have found a wonderful blessing. When you look forward to heaven even more because you are going to meet God than because you will meet those who lived and died in the faith and fear of Christ, you have found a great blessing.

The fourth blessing, he says, is this: "Your strength is in my heart." My flesh is weak. I may grow old. I may have a difficult old age. I may have some handicap when my godless neighbour does not. But even though my flesh may fail and my heart may fail, you can pick my heart up. Your strength is in my heart.

Paul was saying the same thing when he said, "My outward man is decaying, but my inward man is getting stronger every day." These are blessings the man of God has that the godless man does not have. You do not realise it until you go to worship maybe; until you think about these things and stop thinking about the other things for an hour, and think about your future and theirs.

The first comparison led the psalmist to envy. It led him to envy those whose life was so easy and so nice, but the second comparison leads to something quite different. It leads to evangelism. The epilogue in vv. 27–28 gives us his conclusions. Those who are far from God are facing retribution in God. Those who are near to God find in him a refuge. Those who are far from God need to run further *from* him because retribution comes from him; those who are near to him run *to* him. Therefore, the real thing that he wants to do now is not to run away from it all; not to say, "It's not worth it. It's just too much trouble to try and live the life of faith"; not to run away and get far from God, because that way lies punishment; that way lies perishing.

Look at it, "For lo, those who are far from thee shall perish. Thou dost put an end to those who are false to thee." But he is not going to run away; he is going to run back to God. He is not going to hide from him, he is going to hide in him.

Then he says, and this is the lovely conclusion, "... that I may tell of all your works".

We can apply this to ourselves and say: I am going to tell my neighbour: I have got something that you haven't got, but I want you to have it. I've got blessings that you know nothing about, but I want you to share them. I want you to know what God has done for me, and how he has held my right hand, and how he has been with me all the time, even when I didn't realise it; how he guided me; how he brought me back again, and how he is preparing glory for me. I want to tell everybody of his works. When I was envious I could not speak. It would have hurt people to talk about God as

I felt then. But now that I have seen it all from a different light – now that I have seen it all properly – I want to tell the whole world about God.

This Psalm is full of honest, personal, spiritual experience. This man Asaph has been dead and gone these three thousand years. Though he is in glory – he said he would be and I am quite sure he is. Yet through those three thousand years this man speaks to people who have felt just the same, and who wondered if it was all worth it. Then they came to the sanctuary and they heard that it was wonderfully worth it, and that God wants them to go and tell others of his blessing.

READ PSALM 90

Psalm 90 is written by an old man, that is obvious. Young men don't talk like Psalm 90; they don't talk about the brevity of life. They don't talk about three score years and ten, and if it's four score yet is their span but toil and trouble. You have never heard a teenager pen words like that. It comes from a man at the end of a tough life, a man who lived in the desert, a man who was responsible for a group of people, two and a half million strong, a man who had to lead them through a wilderness when he had no food for any of them and no water for them to drink, a man who got them through after forty years, but died before he reached his goal. It is the Psalm of a tired man too, a man who is a bit weary with life, feeling his age.

A wonderful old doctor who lived in Yorkshire, Dr Vines, when he was in his eighties, or early nineties, was invited to go and speak to the local youth club. He went and spoke to them. When he had finished, a girl in a mini-skirt got up and said, "Oh Doctor Vines, you are old fashioned."

He said, "My dear young lady, you came into this world an old fashioned way and you will go out of it an old fashioned way."

What a brilliant answer! This Psalm is for people who realise that life is short. I don't know when you first really realised this. I can remember two peaks in my life. One, when a friend of mine was drowned. Brian was swept out to sea and didn't come back; his body was washed up two days later. I can remember as a young teenage boy lying awake and thinking, "Where is he now? Is he anywhere?

Is he alive? Is he dead? Is he gone? Has he just gone out like a light?" Then I can remember at the age of thirty or thereabouts when a very big change occurred in my life. I remember thinking then, "My, I could be over the top." I remember realising then, at depth, that I only had one life to live and that the decisions I was making at that time were so important because I could waste the rest of my life by making the wrong decision.

From time to time since, the thought has come flooding through, "Your life is going." Men between fifty and sixty tend to go through a real phase of looking back and saying, "What have I done? What have I left behind? What have I achieved?" Moses was writing a Psalm feeling like that. He is looking back over the years: Lord, you are secure; you have been there all along; you have been our dwelling place in all generations.

For, you know, a real man of God never talks privately. He can't, he is part of a family. A real man of God says "our", he doesn't just say "my". There will be personal moments when there will burst from his lips a very personal prayer or praise. But the man of God says, "Lord, you have been our dwelling place". The first thing about a man of God is his address, and you will always find him at it. His dwelling place is God.

I said to my congregation: "This church is not the church of God in Guildford, it is the church of Guildford in God." That was our address. I remember meeting a German who had been brought into the Hitler Youth in the 1930s. They put him on the mat and questioned him, asking: "Where do you live?" He said, "Stuttgart." "Wrong answer. Where do you live?"

"Germany."

"Wrong answer. Where do you live?"

"The Third Reich."

"Wrong answer, where do you live?"

He said, "I don't know what answer you want."

They said, "When we ask you 'Where do you live,' you say, 'I live in Hitler.' That's your address. That's where you live from now on. You live in him."

That man became a Christian in a prisoner of war camp in Britain because a Christian in this country pushed sandwiches through the barbed wire to him. He says, "Now I live in Christ" – that is where he lives, wherever he goes.

Wherever we are, the Lord is our dwelling place in all generations. I want to emphasise this because far too many people just "visit" God. Do you know what I mean by that? Some people just visit God when they are in an emergency. When they are in real trouble and no one else can help them they say, "Oh God," and it is just paying a visit. Some people just pay visits occasionally to the Lord's people to worship. As some put it, "they go there to be hatched, matched, and dispatched." Or, as one man said to me: "Every time I go to church they throw something at me; they either throw water or confetti or ground." Well that was his fault for only going on those occasions, but that is just visiting God.

Even those of us who come every Sunday to church can still be visiting God. The point is: where do you live on Monday and Tuesday and Wednesday? "God is our dwelling place" – that means that is where I stay. I don't just visit him. I don't just go and see him now and again.

The word "dwelling place" could be translated "refuge". A word that combines both meanings would be "haven". God is our haven. Home is a haven. To come to God is like coming home. Many people have found, praise God, through a Christian fellowship that coming to God is coming home, a haven, someone to turn to, someone who is there, someone who cares about the troubles, someone to whom you can come. That is how this Psalm opens. Here is a man of God.

It says at the beginning of the Psalm: "A prayer of Moses, the man of God." The first thing a man of God is is someone who lives in God – not just visits him but lives in him.

But the rest of the Psalm is what I want to draw your attention to now. I want to divide it up into three simple points and they are these. If you are going to be a man of God you have to face facts. There is no room for fantasy in religion. It has to be real; it has to be based on fact. When you meet God and when he becomes your dwelling place you have to face up sternly to three stark facts which the world refuses to face. It is difficult enough for us to, but if you are going to meet God and if you are going to live in him, you have to live with these three facts about yourself. Fact number one: our insecurity in God. Now that is a strange word and I will tell you what it means shortly. Fact number two: our iniquity before God. Fact number three: our inability without God.

Let us take the first: our insecurity. If there is one thing as clear as that God is there, it is that we will not be here much longer. In four vivid pictures Moses says that human life is like dust. What happens to dust? Blow it away, wipe it away – it has gone. He says human life is not only like dust, it is like driftwood: you sweep men away as on a flood. Have you ever watched the Thames in flood and seen a bit of driftwood just going down the stream and disappearing from view? That is human life. He says human life is like a dream. I might sometimes remember a dream but only little bits of it, and then it has almost gone.

He says that life is like a desert. I have lived in the Arabian Desert and when it rains the grass springs up in hours. Its like a greenhouse and barren hills of Aden can go green in hours. Then the hot sirocco wind from the desert comes and the green disappears and the grass withers and goes by evening. I have seen it happen, and that is human life too. We grow up and we flourish, then we wither and we are gone, and our place knows us no more. It is God who does that to us. Let us make no mistake about it. Death is not a natural event for man. It is a supernatural event. It is something that God does. The Lord gave and the Lord takes away. Therefore, one of the first things the man of God discovers is that his life is not his own, it is on loan to him. God gave it to him for a brief period and will take it back again and will ask him what he has done with it. It is not his, it is God's.

The first thing we need to learn if we are going to be men of God is the insecurity we have in God. He is always there. Before the mountains were brought forth, or before he had formed the world, he was there. From everlasting to everlasting, God was always there. Yet the stark contrast is that we are not always here.

Every year in every church there are some names we cross off our membership roll. They have left us; they have gone. We need to know that. We need to ask a very important question: why? Why does God take our life away from us? Death robs us of all that we cherish. I mentioned that the world won't face facts. One of the facts the world won't face is the fact that your life will be taken from you. How many people are living as if they are here forever? Jesus said "You fool" to the businessman who said, "I'm going to build up a bigger business".

Jesus says, "You fool, tonight your soul will be required of you."

I tell you, we are on the run from death. A doctor in one of my congregations told us: "You know, as people get older their bodies get full of aches and pains and they come to me with them. If I tell them, 'You're getting old,' they laugh and they say, 'Yes, we all are. Born too soon,' and they laugh. But if I tell them, 'you're wearing out' they go all serious." That is not funny. It is a fact of life, which you have to face

– that God gave and God will take it away again. I don't know how long I am here for, and you don't. It is short, and if you are not prepared to face that fact squarely you will never be a man or woman of God.

The question is: why does he take it away? Why does he allow this thing to come since it is not natural to us to die? We know it isn't – we rebel against it. We hide from it, we run away from it. We dress a funeral up like a harvest festival to try and make it life, but we cannot disguise it. Why does God do it? The answer is in the second fact of life. Our insecurity in God is due to our iniquity before God. The stark truth is: we are not fit to live forever. You see, no scientist has ever been able to discover why we die. From the moment a baby is born a clock has been started that will tick off the hours. Maybe three-score years and ten, maybe four-score years, maybe even much longer. Whatever it is, the clock has started to tick. If a part of my body is lost or damaged I can replace it. If I rub my hands, there are dead cells of skin dropping on the pulpit, but if I am healthy they are replaced. If I get exercise and air and food I can go on replacing. Why can't that not go on happening? I will tell you why – death is not an event, it is an execution. When God made the world he looked at it and said: now that is very good. His message to man was: I have put you in there to enjoy it but don't you spoil it. In the day that you start disobeying me, I will have to put a sentence of death on you; I am not going to allow evil to spoil my world forever. That is exactly what happened.

From Adam onwards, that same sentence of death has been passed on to every generation because it is in our nature, because we have spoiled God's world and it makes him angry. The next section of the Psalm, "Who considers the anger of God?" Well, who considers God anyway? But if they consider God, they just want a God of love and comfort, a kind of almighty hot water bottle just to warm them up when they are cold, to comfort them when they are lonely. But who considers the power of his anger? But you know, if you had spent your love and created something beautiful and somebody came along and smashed it or marked it and just ruined it as a sheer vandal, wouldn't you be angry? God is angry – he looks at his world and what does he see? He sees a world that is wrecked.

At least two-thirds of the news headlines are bad news, often more. Sometimes I have picked up my morning newspaper and I haven't been able to find a bit of good news in it. God looks not only at the outside, he looks at the inside of the human heart. I wonder how many people would still be your friends if they could see everything inside you, and God can. God looks down and he is so angry. He says: I can't let those people live forever; I can't let them go on spoiling my world – I'll give them seventy, eighty years but I can't give them more than that. It is going to spoil my whole plan and purpose to let them live forever." So it is God who withdrew life and he did it for a moral reason.

Death is not so much caused by a physical thing. Whatever appears on your death certificate – hardening of arteries, coronary, whatever, that is not the cause of your death; it is the occasion of it. The cause of your death is sin. The Bible makes that quite clear. You are not fit to live forever. A man of God is someone who has faced up to that very squarely and realised that he has done things which make God angry, and that by nature he is a child of God's wrath, and that he has done many things to make God cross. The life that God gave me, what have I done with it?

The third fact which the man or woman of God must face is his inability without God. What would you say would fulfil and satisfy you when you reach the end of your life? I think most people I talk to, whether they are Christians or not, would probably agree that if you could reach the end of life's journey and say just one thing – "I have lived a happy and a useful life", that that would be satisfying. Would you agree? I have lived a happy and a useful life. Now let me tell you that Moses would agree with you entirely. The final section of the Psalm is concerned with how to live a happy and a useful life. Moses, being a man of God, realised that he could not have either without God. So he asked God to help him with both. The world thinks it can be happy without God. Indeed, the world thinks it is easier to be happy without God.

Alas, sometimes they have been to church and been confirmed in that impression – that if you find God, life is a misery. God forgive us for that libel on his nature, but having said that, Moses was wise. He knew that he could have enjoyed the pleasures of sin for a season, but he knew that is as long as it lasts. He knew that there are many pleasures away from God, there are many enjoyments away from God, but none of them last. The important thing is to find lasting happiness. So Moses prays: "Lord, have pity on us. Satisfy us in the morning so that we can be glad all our days." Some people have thought he meant, "Satisfy us early each morning and then we can celebrate all the day," but I think he meant the morning of life. "So teach us to number our days" – that is wisdom, to count up where you are on the scale.

It may shake you but I am going to try to help you to do that. Let seventy-two years equal twenty-four hours, the day of life (taking seventy-two as an average). One year of your life equals twenty minutes of the day. What time of day are you at now? If you are thirty-six you are at high noon. If you are sixty, you are already living at eight o'clock at night. Now number your days. Work out what time of day it is on your clock. Teach us to number our days, and Lord, satisfy us in the morning that we may be glad all our days.

There was a dear old man in my grandfather's church. He had a long beard and an old wrinkled face, and he came to every service and every prayer meeting, and the women's meeting, and the men's meeting, and the boy scouts, and the girl guides, and the Sunday school, and everything. My grandfather was told to go and stop him coming to some of these things. It was embarrassing. He asked the old man, "Why do you need to come to all of this? If you come to the services, and the prayer, and the fellowship that is enough."

The old man replied, "Look," he said, "I was sixty-seven before I found Christ, and I'm trying to catch up on lost time." Teach us to number our days....

One of the criticisms that comes through in some churches is that they are so geared to the young people. I want to stand firmly and say: Praise God that they are being satisfied in the morning of their life, and that they won't have the regrets that many have had that they only found Christ late. Pray for the Sunday school work, "Oh, satisfy us in the morning." Or if you are not satisfied in the morning, then you could pray: "Lord, give me as many days of joy as I've seen sadness. Give me as many days of happiness as I've seen evil." Moses prayed that. A man in one church came to the Lord at the age of forty and said, "Lord, I've wasted forty years, just give me forty more of service for you." The Lord gave him forty more of service in the fellowship, and he retired from service when he was eighty. "Oh make us glad as many days as you've afflicted us. We've lived under your wrath, may I live as long under your love" – what a prayer.

What time is it on your clock? God wants you to get that time and then look at what is left, that it may be filled with his happiness. You will never be happy unless God has mercy on you and shows you his love. So Moses said: "Lord, have pity on your children, return! How long?" In other words, if you want to live a happy life get God back into it. It is the only way. As long as God is not in it then it is not a happy life. What about usefulness? Well, there are plenty of humanists and plenty of unbelievers trying to help others, but lasting usefulness? Don't we all want to do something *worthwhile* with life? Isn't that word interesting? Don't we all want to do something that is going to be worth something for a while, that is going to last? How we want to do something that is going to last on after us. If we are nobodies we might scratch our names on a monument with a pencil and hope that we can say after we are gone, "Well, my name's scratched on a monument somewhere in the lake district. I wrote it up myself: 'I was here'." You know, we are trying to have a monument to ourselves. Some get their names on brass plates or stones but frankly that is not the way to something that is lasting; that is not lasting usefulness.

I will tell you how to be useful in a lasting way. First of all, let God do something to you, "Let your work appear to us, let your glorious power be manifest to us," says Moses. In other words, before you can be useful you have got to be usable. Before you can do lasting work, God has to do a lasting work with you – that is the Bible teaching. Before you can do anything that will last in God's sight, God has to work with you. So the first prayer for usefulness is, "Let your work appear. You do something with us," says the man of God, "And then establish what we do for you." That is how to live a lastingly useful life, so that you can still at the very end of your life be doing something that is of lasting value. I know saints who have been doing that right until the last, in physical weakness maybe, but to the last they have done something of lasting value.

I think of a wife of a predecessor of mine, a pastor in Chalfont Saint Peter. She died at the age of twenty-one of typhoid. But as she lay dying in her bed she saw everybody in the church and all the young people of the district; she saw them one by one and she sought to lead them to the Saviour. To the last minute she was doing something of lasting value. Moses said: "Lord, let your work appear to us, and then establish our work for you."

Lasting work begins with what God does. When I looked back over the (then) 150 years of history of a church where I served, I thought of how many thousands of meetings had been held, how many thousands of hymns had been sung. The statistics would have overwhelmed, but the vital thing is what lasted would have been begun by what God had done in that fellowship – when his work appeared.

What we have been studying in this Psalm was written in the Old Testament, not the New. We are not living BC, we are living AD. A Christian would not write this Psalm today. He would use it, he would build on it, and you cannot have the New Testament until you have really got a grip of the Old, I believe. To put it differently, you have got to understand God's anger and wrath if you are ever going to find his love. The problem with much Christian living today is that people are trying to find his love without facing up to his wrath and their own iniquity. So the Old Testament is a vital preparation. I have laid a foundation with Psalm 90, but it is melancholy, not merry. It is melancholy because it was written BC. How would a Christian write it? Instead of "a man of God" at the top it would be "a man in Christ".

Someone who is in Christ faces squarely the three facts I have mentioned. But over against them they set three other facts. They face squarely their insecurity in God, but against that they place the resurrection of Jesus from the dead and say: everlasting life is mine and so I am not afraid to die; I am not melancholy – I know that because he lives I shall live also, and I have real life in him. The fact of the resurrection of Jesus answers the fact of insecurity, and a Christian faces both. Praise God that Moses faced the first even before he had the second. Plenty of people won't do that. But as Christians we have no excuse for not facing the first fact when we have got the second, which overwhelms and neutralises the fear of the first.

Against the fact of my iniquity in God's sight and my secret sins which he exposes, I set the death of Jesus. He shed his blood on the cross and paid the penalty. The wrath of God and the anger of God against what I had done, he turned away from me and took into his own body on the tree and that is a fact. So I am no longer a child of wrath, but a child of the Son of his love. Against my inability to live a happy and useful life by myself, I set the fact of the Spirit of Jesus Christ. The Holy Spirit given to me brings the joy (not the pleasure, not the happiness) that is deeper still, and brings to me that usefulness so that I know that where Moses prayed, "May your glorious power be seen," I know that that glorious power is the power of the Holy Spirit. It is he who will begin a good work in me and continue it until it is complete.

Therefore, I know that if my name is forgotten tomorrow, my labours in the Lord are not in vain and that he will establish the work that he has done. Isn't that thrilling? Man may forget but God never does. "Blessed are the dead who die in the Lord. They rest from their labours and their works follow them".

READ PSALM 92

I have observed a revival of interest in poetry in my lifetime. When I was at school, if a boy wrote poetry he was written off, but now it is the done thing and poetry really has come back into its own. That may be one of the reasons why the book of Psalms is again becoming more popular. There are many other reasons too, but much of the Word of God came to us not in prose but in poetry. Most of the prophecies came in poetry.

Now I want just to say a little about Hebrew poetry so that you can understand it and get the feel of it. It is not like English poetry. It is not based on rhythm so much as our poetry is and it is not based on rhyming. Hebrew poetry is very different. It is based rather on what I would call "thought rhythm", and instead of rhyming the sounds it rhymes the thoughts.

So most Hebrew poetry is based on the simple idea of a couplet, in which you state in one sentence a thought and then you repeat the thought in another sentence of almost equal length. You will find that this runs right through prophecy and right through the Psalms, and once you get it, it opens up a whole new field of poetry for you. It is not monotonous – not merely finding a synonym to say the same thing twice. Sometimes the same thought is repeated in the second half. Sometimes there is one alteration made in the thought. For example, "Declare thy steadfast love in the morning, and thy faithfulness at night." There is the same thought but a change of time. Sometimes there is a contrast between the two thoughts, so that they are opposite to each other and reflect each other. That is why the Psalms are best sung antiphonally – half a choir in one position in a room, and half in another, and for half to sing the first line of each couplet, and the other to sing the second as a kind of echo. You hear the thing twice in different words and music. Usually it is in a kind of three-three rhythm in the Hebrew, though you get three-two and four-four, but there is this kind of coupling of thoughts. The real rhythm of the poetry is not in the rhyming of the words or even the rhythm of the words, though it is there, but in the rhythm of the thought.

Now do you realise one very significant thing about this? Hebrew poetry will translate into almost any other language and keep the poetry. It is as if God said, "I want the poetry I give to this nation to be available to the whole world. I want to set the whole world singing." Whatever translation, whatever language the Psalms go into, the poetry comes through, and you can sense it. Look at these first four verses here:

It is good to give thanks to the Lord,
and to sing praises to thy name, O Most High;

To declare thy steadfast love in the morning,
and thy faithfulness by night,

To the music of the lute and the harp,
and to the melody of the lyre.

For thou, O Lord, hast made me glad by thy work;
at the works of thy hands I sing for joy

Do you get the poetry? It comes across, even in English. Though it has lost the rhythm of the Hebrew words, the poetry is there and the echo is there, and the response is there.

Having said all that about the technical side of the poetry, we can say that the first four verses of this Psalm are well nigh perfect Hebrew poetry. I want you to get the feeling of the poetry in your heart as we study it, and realise that God was not just saying something that he wanted us to accept in bold prose. I am afraid most of this chapter is going to be in prose, so it is going to lose something, but I want you to recapture the poetry and the song in this. "Sweet is the work my God, my King" – that recaptures the poetry in English.

Now this is a song for the Sabbath. It is meant to be sung weekly, on the seventh day, the day they gave to worship. Therefore, in a sense for us we can turn this into a song for Sunday. It is the sort of song we should think about once a week. It tells us what to do on the Lord's day, and how to do it, and why to do it, and when to do it, and where to do it. You will find all these questions answered in this Psalm. I have divided it into two halves. The first, by way of introduction, simply talks about the worship of God – how we are to do it, why we are to do it, where we are to do it, when we are to do it. It is giving us instructions for how to spend our Sunday. We have spent six days largely on ourselves and other people. Now this Psalm is saying: here is how to spend one day in the week on God. I hope you haven't exclusively spent the week on yourself, but we have had to be engaged in our daily work in the affairs of the community. But now this Psalm says: here is a day when you can give something to God, when you can concentrate on him.

The first verse tells us that it is a good thing to do. Why should it be a good thing to sing praises and to give thanks to God? I can think of many reasons. First of all, basically, it is a morally good thing, because it is courtesy. If anybody else had done as much for you as God, you would never cease to thank them. If anybody else had given you health and food and clothes and every blessing you have had this week, you would say, "Thank you, thank you, thank you." If you had not sent a letter by now to thank them you would be feeling guilty. Yet we can take all these things for granted and just forget to give thanks to God.

Sometimes I am told that there are many good people outside the church who never worship and who never call themselves Christians. Well, they may be good to their neighbour, but I want to ask you, are they good to God? Do they give thanks to him? Do they do this good thing, which is more important than all the good things you do for your neighbour, and that is to do good towards God and to give thanks to him? It is a good thing. Call no-one good if he does not give praise to God.

A good person does good things, and that includes giving praise, but it is not only a good thing in itself morally, it is a good thing for us. It is a healthy exercise.

One preacher, a well-known minister who had a remarkable ministry in India and this country, and in Africa was sent out to take up C.T. Studd's work in Africa when Studd became too elderly to manage it himself. This minister once said to me, "You know, if ever I feel physically under par, if ever I'm run down, you know what I do? I try and get a preaching appointment. I get up and preach for an hour about God, and I feel wonderfully fit afterwards. It is good for me." That was how he recovered, and that was how he kept his health up.

It is good for you to sing praises; it is good in so many ways. For one thing, it is awfully good for you to give thanks. It stops grumbling. It makes you a contented person – very good for you. It is good for you to develop what you were meant to do. You were put on this earth to the praise of his glory, and to give thanks and sing praises is good for you. You are doing exactly what you were meant to do. You were made for that. It is not only good for that, but it gets us out of ourselves. All the week we have maybe been troubled by the cost of housekeeping going up, and thinking, "How am I ever going to get that thing done for the boss by Friday?" And we have been troubled by many things. But to come and give thanks and sing praises is good. It gets us right out of ourselves, and that is healthy for us – a good thing.

It is a good thing for God too, and the Lord loves the praises of his people. It is a good thing from every point of view. Is it not wonderful when duty and delight are the same thing? There are some things that are our duty but not our delight, and there are some things that are our delight that we should not do. But there are some things that can become a duty and a delight, and singing God's praises is one of them. If your heart enters into the praise of God with your mouth then it is a delight as well as a duty. It is a good thing all around, so you can use the word "good" in whatever sense you wish and it will fit this first verse.

The second verse moves on to a deeper question, as to *why* we are praising God. What is the essential quality about God that deserves our thanks? The answer is his love or his loyalty. I am going to use the word "loyalty" to sum up the first and second halves of the verse, because this is a quality that is strangely lacking in our modern society but is right there in God. The word "love" has been so debased now that I doubt whether we can still use it in the simple sentence, "God is love" and not be misunderstood. I think we have got to put in an adjective before the word "love" now, because people use this word "love" in so many ways that just to say "God is love" you have almost killed their thoughts before you start. I went to a youth club once and the youth club leader said, "If you are talking to these youngsters about God, don't use the word 'Father' and don't use the word 'love,' if you'll take my advice." I made the mistake of using the word "love" and got an obscene gesture from a teenage girl in the front row immediately. I realised then just why he had said it. The word "love" has gone down and down. That is why so many people have problems like this. A man rings me up and says: "If God is a God of love how can..." and then he produces the problem. The real reason was that his understanding of the word "love" created the problem. Do you see? He had no real grasp that the word "love" really meant something far deeper than that – that it meant something that could punish, for example; something that had an opposite side to it.

Therefore, we have to say "God's holy love" or "God's steadfast love", or "God's something love". We have got to put an adjective in. So here, praise God for his *steadfast* love. That double word is translating a single Hebrew word for which we have no equivalent in the English language, *chesed*, which means loyalty. It is translated "loving kindness" in the Authorized Version and "steadfast love" in the Revised Version. It means not just to fall in love with someone, but to remain loyal to them at whatever cost – God's covenant love.

What is happening when two young people get married in church? Why don't they just, since they love each other, go away and live together if all that you need is love towards each other? The answer is: you need more than that to create a marriage. Love is not a sufficient foundation for marriage. When two young people stand together, we know they love each other or they would not be standing there. We know they have loved each other for some time before this. What are we doing in a wedding? We are saying, "Are you prepared to add the dimension of loyalty to your love? Are you prepared to say, not 'I love this person' but 'I will', for better or for worse, for richer for poorer, in sickness and in health—are you prepared to stay with them through thick and thin, until death us do part? Are you prepared to turn your love into loyalty? If you are, then make the promise." That is marriage in God's sight. It is a covenant. It has loyalty in it, as well as love. Even if one of you falls out of love with the other, and even if one of you finds someone else you love better, it is the loyalty that makes the marriage. Thank God that he is not a God of human love, who has fallen in love with us and could fall out of love with us. He is a God who has got loyalty. He is a God of steadfast love, and when you have steadfast love, that issues in faithfulness. That is what we have to praise God for – a God whose love is *chesed*, loyalty, loving-kindness, steadfast love.

One writer told of a man whose wife, shortly after their wedding, got into bad ways. She went rapidly from bad to worse. Finally, she was making his life so difficult that all his friends and relatives said, "Why don't you divorce her? Why don't you separate from her? She's no good for you. She hasn't a spark of love for you. She's ruining your life." He turned round on these friends with anger and he said, "Never speak to me like that about my wife. I love her, and I shall love her as long as there's breath in her body," and he did. She died a few years later as a result of her sin with his hands spread over her in love. That is loyalty. That is steadfast love that issues in faithfulness. That is what covenants are all about and that is what marriage is all about. They are not about love, they are about loyalty, and that is something far, far deeper. So we are to praise God every morning, that the rest of the day God will be loyal to us, and we can praise God in the evening that he has been loyal to us. So praise God for his steadfast love in the morning and when you get to the end of the day look back and praise him that that has issued in faithfulness.

The Psalm continues, linking hands and mouth in praise. Why not enrich our praise with instrumental music? Now because there is a silence in the New Testament about instruments, some Christians have thought that all instrumental music belongs to the Old Testament and is un-Christian. There were gigantic battles in this country over the introduction of organs or harmoniums to public worship.

Nevertheless, I believe that all arguments from silence are difficult arguments. We must argue from what the Bible says, not from what it doesn't say. I believe that the early Christians continued in the temple worship, the prayers and the praise, which was instrumental. You will find that in the New Testament, and how a musical accompaniment can enrich your praise, so that hands can be used as well as mouths.

Martin Luther was one of those Christians who found that instrumental music was helpful in private devotions. In these days of recordings, when so much music is available to us, may I suggest you consider using music at home for your private devotions, to enrich and stimulate your own praise to God? If it is right in public then it is right in private as well.

Regarding public worship, the psalmist says, "Praise him!" But there is a danger with all instrumental music. The danger is that it can become an end in itself, rather than a means. It has aesthetic appeal to us. It can move us of itself. Therefore, David puts in a word in the Hebrew, which does not quite come out clearly in translation. He says, "Muse with music". Or literally, meditate while you play. The content of your heart, your thought life, is important while the music is on. If it is just touching your feelings and just moving you as music, then it is not praise. But if there is meditation in it, if the thoughts of your mind are towards your Maker, if the music is enriching and drawing out those thoughts, then that is the kind of praise that God wants. So it is music and meditation. There must be musing if it is to be music for the Lord. The word is translated in the Authorized Version :"Make a solemn sound". That "solemn sound" means "meditate". Let there be thoughts towards God with the music, because the world can be moved aesthetically by music by itself, but let their thoughts be toward the Lord.

One hymn puts it beautifully: "O, may my heart in tune be found like David's harp of solemn sound." Somebody has said: "Music without devotion is but a splendid garment on a corpse." How easy it is to tell when it is just music without the devotion of the heart. It is like a beautiful garment on a corpse.

As the Psalm continues, I want you to notice that praise should be happy. There is a time for mourning as well as a time for laughing. There is a time for rejoicing and a time for weeping. The time for weeping is when we confess our sins. The time for mourning is when we consider our sin. But when you are praising God's love and his faithfulness, that should not be like a funeral. From time to time many Christians have got this wrong – that somehow God is pleased when we are all dressed in black and when we have a long face but have you ever tried to say the word, "Hallelujah" with a long face? You just try it sometime. It cannot be done. In fact, this idea is just wide of the mark. If you are going to give thanks to God, if you are going to sing praises, then let it be with joy. "My heart is glad," says the psalmist – "I want to sing for joy."

What makes us so happy? The answer is: not because of anything we have done, but because of what the Lord has done. If you have seen God do things in the week then you are happy to praise him in worship. Every week he is doing things – sometimes in a spectacular way, sometimes in a quiet way. Now bear in mind that when God does something it is because he has thought about it first. God is not a thoughtless God, and he doesn't act before he thinks. When God does something he has planned it carefully. It is always there in his mind before it is there in his hands. Therefore, we are not only thrilled with what God does, but with the thoughts behind what he does. His works are great, but his thoughts are deep, and that is the next verse (v. 5).

It is those who not only see his works but understand his thoughts who are going to be glad, who get behind what he is doing to understand what is in his mind. This is something very difficult to do. Such thoughts of God are way above our thoughts, and spiritually discerned, and it is not easy for us to think his thoughts after him. The brutish man knows not, the fool doesn't understand and there are hundreds of people in your town who have not seen a thing of God's work and don't understand a single thought he has had this week because they are living life at the level of an animal. They are living as if they are only physical bodies that need feeding and clothing and sleeping. So they don't understand, they don't know.

There are fools who have only got one life to live but refuse to talk about death, refuse to ask the real questions about what life is for. I was talking to someone and I asked them, "What do you think life is for? What do you think you are here for?"

"I hadn't thought about it," came the reply. This was an adult in a good job, very intelligent – never thought about it. You don't understand God's thoughts like that. You don't see his works like that. So there are many people who don't even see his works, and certainly don't go beyond that to understand his thoughts. These are spiritually conditioned.

But where you have understood what God is thinking and see what he is doing, you can read your daily newspaper with new eyes. You see what God is doing. You don't just say, "Oh, there's trouble in the Middle East again." You say, "Look what God is doing. Can't you see God's plan unfolding? Can't you understand what he is about?" So the psalmist says, "Oh, how great are your works, and how deep your thoughts." The rest of the Psalm is all about what he has understood.

Here comes the biggest surprise. You might think that the psalmist would go on to talk of creation, and the beauty that God has put in nature. Praise God for his work in creation, but he doesn't. There are other Psalms about that: "When I consider the heavens, the moon and the stars, the work of your fingers...." Nor, here, does he praise God for his work of redemption. There are other Psalms where he does that, how he brought Israel through the Red Sea and out of bondage in Egypt.... What is the work of God that is occupying his mind at this stage, and what are the thoughts of God that are thrilling him with praise?

The answer is God's work in judgment. You have really got to know God well to be able to praise him for his judgment and to understand. Let me try and convey to you what I believe David is saying. The world's opinion is that this universe in which we live is not moral or immoral but amoral, which means indifferent to moral values; that therefore the wicked can prosper and the innocent can suffer; the whole thing is chance; there is no point in trying to be good – it doesn't pay; wickedness can pay. In fact, now in England we have reached the point where crime does pay, because more than fifty percent of the known crimes in this country are never solved. Therefore, crime now does pay in England.

So people say, "This world is not a moral universe. There are no moral principles in it. No one's going to stand up for you if you're right, so you'll have to stand up for yourself. The chances are that a good man can finish in disaster and an evil man can die in peace in his old age. There's just no morality in the universe. Therefore, there need be no morals. You can write your own." Now that's the world's observation but David praises God that this is not true. There is a God in heaven, and that God is a moral, righteous God, and it does matter how you live. The end of your life is directly related to how you lived it. He is so thrilled that this universe is a moral universe where moral values matter, and where the wicked and the righteous do not go to the same place, and where they are not even in the same condition in this life. He is going to praise God that God is revealing to those who understand his thoughts, to those who can discern his works, God is revealing that the wicked perish and that the righteous flourish.

Now that is what is going to occupy us for the rest of the Psalm. It is an exciting and thrilling thought that, in fact, moral values do count in this universe, and that is what makes us glad. Because if they didn't count, if we all ended up the same way, and if it was purely a matter of chance whether you flourished or perished, then frankly the situation is hopeless. But thank God that is not true. Praise God that he is in charge of the universe, and therefore moral laws are written into it.

Now let us look at the two facts that David spreads over the rest of the Psalm. Number one: the wicked are like perishing grass. Number two: the righteous are like flourishing trees. I do not know if you can get the flavour of those similes, those pictures. Here in England's green and pleasant land we cannot stop grass growing, and it is an enemy in every flower bed. I remember the days on the farm, long ago, before we ever thought of silage or artificial machines to dry grass, we tried to make hay in the British climate and it was all we could do to dry it. Sometimes you just did not get it dried.

It is very difficult for us therefore to realise that grass is a picture in the Bible of anything that is short-lived. Go out to the Middle East and you have got a region where when the wind blows from the west it brings moisture and it falls, and the grass springs up, and it flourishes, and it grows, and it is green and thick. But as soon as the wind swings round to the east and the hot sirocco from the desert hits it, it withers and it is gone. If ever you have been through Aden you will know how barren it is, and as I said earlier we lived there for just under two years. I remember one day it rained. When it rained the whole of the barren rocks of Aden turned green. There was grass there, there were plants there in the rock, and a little bit of water brought them out. But two days later, back to the barren volcanic rocks of Aden. In the Middle East grass grows up and it can die out in a matter of hours. It never lasts the year through. When the dry season comes the grass goes.

So if you go to Galilee at the right time of the year, green hills lead down to that lovely blue lake. But go in July: brown, barren hills; the grass is all gone. Now that is the picture. Grass grows up and it goes. It may flourish, it may look green and strong, but its death sentence is on it in the Middle East. Its life is limited. It will be gone, and the shepherd may have to lead his sheep fifteen miles to find some more. Grass is a picture of the fleeting and, "the wicked are like grass" says the psalmist. They may flourish for a moment. They may look as if they are getting on well now, but they are doomed. Now how does he know that? He knows it in two ways: deduction and observation. This is the right order for the Christian to have his convictions. He must first of all have them by deduction, from the facts of God. Here are the facts of God: God is righteous. Number two: God is the Most High. Number three: God is forever. If God is good and Most High and forever, then the wicked are doomed. For God must have the last word. If he is Most High, he is in charge. If he is forever, then he will outlast them. Therefore, he must have the last word. By a matter of simple deduction, if God is what he is then the wicked are doomed. They will not get away with it. God will settle his accounts. He may take a little time to do so, but every person will have to render an account to the Most High, who is there forever. The wicked live as if they have outlived God and they say, "God is dead." Look, he is the Most High forever. Therefore, by deduction, the wicked will go and the righteous will not, but it is not only by deduction, it is by observation – his own experience and testimony.

Here comes the shepherd and the soldier. This is his experience. There had been days, of course, when David could not understand God's thoughts – when standing for the right he was persecuted and attacked; when he felt all was lost and his soul was disquieted within him, and he was cast down. Why? Because his enemies were pressing on him and they were prospering. He said, "My God, my God, why have you forsaken me?" He was the first to use those words. In the early Psalms you see this despair – in his early life when his enemies had the upper hand and were flourishing, and he was a fugitive running from cave to cave. You are a God who hides yourself. Where are you? Why don't you come to my aid? Or as a modern translation has it, "Good Lord, where are you?" But that was a short-term view. Psalm 92 was written a little later in his life, and taking the long-term view he is saying: "I can now see that God is righteous. He lifted up my horn. He anointed me with oil, and my eyes have seen the downfall of my enemies, and my ears have heard it."

Just give God time, that is the answer. The trouble is we are in a hurry and God isn't. If you take the short-term view you get depressed about the state of the world, the wicked do flourish and the innocent do suffer. Take the longer-term view and you will say, "He has lifted up my horn like the wild ox." If ever you have seen a wild bull attacking an enemy, it jerks its head up with its horns. These are its weapons and it has a strong neck, and it jerks its head up, and with that horn is able to attack. That is what the Lord enabled David to do. David was bowed down, but the Lord lifted his horn up, gave him strength, and anointed him with oil.

That is going back to the days when he was a shepherd and a sheep had a wounded head – an enemy had attacked it. Maybe a hyena had bitten its ear or head. The shepherd would have a horn of olive oil and would pour the oil on to seal the wound and keep it free from infection. You have anointed my head with oil. You have lifted my horn up; you have healed the wounds. When I was standing for the right you did this for me, and I saw my enemies go down. With two of his senses, through observation – eye and ear – he saw it happen and heard it happen.

When you have got experience of the Lord you know that that is what he does if you are living in his righteousness. He may take a little time, but he will lift your horn up. He will anoint your wounds and you will say, "My enemies have gone."

Now let us move to the other side of the picture and the last thing in the Psalm: the righteous are like flourishing trees. They grow in the same environment as the grass, but what a difference. I want to give you just a little bit about trees now. What a difference between grass and trees: the height for a start, but more than that, grass in the Middle East comes and goes in a matter of hours, but a tree goes on standing. There is something strong, upright. The two trees that the psalmist speaks of now are the most majestic trees in the Middle East. On the one hand is the palm, that strong stem that reaches up into the sky and is such a welcome sight in the barren areas of the Middle East. Going through the desert you see a palm, as the children of Israel came to Elam and saw seventy palm trees – what a sight. A palm is so majestic, it can stand drought, it can stand intense heat and still it stands. The grass is all faded and gone, but the palm tree is still there.

Then to take an opposite extreme, if the palm tree can stand dryness and heat, there is a tree that can stand intense cold and wet. You will find it high on the mountains of Lebanon – a majestic, upright tree: the cedar of Lebanon. Both the palm and the cedar are evergreens. This is the contrast with the wicked. The wicked may flourish, but just like grass; but the righteous flourish like trees.

Psalm 1 says the same thing: "Like a tree planted by a river". In this case the trees are planted in courtyards and that is where palm trees do best. If you go out to the Middle East, often outside a palace there is a courtyard and there are palm trees in the courtyard reaching up to heaven, sheltered by the walls and therefore at their very best. The trees of the righteous are planted in the courts of the Lord. In the Old Testament, that would be in the temple worship. In the New Testament it means in the fellowship of the church. I am quite sure that the trees grow tall when they are rooted and grounded in the soil of the courts, the temple of the Lord, which is now his people. You will find trees like this planted in every fellowship. What a godsend they are, how beautiful they are.

But now comes this lovely verse. For all those over sixty, you may think a lot in your church is for young people, well here is something just for you and it is a wonderful promise: that in your old age you are still green. A tree can be gnarled, wrinkled and grey and look absolutely dead on the outside. But if it were to be cut through you would find the sap is still there, and it is still green on the inside, and that is what the righteous are like, says the psalmist. There are olive trees a thousand years old in the Garden of Gethsemane, and they are still bearing fruit. An oak tree at Hebron is propped up with posts, and there is a corrugated iron roof over it to protect it, but it is still bearing leaves, and it is centuries old. Go to California and you will see Californian redwoods whose girth is huge. You find that those redwoods were planted before the time of Christ and they are still bearing fruit. Praise God for the old people who are righteous before the Lord and who still have as much life in them as they had when they were first converted, and more.

It does not come automatically. It does not follow that because you are a church member you are like this – it is the righteous; and praise God for the righteous among us who have as much life in them in their old age. The outside may be decaying, the outward man may be decaying but the inward man is being renewed every day, and there is life, and they still bear fruit in their old age. Now this is true of cedars and palms. They may be very old, but the palms still bear up to a hundredweight of dates a year, and a cedar may be old but it still produces lots of seeds.

Within the dates and within the seeds the tree is reproducing itself. Each of those seeds can produce another tree like it. This is the fruitfulness of the righteous in their old age. I thank God I have known many people like that who are still bringing people to Christ in their old age. They are not leaving it to the young people. They are still flourishing, and even though they are old and grey-haired they still have spiritual babies. They still reproduce themselves in new Christian lives; they still have children. Isn't that exciting?

I would not mind a church that had nothing in it but old age pensioners if they were all like this, if they were all winning people for Christ and all still sappy and green. It would be wonderful, wouldn't it? So there's the promise: the righteous are like trees. This fruitfulness in their old age is not to be a glory for them; it is not to be a testimony to them, it is to show that the Lord is upright. These upright people, like a palm or a cedar in their old age, still bearing fruit, are a demonstration that the Lord is upright and that he is still honouring their uprightness.

So some people are like grass, they flourish and then they are gone. Their doom is certain. They neither know nor understand the thoughts of the Lord. They cannot discern the doings of the Lord and their life is wasted. Some people are like trees, even after years of walking with the Lord, still enjoying the Lord.

But the Lord is neither grass nor a tree. The grass goes and even trees have to go – they do not live forever. When all the grass is gone and when the trees have gone, do you know what is left in the Middle East? Rock – and it is still there. The rocks of the Middle East were there in Christ's time. They were there when the foundations of the earth were laid. The rock is the abiding feature of the landscape. So the psalmist, being a naturalist and being so keen an observer of nature, says, finally: the Lord is my rock. Why? Because he is solid righteousness.

You see, the word "righteous", as applied to human beings, is always a relative word. Even King David was a righteous man, but he had sinned. He had needed forgiveness, he had needed cleansing, he had need of the Holy Spirit to give him the righteousness of the Lord. So "righteous" was a relative word, it wasn't inherent in him. But when you look at the Lord—the Lord has never sinned; the Lord has never needed forgiveness. The only way that you and I will ever be righteous is to come to the Lord who is the rock.

Ask yourself one question. If you are either "grass" or "tree", which category have you put yourself in whilst thinking about this Psalm? You are one or the other. In God's sight you are either wicked or righteous – there is nothing in between. Now just say, "Where do I fit into that picture? Am I just grass and one day will they dig up the turf and put me under and replace the grass on top? Or am I a tree? Am I a tree planted by the river producing fruit even to my old age?" I tell you, the one thing that will decide the difference is whether you can say: "Rock of ages, cleft for me, let me hide myself in thee." It is when you come to the Rock that you become a tree. It may be bad horticulture, but it is good theology and it is wonderful experience.

READ PSALM 103

Some people say that talking to yourself is one of the first signs of weakness. I don't agree. It depends entirely on what you say to yourself. You might be talking nonsense. On the other hand, you might be saying something very wonderful. You can often have a very intelligent conversation with yourself because at least you understand what you are saying. But this Psalm is of a man talking to himself, and this is the right way to do it and it is not a sign of weakness, but a sign of strength.

Charles Haddon Spurgeon, a great preacher in London, used to say that Psalm 103 would suffice for the hymnbook of the Church – that if we just had this Psalm we would have enough to sing every Sunday. In the light of that, we are going to look at a Psalm that doesn't ask God for a thing – no shopping list; nothing to ask from God. The reason is that David wants to bless the Lord. Now this is an extraordinary idea. Most people are familiar with the thought that God could bless us. In fact, the very term "God bless you", which is used by some people with meaning and by some people without meaning, is a familiar idea.

I am amazed how many television entertainers finish off their act with the words "God bless you". Even they seem to understand what this means. But I have never yet heard anybody say, "You bless God", and that is what is happening here. The idea that I could give God a blessing today is an idea that would never have occurred to me unless I had read about it in the Bible. Do you realise that you could give God a wonderful blessing? Now, what could you give? Well, as I have mentioned before, there is only one thing that you can give God that he did not give you first. You cannot bless him with money because all the money in the world belongs to him anyway. You cannot bless him with health because he does not need health.

You cannot bless him with anything that you have to give except one thing and that is to give him your thanks and praise. That is all you have got to give that could bless him now. Everything else that is given this morning will be given to you; it will be a blessing to you. Even when you bring your money that is a blessing to you. But if you bring your praise and your thanks you are going to give God a tremendous blessing. In fact, that is the ultimate test as to whether a service of worship has been worthwhile.

David, talking to himself, tells himself to bless the Lord and realises that if he is going to do this he must do it in three ways. He must do it individually, inwardly and intelligently. True worship must combine these three things. When teaching on the Lord's Prayer I have mentioned that even when you pray in private you should bring the *public* aspect into your prayer to *our* Father. Now when you pray in public you should also remember the private aspect. Do you see how Scripture dovetails and balances out?

This Psalm was written to be used by hundreds of people in public services of worship. Yet it begins with an intensely personal, "Bless the Lord, O my soul". There is something very healthy in the time of private prayer that begins and ends a service. What do you say in the silence? May I suggest that a very good thing to do at the beginning and end of a service is to say: "Bless the Lord, O my soul". In other words, don't bother about the people around you for a moment. The congregation is together, but I must bless the Lord this morning. It has to be an individual thing. I have something to offer to God. At the beginning of worship in the private prayer moment, you could start with, "Bless the Lord, O my soul, and all that is within me, bless his holy name."

However big the crowd there may be in a service, God looks at each individual. Therefore, one person who is not worshipping can help to spoil a service. One person who is not seeking to bless the Lord is taking away from the whole worship. Therefore, the psalmist begins with this reminder. Secondly, if you are going to worship properly, even when you are with a crowd, you must do it inwardly. The Lord is not really interested in the outside of us. The religion of the Bible is a religion of the heart. It must come from the inside. It is an inward thing. Whatever we do with our bodies – stand up, sit down, kneel, or what have you; shut eyes, open eyes, whether we put our hands together or not, whatever we do with our lips and our mouth, and we do quite a bit, whatever we do with our ears – the most important thing is what happens within me; what I am thinking about when the prayer is being offered. Where are my thoughts going during the sermon? Did I leave the gas on? Was that a good football match yesterday? What is happening within me? The Lord knows what is happening within me. He doesn't look at the outward appearance; he looks at the heart.

The true test of my blessing the Lord in worship will be what is going on inside me, what I am really feeling, what I am really thinking. I may not tell anybody else what I am thinking in the service or how I am feeling, though usually we can show something on our faces, but God does not even look at that. It may be that even a facial expression is misleading and not really telling you what a person is thinking, but deep down what is happening within me is what will make the worship. If I am full of love and joy and peace in the service, I am going to help that service tremendously. If I am all twisted up inside, if I am worried and anxious or resentful or unhappy, then that is going to affect it too. "Bless the Lord, O my soul" – that is the individual part of public worship; "and all that is within me, bless his holy name" – that is what is meant by loving God with all your heart and your mind and your soul and your strength. All those are within you, and that is what God is desiring.

Now the third thing is that we are to bless the Lord intelligently. It requires a conscious mental effort. Now for better or worse the most frequent comment I ever get after I have preached is, "Well, you've given me something to think about." Sometimes it is said in a tone of appreciation and sometimes it is said in a tone of resentment, as if that is the last thing somebody came to church to do. The person who said, "The greatest unexplored territory in the world is right underneath your hat," was making a very profound statement. We are to worship God with all our mind intelligently.

One of the gifts God has given to you is the gift of memory. Thank God for the gift of memory. Do you realise how little is possible once you lose that gift? It is a tragic possibility towards the end of life particularly, that your memory begins to forsake you. Don't worry – as soon as you get to glory it will all be restored and transformed. But the memory is a vital part of life, all the things that we do. Your memory is going to help you do so much.

Worship surrounds memory. What is the central act of Christian worship? The Lord's Supper, breaking of bread. Why do we do that? "Do this in remembrance of me". Memories will help you to worship. How good is your memory? The psalmist knows that he must make a conscious, intelligent effort when he blesses the Lord to remember the benefits that he has received during the past week.

Use your memory, forget not his benefits, and go back over the week. All of us can remember the benefits of belonging to God.

I like the word "benefits". The last time I read it was in a life assurance policy. They told me all the benefits I would have, what would happen to me or my wife or my children, and so on. It was a little depressing to realise that these benefits would not be mine unless something happened to me. But nevertheless, there was a list of benefits. I thank God for life assurance policies from God that give me my benefits now, every week.

Indeed, at a very crude level I get far more from God than he ever gets from me. The benefits of belonging to God are so huge but you can forget them and you can grumble and complain, and when you do you are forgetting all his benefits. So we come to bless God in a service, and if we do it individually, if every one of us does it, if we do it inwardly and think about our thoughts and feelings, and if we do it intelligently by consciously making an effort to go back over the week and remember, then God is going to get a blessing from that service.

Now let us look at all the blessings David remembers. Remember this is his list, not ours but we may share it. "Count your blessings, name them one by one, and it will surprise you what the Lord has done." I know that hymn is considered bad poetry and the tune is considered poor music but it is good Christianity, which is my main concern. I am sorry we have lost that hymn. I would think that you could fill up three foolscap sheets of single space typing from just one week if you stopped to count your blessings.

David does this and he reels them off so quickly he cannot even spare a whole sentence for each one, just a phrase. "Who forgives" – now that is the first thing that he mentions as if that is the biggest thing in the whole memory that he has of God's dealings with him; the very first blessing he thinks of. I think it is helpful to ask myself, "What would be the first blessing I would think of this last week? Forgiveness?" Who forgives all your iniquities—there is no blessing like this.

Someone being interviewed on television was asked what the greatest things in life were. He said two things: health and peace of mind. He was reflecting a philosophy that you will find in many people: health first, peace of mind second. David would say forgiveness first – that is a person's biggest need. It is a greater need than food; it is a greater need than health, and it comes first. This Psalm is so full of forgiveness that David keeps coming back to it. The reason he does is this: it is the one blessing that only God can give you. No man can forgive all your iniquities; only God can do this. There is no relief like the relief of knowing that you have been forgiven. There is no joy like the joy of knowing that what was wrong has been put right and forgotten.

Now the second phrase, which I appreciate: "who heals all your diseases". I think of the number of times that germs touched my body and they did not win the battle; the number of times I could have been very ill and was not; the number of days I have enjoyed health; the number of times things could have gone wrong and they didn't. I bless the Lord for the times I have got better. Have you ever counted up the number of times you got better from something? It is an amazing number when you add it up. I also thank God for the times I have got better through the help of surgery and medicine.

The next thing is: "who redeems your life from the pit". I remember headline news in county Durham. Some miners were trapped fifteen hundred feet below the surface, down in the pit, and they were going to die. The whole community would gather at the pithead, and they would wait, and they would pray, and they would work, and men would go down to rescue them. Then the men would be brought up on stretchers and taken to a hospital and recover. They knew what it was to be redeemed from the pit at a very down-to-earth level.

If you have ever been in a mining community you know the drama and the relief when people are rescued from the pit. David is saying: many times I have been in danger of death and the Lord has rescued me. Maybe you could say: "That's my blessing. I've been very near to death, I've been in danger and the Lord rescued me." We can all say that some day he will rescue us from the pit. He not only rescues us from death, but from hell. He redeems your life from the pit.

David the king says in the second part of v. 4: "I feel like a king; he has crowned me." He is not talking about the robes or the throne or the crown that he wore as king of Israel. He feels like a king, like a member of the royal family, like a prince of God. The reason is that God has crowned him with steadfast love and mercy. I will tell you what makes you feel like a king: mercy; to wake up in the morning and know that God's love and mercy are on you – you get up like a king. He crowns you. That is David the king saying the Lord makes him feel like a king.

Now look at the next little blessing. This is perhaps the most amazing of all, and the younger generation just would not believe it: "... who satisfies you with good as long as you live". Every part of that sentence is remarkable. First of all, we live in a world which is terribly dissatisfied. People are trying this, that and the other. But evil does nor satisfy. There is only one thing which satisfies and that is good. Some people take a lot of convincing to persuade them that it is goodness which satisfies, because the world seems to say: try something evil, that is satisfying. Well, it might seem so for a time, but you cannot add "as long as you live". If one thing is written on the stage of human affairs it is this: there is nothing this world offers that satisfies you as long as you live. Whatever hobbies or interests you take up will satisfy you for a time but there will come a day when they no longer do so.

Even healthy things can fail to satisfy deep down. Why? Because God made us for himself and he made us for goodness. "Godliness with contentment is great gain". To satisfy you as long as you live. He will not satisfy you with many things, he will not satisfy you with expensive things, but he will satisfy with good things. If you think back over the past week, it is the good things that satisfied you.

Finally: "so that your youth is renewed like the eagle's", he renews you. Have you ever visited an elderly saint and felt that they were younger than most teenagers? Have you ever visited someone who has walked with the Lord for forty years and yet they seemed just at the beginning of exciting possibilities? Why? What was happening? Well the eagle has a unique moulting which renews itself so that it looks like a young eagle again. David, who was a keen observer of nature, often likened himself to birds. Look at Psalm 102:6f. "I am like a vulture of the wilderness, like an owl of the waste places; I lie awake; I am like a lonely bird on the housetop." A vulture and an owl in Psalm 102, but now an eagle – the most majestic bird of all. It soars with vigour, majesty and life. No wonder the United States chose it as a symbol, as Rome did before that, as many nations have done. Here David is saying: I don't feel like a vulture or an owl any more.

Bear in mind that the list of blessings is David's list, not yours and not mine. Make your list as he made his. If there are certain things that you are not enjoying, then ask yourself whether it is true of you as it was of David that you are *a person after God's own heart*, because if you are not then you are not likely to enjoy the blessings to the same degree – but this was his list.

From looking at God's activity on his behalf he begins to think what lies behind this – not only what God does but why he does it. What kind of a person is he? What are the attributes of his character that make him behave in this way toward me? There are three headings here, and under each of them is a contrast. First of all, God is a God of justice—that is why he does certain things. Second, God is a God of mercy—that is why he does certain other things. Thirdly, he is a God of pity—that is why he does other things.

We look at these three lovely things: justice, mercy, and pity. The first thing is: when God relieves people's troubles it is often because of his justice. God hates those who exploit others. God is troubled, and he cares about the downtrodden, the oppressed, and those who through no fault of their own are suffering from others, and God vindicates such.

The most outstanding example of this is in history. There was a group of people who were in slavery – they were in chains. They were being forced to build huge buildings, the ruins of which you can see today, four thousand years later, and God cared. His justice cared about these people who were dying, who were being whipped to death, who were being killed off, who were being worked to death. God did something about it.

Notice how he does it: he told an individual, then he showed a nation. He told one man what he was going to do and then he did it. This is always his method of working. He tells a man what he is going to do and then he does it. He gives it to the ear first and then to the eye. He made known his ways to Moses and then his acts to the people of Israel. God always says what he is going to do before he does it. He tells an individual then helps the multitude. This is his invariable way of doing it. Why? Because he wants to elicit faith; that is why he tells you what he is going to do before he does it. Every single thing in the life of Jesus, God told someone before it happened. He said, "There's going to be a baby born in Bethlehem of Judea," long before it happened. He said that he was going to die on a cross long before it happened; that he would rise again, long before it happened, so that people might believe. "Moses, I'm going to come and get you out of Egypt. Tell them this that they may believe it." Then one day on the shores of the Red Sea Moses stood and said, "Stand still and see what the Lord is going to do."

Whenever God is going to relieve the oppressed, that is how he does it. He tells a man and then through that man's faith, and those who come to share it, he relieves the need. Think that through – that is his justice putting things right. But if God was only justice then we would be in trouble. The second thing mentioned in v. 8 is mercy. God can be very angry, and is when we sin. But God's anger is not like my anger in two regards. One, he is very slow to get angry and I am very quick. Two, he is only angry for a short time and I stay angry for a long time. He is slow to anger and he will not keep his anger forever. When I do wrong, God is angry, no question about that. He will chide me; he will tell me that it is wrong but then he will bring his mercy.

At this point David returns to forgiveness. You know the reason why he does, from Psalm 51. He wants to bless God for a negative thing and a positive thing. The negative thing, that God did not do what he should have done; that God did not do what he might have done. When people say to me, "What have I done to deserve this?" my immediate reaction inside, though it doesn't always come out, is to say, "Just stop for a moment and ask the question: Just suppose that I got everything I deserved. Just look at it that way."

I can tell you what you would get if you got everything you deserved – you would be in your coffin right now. It is of his mercies that we are not consumed. You do not deserve even to live in God's good Earth, and neither do I. This lovely land and the sky. Who has spoiled all this? Who is polluting it all? Not just with physical waste but with moral and spiritual waste. Who is doing it? Every single one of us has spoiled

God's earth. If we got what we deserve we would not be here. I bless God that he did not deal with me according to my iniquities, or I wouldn't be alive – that is the negative side. Did you ever bless God for not doing what he might have done, for what he hasn't done to you?

Now the positive side: "as far as the east is from the west". Now here are the dimensions of forgiveness. How high is love? Sometimes I used to say to my children when they were small: how much does God love you? As high as the heaven is above the earth. In other words, the biggest vertical dimension you can think of. Go out into space as far as you can, and that is still not as big as God's love for you. Therefore: how far does he remove your sin from you? As far as the east is from the west. I found myself thinking about that and came to this conclusion. When you have done wrong, is the best thing you can do for yourself to get as far away from the crime as possible – make your getaway? That is precisely the opposite of God's method of dealing with your sin. God's method is to say: you stay right where you are, we will take your crime away. In other words, removing the crime from the criminal is the real way to deal with it. If you try to remove the criminal from the crime, sooner or later he will be caught. You cannot escape from God, even if you could escape from people. But God takes the crime as far away as it can possibly get, so that you will never meet it again, never have to face it again, never have to live with it again. It has gone. That is forgiveness and that is mercy.

Finally, God is a God of pity. Why? Because he remembers that we are dust. He remembers that we are like some flowers which in a week's time will be dead and gone. A human being is like a flower – we come, we flourish, and then the place of that person knows him no more.

When you go to worship, do you realise that you are sitting on a seat that has been occupied by someone who is now dead and gone and the place where they sat knows them no more? God pities us. It is not that he made us for that. No, it was our sin that did this for us. It spoiled our life. God does a lot of things out of sheer pity for us. Thank God that he is a God of pity. He knows that we are here today and gone tomorrow. How does he help us? He tells us: my love goes on; my love is an everlasting love. It will go on to your children and your children's children. Man's life is so transient, but God remembers this. Into our fleeting lives he injects a love that goes on, and therefore a love that will keep us going on. He offers us the hope of eternal life. At the end of verses 11, 13 and 17, we read: *those who fear him*. There is nothing automatic about the love of God, nothing automatic about his mercy and his pity. It comes to a particular group of people only: those who fear him. Some tell us that fear is a bad emotion and that it sets up inhibitions and all kinds of things. Well there can be phobias that are unhealthy fears, but there is one fear that is healthy: the fear of the Lord.

I would to God that those who are causing children to die of starvation would fear God. I would to God that those responsible for the entertainment of our country would fear God. I would to God that those who are in positions of responsibility and in politics would fear God. I would to God that those who are in education and science, playing with people's minds and with their futures, would fear God. To those who fear God, his mercy and pity come. There is nothing wrong with fearing God. It is a fear that is the first wise thing you ever did – not to be frightened of God, but to fear grieving his holiness, to fear his anger, to fear displeasing your Maker. So it is not unconditional. All these things come to those who remember. Here is the memory again: remember to do his commandments, to live his way.

Finally, the psalmist broadens out. He is already thinking about others, his grandchildren, but now he is thinking about everybody who is going to sing the Psalm. He is thinking about more than that and he realises that God is king over all. Do you know what made David a great king? The answer is that he acknowledged a greater king. All the world's greatest rulers have been those who have acknowledged a greater ruler. The world's worst dictators are those who did not acknowledge anybody above themselves. The Lord has established his throne in the heavens; his kingdom is over all, therefore, everybody come and join me in blessing the Lord. You angels up there, you give him your obedience then give him your praise. Join us in this. Bless the Lord, you angels of his! And you people in the temple with me; all his host and his ministers, you bless the Lord!

Then he looks at nature around, and the horizons that stretch out from Jerusalem, and he calls on the hills, and all his works, and all his dominion: angels, all you his hosts, all the horizons around us, all his works, bless the Lord!

Then David finishes where he began. Say to yourself: "Bless the Lord, O my soul!"

READ PSALM 104

Harvest festivals have lost their original meaning. In some cases they are a kind of vestige of the days when most people in Britain lived very close to the land – a kind of nostalgic dream of country life that comes out in so many ways. We dream of a little cottage in the country or a caravan or a trip to the country. There is something in all of us that wants to get back to the land. The hard fact is that over the last one hundred and fifty years in this country, people have been increasingly alienated from nature. Man and nature have been drawing further and further apart.

There have been three stages or steps or aspects in this alienation. First, the great drift to the towns began in the industrial revolution. More and more farm labourers left the land and went to live in the towns where there were better wages, even though there were poorer living conditions. The population moved from country to town until now the majority of our people live in the towns. Many young people have never seen a farm where food is produced.

We have crowded into the towns, and because the towns have got so crowded we have had to build upwards. Increasingly, most of the world's population are living in urban areas. With increasing mechanisation, and the huge farms of today, fewer labourers are needed and so the drift goes on.

The second reason is that man has exploited nature. We have not yet learned that there is a natural law that if you take out you must put back. It is a good farmer that has learned that law; a bad farmer does not learn it. Do you know that something like five thousand million acres of once useful farming land is now desert and dustbowl? That is a fantastic area of land and it is because we have exploited nature. Not only in agriculture but in industry and in the very development of cities. Something like one million acres a year are paved over with cement or tarmac, and we are left with what has come to be called the "concrete jungle".

We are using up fossil fuels at an increasingly rapid rate. We have taken, and taken, without realising what we were doing. You cannot have a good relationship with anyone unless you are giving as well as taking, and you cannot have a good relationship with nature unless you are giving as well as receiving.

The third factor is that we have been polluting nature to an extent hitherto unknown. We now realise that this little globe of ours is nothing more than a space capsule, and that its resources of air, water and power are limited. I needn't dwell on the figures but the biological time bomb is with us and somebody has said, "We've been through the Stone Age, the Ice Age, the Iron Age, the lot but we've now reached the garb-age." It sums the fact that Thor Heyerdahl, when he crossed the Pacific could use the water of the ocean for washing, but when he crossed the Atlantic a few years ago on a second raft he found plastic bottles, and rubbish, and pollution floating around.

Now that sets the scene and the result is we have become alienated from nature. The problem is worldwide. Because of that we have woken up to the fact that we have got alienated from God's creation, though that is not how everybody puts it. There is a cry now of "back to nature" but we don't quite know how to get back. Some decades it could be said that the young generation were more concerned about pollution than older people, but now all ages are concerned, as are many international organisations.

I want to describe first of all, wrong relationships to nature which are appearing in our country, in our day. Number one I call the attitude of romance. I am not just thinking about the kind of poetry that William Wordsworth wrote in the Lake District. I am thinking of the view that says the relationship between man and nature is that they are equals – that man is solely a part of nature and therefore he must respect the other part of him. It is fostered largely by evolutionary thinking which regards man as no more than an animal, and that therefore he ought to regard other animals and plants as equal to himself and give them the respect due to equals. There are two dangers of this outlook, which is far removed from the biblical outlook on nature. The one danger is that you have too high a view of nature. You start attributing human feelings to trees. "How would you like it to be chopped down?" You begin to have a humanised view of nature. Here is where St. Francis, who was making his own protest, just slipped over the line into romance when he talked of "Brother Ass" and "Mother Earth". The Bible never uses personal adjectives in this way. It is too high a view of nature because if that tree is my brother then I cannot possibly ever touch it.

Albert Schweitzer towards the end of his life, slipped over this line in his phrase "Reverence for Life", a phrase which caused intense embarrassment to the colleagues on the medical staff at Lamberéné because it extended to flies, insects, and all forms of life. This is to romanticise nature. If you follow this through logically you finish up in the position where you are unable to swat a fly in your kitchen. It is not the biblical viewpoint; it is an over-romantic view. It has too high a view of nature, treating it as equal to human beings. Therefore, it will have too low a view of human beings as equal to nature. It will describe man in terms of a "naked ape" and society in terms of a "human zoo". Now you can see as soon as I mention these things how prevalent this view is. It is a genuine attempt to get right with nature but it has done it at the cost of a right view of both nature and humanity. The view of romance simply is not the view of the Bible, it is not the way back.

The second view which is wrong I call the view of "reverence", which actually puts man below nature and encourages him to worship nature. Now this view is very common in the East. It is only a short step from the statement "all is beautiful" to the statement "all is divine". This is the view we call "pantheism", which means everything is "god". When you look at a tree, that is "god" you are looking at; when you look at the sky, that is "god" you are looking at. It is not long before you treat nature as sacred. As soon as you treat part of nature as sacred, you treat it as sacrosanct, which means untouchable. The wrong view has kept people hungry and it is not the view of God. When I look at a tree I am not looking at God – that is not God.

It is this view that has become popular under the title of Zen Buddhism. This view reverences nature and puts man below nature and makes him kneel down before it. We are back to the sacred grove of trees again.

Both these views fail to take into account one stark fact of nature, and that is that nature is not universally benevolent. Nature has two faces: sometimes she has a beautiful face and sometimes she doesn't. William Wordsworth, on a summer day looking at the daffodils near Rydal Water, could write poetry. I wonder if he would have written poetry if he had been in the Delta in Bangladesh when the floods came in. You see nature is not a one-face thing. Sometimes nature is good, other times nature is not so good, and we have to come to terms with that fact. If you romanticise nature you can only do so by selecting the beautiful and the good, and the beneficial, and shutting your eyes deliberately to that in nature which is against man: the typhoon and the earthquake.

The reverence view likewise means that you are worshipping a God with two faces: a God who is kind to you sometimes and not so kind other times. If you worship nature as God, you are worshipping a two-faced God and you cannot be sure what his attitude is towards you.

Let me now become positive. I have been critical and I have tried to make you think. Now let me come to the Bible: here we have the book written by the Maker who made nature, and he ought to know how we can integrate with the universe around us. The first thing the Bible tells us is never to get God confused with nature. It is idolatry to worship the creature rather than the Creator. It is possible to be worshipping his garden on Sunday rather than God, and that is idolatry. However beautiful our gardens may be, we must never worship them. We must never give them prior claim; we must never give them prior affection and attention. My garden is not God. God made the flowers, yes, but those flowers are not God. You can worship flowers but you are committing idolatry if you do, and idolatry shows mental and moral confusion.

So the first thing the Bible makes clear is that nature is not an extension of God; it is in the same relation to God as a chair and a table was to Jesus in Nazareth. If you wanted to go and talk to Jesus you would not talk to the table and the chair. The two wrong attitudes are: romance, which said that man is equal with nature; reverence, which said that man is below nature. Now here are two right attitudes. The first is regency, which means that man is above nature – that is the first insight that we get. Make no mistake about it, the Bible says that you are more important than any part of nature at all. It means that the sacrifice of any part of nature is justified for your sake. That is a revolutionary biblical insight, the implications of which we have to think through. It means, for example, that Jesus was prepared to sacrifice hundreds of pigs for the sanity of one man—that puts it in perspective.

Therefore, I do not think it is unchristian to use monkeys and guinea pigs to discover how to help men and women. I think it is a naïve view to say that is "un-christian". That is not to say that one justifies unnecessary cruelty. But if you have ever seen a pig drown, you know that those pigs that rushed down the slopes of Galilee did not drown in a very pleasant manner, but Jesus saw the sanity of one man as more important than hundreds of pigs. That puts nature and man in the relationship of regency.

There is a difference between you and the ape. You are made in the image of God and that puts you above every part of nature. There is no planet circling the heavens that is more important than you, which God would not sacrifice for your salvation, not one part of nature more important. Therefore God says to man: you have dominion over nature. You are a regent; you can reign or rule over nature. That allows us to do three things. It allows us to manipulate nature. It is interesting that the whole of modern science began in Christian thinking with a rediscovery of the Bible at the time of the Reformation. If you read Professor Herbert Butterfield's books on modern science you will see how he reveals that it was the belief that God had given us dominion over nature which led to the burst of modern science and technology which now we experience. I believe science is basically a Christian thing. It not only means we can manipulate nature it gives us authority to destroy nature. It gives us authority to use that axe against a tree, which the "romance" view and the "reverence" view do not. It means that God would rather we did chop down a tree if it is going to help a human being. It does not mean that he allows wanton destruction, but it does mean you can destroy part of nature if a good purpose for man is involved.

I believe it is God's will that we manipulate nature. No cow was ever intended to give a thousand gallons of milk but we have manipulated nature. All farming is manipulation of nature and God gave us the authority to do so. It has been argued that this is the cause of pollution, that the Christian permission to dominate nature has been the cause of man's exploitation. That is a libel on the Christian faith. Because the Christian faith says that there are two things in our attitude to nature. Number one: regency, but I use that term rather than royalty for this reason – that the regent is not the absolute king. For the second word I want to use is respect, for man is below the Creator. That will give us the right attitude: above nature but below God; above the creature but below the Creator – and therefore we shall develop not only regency toward nature but respect.

We should not knowingly or wantonly destroy, for nature does not belong to man; it is God's. Just as you would behave properly in someone else's garden, that is what you are in on earth. This is God's garden. He clothes the grass of the field and he feeds the birds of the air. Whatever you touch in nature, you are touching God's property and he will call you to answer for it one day. If you have wantonly destroyed any part of God's garden without an adequate reason, one day you stand before God. This is what puts the brake on. God makes us responsible to him. This creates the sense of responsibility. If you love God, you love what he has made. You have respect for the tree. You have respect for the flower. You love God; you love his creatures.

What I am trying to explain is this: God gave us our brains to use, and the greatest unexplored territory in the world is underneath your hat. He calls us to think these things through. A right relationship to nature is utterly bound up in a right relationship to God, and the reason why we have become alienated from nature is because we are alienated from God, and I see no hope of solving this. Even if we were all to go barefoot and live in caves and stick flowers in our hair, we still would not become reconciled properly to nature. We would fall into one of those other things, maybe becoming mystics, Zen Buddhists, romanticists, the lot. But let us return to God and say, "God, I'm under you; therefore, though I will not abuse my regency, I will respect what you have made and what you love."

The glory to me is that God has not made a utilitarian world. There are lots of things that God has made that are no use at all for food. There are plants that would poison you; there are plants that have no goodness in them that you could cope with, with your digestive system. Why did God make these things? Because he is not just treating us as animals, because he has made us in his image and he likes beauty. The flowers that no man ever sees up in the mountains he loves because he is God. He's not only put useful things in the world like grass, he has put things that you can't eat, like chrysanthemums. He likes flowers and he enjoys them. He has created a whole lot of things for beauty as well as usefulness. That is why within us there is a creative urge to have trees as well as corn. There is no moral principle any different between chopping down a corn stalk and chopping down an oak tree. The one can be replaced more quickly than the other but there is no moral difference. You have to justify both on the grounds of human good, and that puts the whole thing in perspective.

There are two things I want to say which will put this back into a biblical setting. First, the Bible predicts a deterioration in man's relationship with nature. The book of Revelation, which unveils the future for us, has some pretty horrible things to say about nature at the end of history. It talks about a third of the trees of earth dying. It talks about the oceans turning to blood. Red tides have been seen, because they are so polluted they turn blood red, and the book of Revelation talks about that. It talks about an increase in earthquakes; it talks about a polluted atmosphere such that the sun is darkened and the moon is blood red. I expect that man's relationship with nature will deteriorate, and I will tell you why: because the number of people who are out of touch with God is increasing and will go on increasing. But I must not finish there. There is another reason why the pollution will go on. Even if all men turn to God, we are told in the Bible that there are things in nature that have gone wrong not because of man's ignorance, folly or sin but because of sin in other intelligent beings in the universe, notably Satan.

The Bible faces squarely that there are things in nature, earthquakes and bacteria, which God never intended and there is something that has gone wrong with nature. Here I come to the positive, optimistic and glorious hope of the Christian: the Bible talks about the whole creation groaning and travailing, wanting to be set free and waiting for the redemption of the sons of God. What does that mean? I will tell you: not only is human nature polluted; nature is polluted too. The whole universe that God made – and when he had finished it, he looked at it and said, "That's good, that's very good" – is no longer very good. It is God's plan to redeem the whole thing, to rescue the whole thing from bondage and decay; to rescue it all from disease and death. This is God's plan. What a tremendous, imaginative scheme, and God decided to redeem the whole universe – not just people but trees and rivers.

So the Bible finishes with a picture of a new heaven and a new earth in which there are trees and rivers, and the whole thing is a re-created nature. Here is the thing that will finally bring us together. My personal redemption or salvation is intimately bound up with the redemption of nature all around me. You see, I am going to be redeemed altogether. God has saved my soul already through Jesus, but he has not saved my body yet. My body is still tied to this polluted nature in which I live. It is a body that is going to die; it is dying as I write this; cells are dying in my body, and my body is tied to this polluted nature. But one day I am going to get a new body with new cells in it, and new cells that will never die, cells that will never get diseased. I am going to have a new body with new hands, new face, new everything in a new redeemed environment.

Do you think God would stop with our bodies? Bodies have got to live somewhere. Bodies have got to have a perfect environment. The body may be perfect but it has to have a perfect surrounding and that is why God has promised us a new earth as well as a new heaven. You hear people talking about heaven and they forget all about the new earth, but that is my notion of salvation. It is God's plan to reverse the original order of creation. When he created this world he made the world first and then he made man and put them in it. Do you know what his order is now? He is making new people now then he is going to make a new world to put them in. Then we are going to be perfectly related to nature. The lion and the lamb will lie down together.

So many promises of the scripture just come flooding back. Do you know, when Noah went into the ark he took seven people with him? Eight people were going to survive the end of that civilisation, the end of that world; it was to be destroyed by water. Eight people escaped and went on into a new world, but do you notice they took nature with them? God wanted the animals saved too. You can read into that what you like, but I just know that the redeeming God who wants to save me wants to save trees, rivers, mountains and stars. There is going to be a new heaven and a new earth – that is the nature I look forward to. When you have got that vision ahead of you, you will get a deeper respect for these things laid out before you now. You will still use them, you may still destroy some of them for a good purpose, but you will respect them and you will no longer be alienated from nature.

I finish these reflections prompted by Psalm 104 by mentioning a man called Jimmy Gilliland. He lived in the north of England in County Durham, and he spent all his waking life apart from work in an iron foundry in Consett, in the pubs, crawling home at night. He never looked at a blade of grass or a leaf of a tree. He was not interested. But many years ago Jesus stepped into his life. Then one of the loveliest experiences you could have with Jimmy was to go and walk with him in the country. Every leaf spoke to him; every flower was beautiful. Now he had not got this romantic view of nature that you mustn't swat a fly, but he had been reconciled to God's creation as well as to the Creator. The alienation had gone, and he was integrated again.

READ PSALM 107

Alexander Duff was the first Church of Scotland missionary to sail for India. He sailed from Ryde in the Isle of Wight on the good ship "Lady Holland" in October 1829. At midnight on February the 13th 1830, as the frail little ship rounded the Cape of Good Hope, it struck the rocks, its back broke, and everything looked as if it would be lost. They couldn't see any land in the darkness but they set off in one boat for the shore to look for land. After searching for many hours they found a shore and landed safely. Then they were able to go back and bring every passenger to the shore. Alexander Duff had led them all the way in prayer and asked God to protect them.

In the morning they gathered some of the bits of wood from the ship on the shore to make a fire and they began to look for all the luggage, but they found none. Everything had been swept away including a very large supply of books, which Alexander Duff was taking to India to start a college and every book was lost. But later that morning two books, and two only, from the entire wreck were washed up on shore: Alexander Duff's Bible and his book of Psalms. Picking up the book of Psalms on the seashore he opened it and it fell open at Psalm 107. His first words, which he read were, "Some went down to the sea in ships." Then v. 28, "Then they cried to the Lord in their trouble and he delivered them from their distress. Let them thank the Lord", which they then proceeded to do, which struck me as being as good an introduction to Psalm 107 as I could possibly get.

This Psalm was written 2500 years ago and more. We

are reading words that are as relevant and as helpful today. Many could say: this very week I have cried to the Lord and he has delivered me. Let them thank and praise the Lord. Verses 1–3 are a kind of prologue telling us the theme of the whole Psalm, and the theme is: "Let the redeemed give thanks." If God has done anything for you at all, this Psalm is a reminder to you to have at least the courtesy to come and say thank you.

Now we are forever telling children to say thank you. Sometimes at a meal table I used to pass something to my children and hang onto the plate or just go on holding it in front of their face. They would look a bit surprised and say, "I've got it," and I would go on holding it. Finally it dawned, the penny dropped, and they would say, "Thank you". You may have had to do that with children. The funny thing is we have to do it with adults, which is why the Bible repeatedly tells you to say thank you.

If you have received anything from God, then say, "Thank you." That is what the psalmist is saying. This implies a number of things and the first thing is that we usually forget to do this. Otherwise we would not need to be told. The number of things we take from God's hand – crises we go through, and a month later we have forgotten to say, "Thank you".

What are we to thank God for? There are two things mentioned in the prologue. First: for who he is; secondly for what he does. Everything that we thank God for comes under these two heads. If you examine your thanksgiving, it is so often for what he does, but we are to begin by giving thanks to the Lord *for he is good*.

We may have been brought up in a Christian country where it is taken for granted that God is good. That is why people ask questions like, "Why does God allow suffering if he's good?" Everybody in England pretty well assumed that God is good. We do not know what it is like to live in a land where they believe that God is bad, where he is a bad tempered God and you are never quite sure whether you are on his right side or not. The relief of believing that God is good is tremendous and it is a thing we take for granted.

Just supposing that God was moody, changeable; just supposing he was a bad deity – you would be frightened stiff of him. You would not know what to do with him. Give thanks to God because he is a good God. For some people the phrase "Good God" is an expletive that they use when they hear some sudden news, but to me those two words are the most remarkable words in the universe in a sense. They belong together, and the fact that they belong together we owe to the Bible and to nothing else.

"Oh give thanks to the Lord for he is good" – only then, having given thanks to God for what he is, can we go on to thank him for what he does. So the Psalm moves on: "Let the redeemed of the Lord say so, whom he has redeemed" – which means: whom he has rescued, saved from some trouble or distress that otherwise they would have known. Thank him for what he is; thank him for what he does. The only thing that you can ever give to God that he did not give to you first is your thanks. It is the least you can give and it is all that you can give.

Now we turn to the main body of the Psalm to see how it expands this theme of giving thanks to the Lord. The first part of the Psalm, the main part, from vv. 4–32 is concerned with people – their suffering and fickleness; how changeable they are; how quickly they forget; how up and down they go. Then, in contrast to that, in the last part of the Psalm we look at God.

Consider the completely different attitude we have to God when we are in suffering to the attitude we have to God when we get out of it. This is the fickleness here. We are calling on God and praying to him and thinking of him when we are in trouble, but then when we are out of it we change. Now we can get on without him and we forget him. That is human fickleness when we are faced with suffering. Let us be absolutely honest with ourselves: do I pray more earnestly when I am in trouble than when I am out of trouble? Do I talk to God most when things are going badly or when things are going well?

Now I am going to approach this major part of the Psalm from a number of different angles. First of all let us look at the fact that we have here four different kinds of suffering mentioned. The first mentions a desert and wandering alone in a desert. Now I would not have thought that suffering comes to you very often, but getting lost in a desert is a frightening experience. I have once been lost in the Arabian Desert and I know what it is like. Everywhere you look there is sand. The sun at midday is straight up; you cannot even tell any direction from the sun. There is no shadow cast; it is around your feet. You stand there and you just cannot tell which way you are looking. You look this way, that way, the other way; you climb a sand dune to try to see a bit further and you just see another sand dune. If you go on walking you will discover sooner or later that you walk in a circle. (I don't know if it's something to do with the fact that your body is usually more developed on one side than the other.) You finish up where you started. It is a most frightening experience. Many people have got lost in the desert. The Egyptian army suffered this way during the Six Day War in the Sinai Desert. So the first picture is of a dying man who cannot find the track. There is no way for him to follow. He is wandering in circles, he is hungry and thirsty, and he doesn't know where to go, which direction. That is the first suffering: wandering in the desert.

The second is a picture of slavery. Not just being in prison but being in bonds, a man who is shackled with iron, and iron seems to have entered into his soul as well, reading these words carefully. In this country we know little of slavery. I used to go regularly and talk to slaves because in Arabia they still had slaves, hundreds of them. A little girl in the marketplace fetched seventy-five pounds back then. There is still slavery in the world, as you probably know. This is a picture of slavery and it is misery. You are just bought and sold like so much goods and chattels.

The third thing mentioned is sickness – a person who is so ill they have lost their appetite. They cannot eat food and they have got to the last stages of physical illness.

The fourth is of sailors at sea being tossed around so helplessly that they are at their wits end as to what to do. Once again, my mind goes back to the Shetland Islands where people lived by fishing, and where they went out at night and faced the elements and some nights they were within inches of death.

None of these sufferings do we experience to a great extent here. Therefore, this Psalm is a bit strange to us. The third is the most likely. But now I want to say that these four things clearly belong to a particular time and place. The Psalm mentions that the Lord has gathered in his redeemed from the east, the west, the north and the south. The interesting thing is that from the Holy Land the four points of the compass lead those people of God into the four troubles mentioned in the Psalm. So these four troubles were not selected at random. Here are the four dangers of living in the Middle East. The danger in the west is going on the sea, and the Jews did not like the sea. They only went on it to do business; the idea of going on it for pleasure would not have occurred to them. The Jews hated the sea. It was dangerous and, indeed, sailing in those days you took your life in your hands.

If they went south to Egypt, into the Nile Delta, the hot,

humid climate as against the cool, healthy climate of the hills of Judea was usually deadly for their health and they succumbed to all manner of disease. If you read the story of the Jews in Egypt you find they suffered from all manner of disease there. If they were taken north it was being taken off into captivity into Babylon and Assyria – into slavery, in chains. If they went east they were into the Arabian Desert where they lost their way in the burning heat. You see this Psalm is written out of real experience.

We locate this Psalm in space – can we locate it in time? The answer is yes. The time is the time of the Exile, when they lost their own land. Some of them fled to Egypt. Some of them went into Arabia. Most were taken into slavery, and a few fled by sea, and they were scattered. Then they cried unto the Lord in their distress. The slaves cried; the people lost in the desert cried; the sick Jews in Egypt cried; those on the sea cried. God brought them back again from the four points of the compass and redeemed them, and they forgot to say "thank you". That is the theme of the Psalm – it is real.

The third thing I want to point out is this: there were religious reasons why they got into trouble. The reasons are clearly stated in this Psalm: they had spurned God's advice and they had sinned against God's laws. Now this does not mean that every bit of trouble you have is due to a religious reason. But it does mean that a lot of the troubles we get into are because we have spurned God's advice or sinned against him. Many of our troubles we could avoid if we stayed with God and were obedient to his will, but we don't.

Therefore, the troubles God sends he sends as a father disciplines his children – to bring us back to the right way, to teach us. Sometimes, occasionally, every father has to apply the board of education to the seat of learning, and apply certain corporal punishment. Why is he doing this? If you love a son you chastise him. If you don't chastise him

I doubt if you love him as you should. It may be occasional but it is a part of discipline and love, and these four things were God's way of disciplining his people.

Now even though this is about his people I think there is a truth on a wider scale; Romans 1 tells us that if a nation turns away from God and gives God up, then God gives the nation up to troubles. There will be a breakdown in family relationships. There will be perverted relationships between men and women. There will be disobedience in children. There will be violence uncontrollable by law. These things follow because men give God up. When you give God up, God gives you up, and he does it for your good, to teach you a lesson. So there were religious reasons.

Now let us come at it from a fourth angle to try to get the heart of the story. Have you noticed that these stories are all parallel? They are all concerned with danger, distress, which is imminent, which is pressing in on people, something about to happen to them which is disastrous. You notice that there is immediate deliverance when they cry. Those in the desert cry and God shows them a track that they had not noticed and it leads straight into a city. Those who are in chains, God bursts the bonds of iron and they are free. Those on the sea find that the sea calms and goes still. Those who are sick unto death recover and start eating food again. They are all the same story—people in danger crying to God, deliverance coming immediately. That is the heart of each story.

So now we are able to look at the main message. It is simply this, and at the head of my Revised Standard Version, it says at the top of this Psalm: "The Lord delivers from trouble." Well that is not quite the main message; it is half of it. The main message is simply summed up: prayer is desperate; it is instinctive when a man is desperate. Praise is not instinctive; it is deliberate. Now let me tell you what I mean: prayer is one of the most natural things in the world.

Everybody prays. Even the atheist who said, "I'm an atheist, thank God" was praying. But it is amazing how people in a real jam say, "Oh God". It is instinctive to pray.

If people do not pray it is because they have had to conquer the instinct; they have had to suppress it – but everybody prays. That does not mean that they are good or that they are Christians. Unbelievers pray. It is natural to pray. If you are in a situation where no human being can do anything to help you it is natural and instinctive to pray. When you are desperate that is what you do, however short or long the prayer. Prayer is therefore natural to the unbeliever. Prayer is not the mark of a Christian; it is the mark of a human being. Everybody prays in some way or another.

The thing that impresses you when you travel around the world and see different religions is this: everybody prays. So when people say to me, "You know I don't want you to think I'm not a Christian; I say my prayers," that does not tell me a thing as to whether they are a Christian or not. Everybody prays more or less, irregularly or regularly, but especially when they are in trouble. But it is not natural to praise. It is instinctive to pray in trouble; it is not instinctive to praise out of trouble.

I have been struck by this: I suppose hundreds of people outside the church, over my years of ministry, have told me that they pray. It is one of the commonest remarks I get. Not one outside the Church has ever told me "I praise". I have never heard the word, "Hallelujah," from an unbeliever. I have never heard an unbeliever say, "Praise God," or "Praise the Lord." Everybody turns to God when they are in trouble, but who comes back afterwards and says "Thank you"?

One of the stories in the Gospels is this: one day ten people cut off from society by a loathsome disease which rotted their flesh and made them repulsive to society came to Jesus and said, "Can you do anything for us?"

He said, "Yes I can and I will." He healed them from their disease and their flesh became like the flesh of little children. They were able to go back to their wives and families and live again a normal life. Out of ten people, only one came back. Jesus said, "Where are the others? Were they healed?" Yes they were, but they didn't want to come back and say thank you. So when people say I can be as good a Christian without going to church as those who do, I ask, "Do you praise God? Do you come back and give thanks? Do you say, 'Praise the Lord,' when you are out of trouble?"

How does it tell you to praise the Lord? It says: Let them come and give thanks in the congregation. In other words, you can help somebody else by coming and giving thanks to the Lord with them. It is God's will to have people come together and say thank you, not just privately but in the congregation, in the assembly of the elders, in the congregation of the people. "Let them extol him and praise him." That is why we meet every Sunday; that is why we go to church. We are told here to give thanks in gift as well as word, to give a thank offering as well as praise, and to bring that, and to give thanks in public. Now that is the theme of the Psalm.

Now we turn briefly to the last section of the Psalm. Against this human fickleness you have divine faithfulness. Against the changeable human nature you have a God who is always loyal in his love, and steadfast. We now see the two things that have been mentioned again and again taken up and explained. Notice in v. 8: "Let them thank the Lord" – for two things: "for his steadfast love and his wonderful works." In v. 15, "Let them thank the Lord for his steadfast love and his wonderful works"; in v. 21, "steadfast love, wonderful works"; in v. 31, "steadfast love, wonderful works." What do these two phrases refer to? Well in the last part of the Psalm we first of all have his wonderful works explained and then we have his steadfast love. I know that some people feel that analysing a poem kills it. I remember at school we took a beautiful poem, we pulled it out and said, "This is a subjunctive clause", or whatever. We pulled it all to bits and analysed it. There was time when I used to think that was a most unhelpful thing to do because it spoiled the poem. I know now they were trying to teach me the deeper truth and value of the poems so that it would not just go over the top of my head but go deep and help me to appreciate it.

Now I know that it may spoil a Psalm for some of you to do all this analysis. It is meant to take you deeper into it and to see the order of the thinking that goes into the Bible. How carefully it is put together, how beautifully it's constructed: a prologue, two main sections, and an epilogue. The second section explains the first and the whole thing unfolds. Well now, look at the wonderful works of God. What do we mean by his wonderful works? We mean by that his control of natural events – his control of the weather, his control of the fields, the gardens, the fruit and the flowers.

He can turn a garden into a desert. In the sands of Arabia sometimes I would come across long tree trunks which told me that some time in the past there used to be a garden there, but it is all desert. The Sahara used to be a garden; it has changed. Israel used to be a desert. Do you know you can check up God's wonderful works? In the Israeli meteorological office. When the Jews got back to their land the rainfall changed. Now Tel Aviv has as much rain as London, and for two thousand years that land was a desert – his wonderful works.

Do you know how God does it in the Middle East? Very simple. When the prevailing wind is west from the Mediterranean it brings rain; when the prevailing wind is east from the Arabian Desert it shrivels everything up. All God did in his wonderful works was to change the wind around.

Elijah prayed and God sent the wind to the east for three and a half years and they had no rain. So Elijah prayed again and he said, "Now Lord send them back the rain," and he climbed Mount Carmel, looked to the west and saw a cloud no bigger than a man's hand but it got bigger and bigger, and the rain came. That is how God brings his wonderful works.

The God who controls the weather, the God who stills the sea, the God who sends the rain. The sun would not have risen this morning if God had not ordained it to. That is the wonderful works of God. He turns the rivers into a desert and he turns the desert into a garden. We are dependent on God and he can change the weather tomorrow and either bring a barren or a fertile land to his people.

What do we mean by his loyal love? We mean two things: his provision and his protection. Here is a little Christian sum for you: provision plus protection equals providence. What do we mean by providence? God provides and God protects. He fills the hungry, gives them enough to eat when they cry to him, and he protects them.

So we come to the epilogue – the last two verses, vv. 42-43. What happens when it is patently obvious that God has rescued people from trouble because they have cried to him? First of all, the upright see it and are glad. You can really rejoice with someone when they say, "Look, I prayed to God and this is what happened." When the upright hear that, they are glad – they rejoice. When the wicked hear that, they have nothing to say. I share some testimonies of rescues privately with one or two unbelievers and their reaction is very interesting: they shut their mouths. They don't know what to say when you tell them how God has answered a prayer, overruled circumstances, changed a situation. The upright are thrilled and they say, "Hallelujah," but the wicked do not know what to say. It is unanswerable, of course. They have no alternative explanation. They are silent because they are desperately trying to think of some other explanation. They are trying to think of a way to get around it. "It couldn't be God; it's just coincidence" – but while they are thinking their mouth is shut.

So v. 43 says: "Whoever is wise let him give heed to these things." Someone has said that experience is a hard school and fools will learn in no other. The school colours are black and blue, and I am afraid most of us learn the hard way, and what a pity that we do. We go through the suffering before we learn. Why do you think the Bible is given to us? Let me tell you: that you may learn from other people's experience without having to go through it. You could go through being lost in the desert, being a slave, and being sick to death, and being in danger of shipwreck. You could go through that and you would learn this lesson. But you can learn it another way if you are wise: you can learn it by giving heed to these things and not going through it.

The wise person is always ready to learn from someone else's experience. The fool must go through it himself. The wise young person says, "I will listen to what older Christians tell me." The foolish young Christian says, "I'm going to try it for myself and see what happens." The new young generation that I talk to is made up of fools like this who say, "We are not going to take from our elders what is right and wrong. We are going to try it for ourselves and find out." They will, alas, and some of them will be dead by forty as a result. They are determined to try everything for themselves, but let him who is wise take heed to these things. They got into trouble because they spurned God and sinned against God. They only got out of it because he helped them out.

Take heed, don't get into these trials, stay with God and you have learned. Let him who is wise take heed and let men consider one thing: the steadfast love of the Lord. He never lets his people down when they cry. Let people then consider this: other people may let you down; God never will. God's people, when they turn to God, find him and he lifts them back again. He gathers them from the north, the south, east and the west. Let people consider that after two thousand years he has gathered Israel back into their land. Let people consider this: that after two thousand years God has not let them down and let them go. Let us give heed and learn from these things.

READ PSALMS 121, 123, 131

When I taught on this group of Psalms, my wife was in Ward 3 at East Grinstead Hospital, and that ward was a very famous place. During the war that was where the Battle of Britain pilots were taken after being trapped in the burning cockpits of their spitfires and hurricanes, and where that incredible surgeon Archie McIndoe developed new techniques for grafting. The first eye graft was done at that ward at that time.

Now we benefit from the experience. The whole ward is now given over to eyes and so, as you go into it, some are totally blindfolded, some partially. You begin to realise what a precious gift sight is, I think, when something goes wrong with it. You also begin to realise that your eyes have many functions, unlike other parts of your body, which only have one or two functions. For example, they have physical functions – that is obvious. They are the communication between your inside and your outside, the environment and your brain; one of the vital links. But they have a function far more than physical. They have a social function. They are part of our relationship with other people. Looks can kill or they can comfort. You can look down on people with contempt or you can look up to them with respect and imagination. So eyes have this social function and our Lord Jesus used his eyes for the social function also; when he looked at the Pharisees with anger, his eyes were his main weapon. When he looked at Peter on the night of the denial, a look was enough without a word to break Peter's heart. But I think it is often overlooked that the eyes have a spiritual function also and they are a vital part of our spiritual life. Jesus said: "The eye is the lamp of the body. If your eyes are healthy, your whole body will be full of light." They have a spiritual function and more than that, we don't realise this function because so often we cut out our eyes when we commune with God. I still wonder whether we should, because the Bible never told us to shut our eyes when we talk to God. It is a tradition that developed and I am beginning to question it very seriously. There is a good motive behind it – we don't want to be distracted by each other and our environment when we talk to God – but it is strange: when they realise the Bible never tells you to shut your eyes to pray, people are shattered. This is something many have taken for granted and just been taught to do. In the Bible the attitude of the eyes when communing with God is to lift them up. Again and again in the Bible we are to lift things up: lift up your hands, lift holy hands, lift your eyes. I think we might sometimes try praying with our eyes lifted up and see what happens. But that is why this phrase, "I will lift up my eyes" keeps coming into the scripture.

Thinking so much about these things, I turned as one always does in times of personal feeling and need to the book of Psalms. For the Psalms reflect so many moods. When you are cast down, there is a Psalm to fit. When you are elated, there is a Psalm to fit. When you have known failure, there is a Psalm to fit. When you have known success, there is another Psalm to fit. Whatever human need you have, the whole gamut of human emotion is reflected in the book of Psalms. Somewhere you find a Psalm that will express for you how you feel and minister to your soul.

Now there are Psalms for when you are cast down – Psalms 42 and 43 are good ones for somebody who is depressed. "Why are you cast down O my soul?" It teaches you to ask the right questions, to think the right thoughts when you are cast down. But there are other Psalms when things are looking up. Isn't that an interesting phrase? Did you notice, "When things are looking up"? Things can't look anyway, but do you notice the meaning of the colloquial phrase – when things are looking up then your eyes look up. I will lift my eyes....

There is a whole series of fifteen Psalms, from Psalm 120 to Psalm 134, which are called "Songs of Ascent", and they are to be used when things are looking up. Throughout those Psalms the phrase keeps coming: "I will lift my eyes up". Those are the Psalms I turn to now. This chapter is rather more personal than perhaps a normal Bible study. I will lift my eyes up; I will look up, things are looking up, so let us look at these Psalms. They have a double meaning: a physical ascent and a spiritual ascent. Originally they were written for the Jews when they went three times a year up to Jerusalem. Jerusalem is unique among the capitals of the world in that it is up in the hills. It is not on a river mouth, not on a plain; it is not on a junction of roads, it has no reason for being there except it is nearest to heaven. So when you go to worship God in his city, it matters not from what direction you go, you go up. Psalms 120 – 134 were written for people as they went up, as things were looking up, to lift their eyes. People live in the valleys and the plains. When you fly over a country you look down, you see where the houses are, where people's businesses are, where the factories are. God invites you to leave that and go up to him; to lift your eyes up; to get above the hurly-burly of the everyday.

So these songs of ascent were written for a physical climb through the Judean hills because people who need help need to look above for that help. Far too many look around for help. The Bible teaches us to look up for help. "I lift my eyes because that's where my help comes from" – and this is one of the secrets of life. If you are burdened today, if you have problems, if you are weighted down, don't look around for help, look above for help. That is a very profound lesson. If you look around you may be disappointed, you may be lost in the crowd, you may go away and say: "Nobody spoke to me."

So there was a physical ascent but also, reading between the lines as their bodies climbed, the Psalms enabled their spirits to climb, lift and soar. In fact, your heart and your eyes are very closely linked. Where one goes the other one will go. Where your heart goes your eyes will follow. Where your eyes go your heart will follow. The two are interlinked and we shall see that in these Psalms.

I want you to join in imagination a group of pilgrims climbing up the Judean hills. They are going up to meet the Lord; they are lifting their eyes, and as they go they sing so their spirits are lifted. I remember going to Israel once and we landed at the airport at midnight, just outside Tel Aviv. We got on a coach. There were seven Presbyterian ministers from Belfast on the coach, and I got in among them. Those who think Presbyterians are cold people ought to have been among that lot because I remember vividly that as we began to climb first the low hills, the Zorah where Samson lived, and then began to see the steeper Judean limestone hills, they were singing, "I will lift up mine eyes to the hills" in a Scottish paraphrase version of the Psalms, and we were lifted. As the bus lifted us, and as our eyes lifted, our spirits soared up until we caught sight of the first houses of Jerusalem right on the hilltop. It was very exciting to go up to Jerusalem that way.

I am only going to take three of the Psalms because these three are linked together with the one phrase which occurs only in these three of the fifteen: I will lift my eyes up. Having been thinking so much about eyes, you can understand how this has shaped my understanding of these Psalms. But it has really been revealed to me. First, though man is the most upright of God's creatures, his eyes are so set in his body that their natural bent is to look horizontally or down. They are at the front of our face and they look those ways naturally. It requires a discipline, a resolution, an effort to lift the eyes. When they are at rest they are either level or down. That's why it is easier to look down. That is why some people prefer to sit at the back of a church than the front. It is more of a strain to look up to a pulpit than to look down to it.

Satan, if he can, will keep our outlook level or down. He will keep us looking at our environment, looking at other people, even looking inward at ourselves, and that is one of the ways he gets us. One of the reasons why people are as they are and why the world is as it is, is because people don't discipline themselves to lift up their eyes. They are too busy looking at the newspaper, looking out at the level of the world and seeing all that is wrong in it. If you want to be distressed, look within; if you want to be defeated, look back; if you want to be distracted, look around; if you want to be dismayed, look ahead; but if you want to be delivered, look up.

My grandfather, if he was ever asked by a child to sign an autograph album, would always write one of two things: "He whose sermon is a godly life will never preach too long" was one thing he wrote; the other was: "When the outlook is bad, try the up-look."

We turn to Psalm 121. Clearly it was for the part of the journey through the Judean hills before you get to Jerusalem because it describes the journey vividly, and the hazards of the journey that the pilgrims made in those days, long before there were coaches and tarmac motorways. So this Psalm 121 describes the journey to Jerusalem. Psalm 122 describes the next stage, "I was glad when they said to me let us go up to the house of the Lord."

So Psalm 121 is not the immediate journey to the temple but the journey to the city. You rise on those hills – tier after tier of hills so that each one you think must be the last peak and then there is another, and your eyes are naturally, in a sense, lifted up.

These pilgrims are coming to Jerusalem for help, for that is what we need. There isn't a single person who doesn't need help of one kind or another. You may have looked around for it and failed to have it. Well now look above for it and come up those hills whence comes my help. Scholars debate as to whether v. 1 is a statement or a question. In the Authorized Version it is a statement, in the Revised Standard Version a question. I think that both are valid translations and both are correct. There is a sense in which your help does come from the hills and a sense in which it doesn't and we ought to get it clear that the hills are a help to us and yet they are not. I would hate to live in a flat place. I have been used all my life to living where there are hills all around me to look up to. I believe that is the environment that God likes us to live in – that is why he put his people in the hills of Judea. He wants us to look up, lift our eyes and have something above us all the time that is yet belonging to earth. So we do lift up our eyes to the hills and our help does come from the hills because God is found in the hills. The hills cannot help us, they can only help us to find help.

Somebody has said, "If you think the hills can help you, that is pantheism, which is only atheism wearing a fig leaf." No, we don't look to the hills; the hills are not God.

If you get bogged down in looking too much at the hills, and not enough at the God who made the hills, you will miss the point. So I will lift mine eyes to the hills; does my help come from there? Yes it comes from there, but not from the hills. The hills are a help to find help because it is the God who made the hills who is my help. This is surely one of the influences that hills can be. There is something very enduring, very solid about the hills.

Now there is a unique difference between pagan temples and the temple of the Lord here. You find that pagan temples are built up in the hills but they always chose the highest hill for the temple. Go to Athens and you will find a totally different situation from Jerusalem. In Athens, in Acropolis, there is the Parthenon right on top of the hill. Man's temple is the very highest point. You find that in pagan worship the high places were chosen so that the temple might be the highest point – not so the temple of God. The temple of God was placed up in the hills but not on the top hill. That is why you cannot see it until you are within two miles of it. Jerusalem is on the hill surrounded by valleys, but it is also surrounded at a radius of about two miles with the circle of hills that are higher than the temple, so that even in the temple, though you are up on a hill, you still look up to the hills from the temple of God. That is the physical layout of Jerusalem. So even when you have got up to the house of the Lord you still lift up your eyes to the hills around – it is still a reminder that God is your Maker. Funnily enough, we have a much more vivid sense of God as Creator from earth than we do from the sky. The sky is so intangible, so ethereal that it is not easy to say that it was made, because it doesn't seem solid enough to be made, but the hills look solid enough and they will remind you of God as the Maker of heaven and earth.

So you need to remember heaven and earth when you worship. That is why the temple of the Lord in Jerusalem is within sight of heaven and earth – The Lord is the Maker of both. It is our Greek thinking that has separated the physical and the spiritual. The Hebrew thought of them as together. We present our bodies as our spiritual worship. We lift up our eyes as an act of appeal for help. God made both heaven and earth. So the hills around Jerusalem still were looked up to. The God who is as solid and reliable as those hills – and even more so because even before the mountains were brought forth, before ever he had formed the world, he was God and he was our dwelling place.

What kind of help can we expect from the God who made these hills around us? You can sum it up in one word and it is a word that occurs six times in the rest of the Psalm: "Keep, keep, keep, keep, keep, keep". That is the kind of help and that is the basic help that we need. That word "keep" means so many things in the English language. It means to hold on to something. It means to keep an eye on something, "I'll keep that for you; I'll keep an eye on it for you."

The word, "keep" here is a strong, castle-kind of word. The Lord is your "keep"; he is your keeper; he will keep you. This is the keyword of Psalm 121. Now there are three things that he will keep us from described in the rest of the Psalm and I will mention them briefly and leave you to meditate on them. Number one: he will keep an eye on the path underfoot as you travel. Number two: he will keep you from the light overhead as you travel. Number three: he will keep you from the danger around as you travel.

Let us take the first: the path underfoot. There were no tarmac roads in those days. If you try using one of the ancient roads, for example, the road from Bethany over the Mount of Olives to Jerusalem, it is today in exactly the same condition as it was in the time of Jesus' earthly ministry. It is rough, stony, the rain washes down it and makes gullies, there are bits of broken limestone lying everywhere. It is so easy to sprain your ankle. It is so easy to trip over; it is so easy to stumble. A pilgrim going up to Jerusalem had to keep his eyes down all the time. That is one of the tragedies of going on a road like that – that you are watching every foot, every step. You know, some people are like that in the road of life. They are so busy watching their own steps that they stumble anyway, because you get tired of watching and the human eye can mislead you and you just miss something and suddenly you have stubbed a toe or fallen over sideways – you have stumbled.

Now there are two ways of walking on a rough road. One is to watch your feet all the time. The other is the way the psalmist discovered. He said, "As I walk up this road to Jerusalem" – and he meant it quite literally – "I'm not going to watch my feet. I'm going to lift my eyes to you and let you watch my feet." That is the other way to tackle the problem — to lift your eyes until you are looking at Jesus and let him watch your feet. The psalmist says, "That is much better than me watching them because the Lord doesn't even doze. He never slumbers nor sleeps. He never misses anything; he never even blinks. His eyes are open all the time – they are watching me."

So it is much better if you are on a rough road and trying to climb the hill called "difficulty". Much better to take your eyes off your own feet, fix them on the Lord, and let him watch your feet. You will not suffer my foot to stumble because you neither slumber nor sleep. In other words, God never shuts his eyes. So lift up your eyes to him and let him watch you – that is the secret. If you are so preoccupied with your own difficulties, your own problems, the dangers around you, you are much more likely to stumble. Those who climb mountains tell me that it is fatal to look down. They must look up if they are going to be safe.

Spiritually, too – lift up your eyes and he protects you from the dangers of the path under your feet. The things that would trip you up – look to him and he will look after them. He won't just let your foot be put in the wrong place lest you dash your foot against a stone. There are promises to this effect throughout scripture. Notice that he watches both individuals and nations. The beginning of v. 3: he who keeps you; v. 4: he who keeps Israel. The Lord can watch every individual of Britain and the whole of Britain, all at the same time. If only we were looking at him and lifting our eyes to him we would not be stumbling as we are, and we really are stumbling.

The second thing he protects us from is the light overhead. Now this is a real hazard of a traveller in the clear skies of the Middle East. He has need of shade and protection of his eyes. Human eyes cannot cope with light from heaven. If there is an eclipse of the sun you must not watch it with your naked eye even though the sun is dark. The rays that peek around the edge can damage your sight. But what is not generally realised in this country where it is often so cloudy at night, and where we sleep indoors and under roofs, is that moonlight is strong enough to damage the eyes very severely. In the Middle East or in the desert the Bedouin, when they sleep at night, take very good care to cover their eyes, because the moon can damage their eyesight while they sleep if they are not aware of the danger. So we are exposed as we travel as pilgrims through this world. There are dangers to which we are exposed – dangers equivalent to the bright light of the tropical sun in the midday, and the glaring clear light of the moon.

The psalmist says, "My eyes are protected because the Lord is my shade at my right hand." That is a lovely phrase – at the right hand. Have you ever noticed that a bride and groom always walk like this? The bride is on the left side of the groom. She has surrendered her right arm; she has put it through his. In that sense she has surrendered her means of protecting herself because in most people the right arm is the stronger one. What she has done is to seize his left arm so that his right arm can fight for her. The Lord is on my right hand; he is my shade, my protection from the sun by day, the moon by night. Whatever I am exposed to as I travel on my journey to Jerusalem, to the heavenly city, then he is on my right hand as a shade.

Moses said, "Let me see your glory Lord." What was he asking? Saul of Tarsus saw it and he was blind for three days. As I said to a congregation: God in his mercy is not showing us his glory in our church service because if he did we would all stagger out of the building trying to lead each other; if we saw his glory now it would be too much for these eyes of ours. One day we will see it but then we shall be fit to do so.

The third thing that we are protected from by God on our journey is the danger around us. Travel was not safe in those days. As late as the 1920s it still was not safe. There were times when the road went through a valley and there were deep shadows. Lurking in those shadows there would be bandits and robbers. If not bandits and robbers, there would be beasts and reptiles. You took your life in your hands when you went on a pilgrimage to Jerusalem in those days. You do today when you get in a car and go on the roads. It is the most dangerous form of transport – far safer in a train and even far safer than that in an aeroplane. If you drive a car, you are putting yourself in great danger. How important it is to ask for journeying mercies. On this journey it says, "The Lord shall preserve your life". You are on a journey to him and so he is going to give journeying mercies. He will preserve your life – your going out, your coming in.

Where it says the Lord is your keeper; he will preserve your life, the Hebrew root word used for "keeper" is the same as the word "eyelid". The eyelid is the eye's protector. Your eyes are protected all the time by your eyelids. They are the keepers of your eye. What the psalmist is saying here is: the Lord is my eyelid.

Now we know that in the Bible it says that the people

of God are the apple of his eye. We get that phrase wrong because in English colloquial usage it means an apple that we look at, and that is not the meaning. Look into your eye in the mirror and you will see that the iris and the pupil look like an apple end on. Have you noticed that? The apple of the eye is the iris of the pupil. The Lord is my eyelid and the people of God are the apple of his eye, the iris, the pupil of his eye, inside his eyelid, and he is the protection. What the eyelid does for your eye, God does for his people as they journey on their pilgrimage.

Does that thought speak to you? It speaks to me very deeply: "The Lord is my eyelid." This whole Psalm is about the eyes. I will lift up my eyes to the hills. He will keep my foot from stumbling because he never shuts his eyes. He neither slumbers nor sleeps. He will protect my eyes from the sun and the moon and he is my eyelid so he will preserve my life until I get there. What a Psalm.

Let us look more briefly to the other two Psalms. Psalm 123 is another song of ascent but now in the temple area. Psalm 122, "Let us go to the house of the Lord. Peace be within your walls security in your towers." He has got to Jerusalem now. He is up in the temple now and still he lifts up his eyes. But now he is lifting them higher still – now in the sense he is even leaving the hills behind because he says, "Now I lift up my eyes to the Lord who is enthroned in the heavens". That is where God is. He dwells in the heavens and he is always at home.

Modern theologians have ridiculed this idea that God is up there or out there. The former Bishop of Woolwich, John Robinson, one of my tutors at Cambridge, took me through the Epistle to the Romans with very great profit to me in those days, but he changed such a lot. He began to say when he brought out the book *Honest to God* that God is not up there; God is not out there; if you want to find God you will have to look down inside your own heart. You are going to find a pretty small God if you just look down there.

One of the things that did was to kill prayer in a lot of people because they did not know where to look. When they looked inside all they could see was their own confusion and their own religiosity. Let us not be robbed of the command to lift up our eyes. God is out there; he is up there, and I will tell you why. People say, "Where is God in the universe?" They have asked the wrong question. The right question is: "Where is the universe in God?" All the heavens, everything you can see, is inside God. That is where he is, therefore he is enthroned – that is where he lives. We can still sing quite happily with children "above the bright, blue sky". It is most helpful to look up and realise that all that is where God is. That is where he is enthroned and he just doesn't come and go. He is there; he dwells there. He is always at home and he is at home throughout the entire heavens, so we look there.

There is nothing wrong with looking up and looking out. But our vision with God changes when we stop looking at the hills. When we look at the hills we see his might, but when we turn away from the hills and look solely into the heavens we see his majesty; the clouds, the clouds of glory, and clouds are associated with the glory of God. There is something infinite about the sky. We know that space is finite but it seems infinite to our little minds. It enlarges our thoughts and we are overcome not so much with the might of our maker but with the majesty of our maker. So the word used here is "enthroned" which means that when we look at God we must look at a King and not just a Creator.

Now if I lift my eyes up I am looking at a throne and I see not my Maker now but my master, as the eyes of a servant are upon his master. We are looking now at our master and this is going to affect how we look at God. Psalm 121 looks for help; Psalm 123 adds something else. I want to use now a word, which has a double meaning and I want to use it deliberately: when we look to God we are to *wait* on God. Servants wait on their masters; maids wait on their mistresses. When I look to my maker I must wait on him as my master also.

This picture taken from domestic service does not click with most people today because we have very little knowledge of this other than from televised period drama. Now people who once served "below stairs" become stars and produce books and write all about it and make a fortune. It is such a rare experience now to be "below stairs" that it has become publishable material. What is a butler's job? It is to use his eyes to watch the hands of his master. As the servant looks to the hand of the master, the maid looks to the hand of the mistress. What does that mean? Well, what does the hand do? What do you do in a restaurant when there is a waitress or a waiter waiting on you? What do you do when you want the bill? They are looking to the hand. A good server is looking intently at the one being served so that the slightest gesture of the hand draws an immediate response of service. In fact they anticipate this. They are watching the customer so closely they can see immediately when they finish the first course and need the second – that is the kind of looking that a waiter does.

Psalm 123 says when you are looking to the Maker for help, remember that you are not only looking to the Maker for help; you are looking to your Master to help him. The kind of looking that there should be in our eyes when we lift them up to the Maker is the kind of looking that says: I am at your disposal; you just need to wave and I will come. I will try to anticipate what you want from me; I am here to serve you. If you give me help, it will be of your mercy not of my deserving. It is very important to realise that we have no right to any help from God. If he gives it to us it is out of consideration as a good master. Yet sometimes we pray and ask for answers to prayers as if at the snap of our fingers God should come running to us with the answer. The situation is totally the reverse. When God snaps his fingers we should come running to him. We should look to him as the servant to the master and as a maid to the mistress.

The psalmist is waiting on you Lord. Then if the master helps the servant it is *mercy*. That is the key word of Psalm 123. Have mercy upon us, Lord. We have no merit whatever to receive help from the God who made the hills. It is of his mercies that we are not consumed, and if he does help you it is his mercy. Not only do you need to wait *on* him but you need to wait *for* him. The servant cannot tell the master when to give help. He must wait, as it says, until he has mercy upon us.

It is very important that we don't treat God like a slot machine: put a coin in and out comes what we want; put a prayer in and out comes God's help. We must be very careful not to do that. We are waiting on God to serve him if he needs us and to wait until he decides to have mercy on us and to serve us. We have no right to expect it. I do not have the right to have one prayer answered. My relationship to my Maker is to wait on him and to look to him with the eyes of a servant.

But you can plead for God's mercy. You can be like the man who went into the temple to pray in the Pharisee and the publican story. It said the publican stood at the back and he wouldn't even lift his eyes to heaven. But he said, "God be merciful to me." You can plead for mercy. You can ask for mercy from your master, and the psalmist does with a very simple and profound ground for pleading. He says, "I've had enough of contempt. I've had enough of people looking down on me with contempt. You look down on me with compassion. I have had enough of the proud and comfortable and easy people considering that I am beneath them. But I look up to you that you may look down on me with pity not pride. That is a very good reason. It is the way to deal with an inferiority complex. Let me lay this heavy on your heart. If you think people look down on you, then you look up to the Lord. That is the cure for it until he has mercy on you. If you think people look down their noses at you, let God look down on you. He will never look down on you in contempt. He won't despise you. So lift up your eyes to him. But do it in a humble, reverent way, as a servant to the master.

Now the third Psalm: too big for your boots and your eyes can go further than your mind. Your sight can travel too high and go beyond your insight. There is a limit. We can see things too big to comprehend and too difficult to understand, and then we become agitated, confused, disturbed. Let me tell you what I mean. I think that through science man has now seen too high, too much. In the Bible days a man could look up and he could only see at most with very good physical sight six thousand stars. Now science with its telescopes and radio telescopes has told me there are millions. To the men in the Bible, the stars seemed a long way off but still much nearer than they seem to us today. We know today light travels at the speed of a hundred and eighty-six thousand miles a second, which means that if you switched on a flashlight, the light from that torch could go around the world over seven times in one second, and travelling at that speed it would take us years to reach the nearest star – and we have seen too much. It has confused our minds and the universe seems to swallow us up and we have seen things too great and too wonderful for us. We have peered through the microscope and the electron microscope into the tiny universe of the atom. We have split it and we have seen too much and we cannot cope with it.

We read in Psalm 131: Lord my heart is not haughty. I will not lift up my eyes too high, not too high or I could see things too great and too wonderful for me to cope with. You can get that way just looking at God. Think of his trinity. If you look at that too much you will get terribly confused and your mind cannot cope with it. You can look at his sovereignty and then you get all bogged down in questions of predestination and freewill. Our minds cannot go as far as our sight. We can lift up our eyes too high.

So though in Psalm 121 and 123 the psalmist says I lift up my eyes, he now acknowledges that he knows his limits. I am not God. I won't lift them too high. I am not going to try and look at things that would not be good for me. To avoid agitation and getting all upset, he has calmed and quieted his soul like a child quieted at its mothers breast. It is a remarkable claim: to be able to calm yourself. Very few people in the world can say that. He did it without tranquillisers, without psychiatrists, without any other help. I have calmed myself; I have quieted myself.

Now I don't believe this Psalm refers to a suckling baby because in fact the word implies something a little older. In fact the Authorized Version says, "Like a child weaned at its mother's breast," and it is an older child here. The Lord never told us to be like babies. He said, "Become as little children," he didn't say become as babies. There are too many of us like babies but little children – that is different.

This Psalm finishes with the same words as the first Psalm. Psalm 121 talks about God keeping us in our going out and coming in, "from this time forth and for evermore". In other words, the help comes from this time forward and forever. I think that just about covers it, don't you? But the end of Psalm 131, the same words: "this time forth and for evermore." But now it is not the help of God, it's the hope of Israel that must match the help of God. In Psalm 121, the help will come from God this time forward and forever. Psalm 131 says: "O Israel, hope in the Lord this time forward and for evermore." God's help must be matched by our hope. We are to reach up in hope and lift up our eyes; and people who have been filled with new hope, have you noticed they lift up their eyes? Have you noticed that they lift up their heads and the downcast eye becomes the uplifted eye?

READ PSALM 126

The first thing that struck me about Psalm 126 is that it is charged with human emotion. Whenever God is real and busy then emotions are released. The cynics and the sceptics cry "emotionalism" and consider that they have made a valid criticism about what God is doing. That is a twentieth century word, and in the eighteenth century the word that they used was "enthusiasm" when they wanted to decry popular religion.

We are told not to let our emotions show. Unfortunately the British will compliment you on not shedding a tear, "How brave she has been." But when God begins to move, emotion is released. Now I am not interested in emotionalism that is something worked up by people.

Why are we frightened of our feelings? The Bible is jammed with emotions. Take the book of Psalms alone and you run the whole gamut of human feelings. Even here in this one Psalm, you have got laughter and tears. When John Wesley in the eighteenth century travelled this country with a horse between his knees and a Bible in his hands, and led three-quarters of a million people to know the Lord Jesus Christ, the cry was "enthusiasm – there is no place for that in dignified English religion". The Bishop of Bristol said to the Reverend John Wesley: "Enthusiasm, sir, is a very horrid thing."

But God loves enthusiasm and does not mind emotions. When he moves as he is going to in this country, there is going to be a good deal of laughter and a good deal more tears than the British are accustomed to. In this Psalm there is laughter, there are tears. People are not afraid to weep and not afraid to laugh. When we can cry and laugh, then the other nations will say of us, "The Lord has done great things for them." They will ask for the explanation of these laughing, singing people. That will be spontaneous evangelism, but let me just say what God's order of emotions is. Yes, God is a God who wants us to cry. He knows what it is to weep himself; his Son wept over Jerusalem.

God also sings. It is those who go out weeping who come back singing. It was the same pattern that was revealed in Jesus Christ himself when he went to the cross and went through the tears and the sorrow. Why? For the joy set before him. That is the true pattern of divine emotion and that is the true pattern of Christian emotion.

This Psalm, charged with emotion, comes out of a particular situation. There is no particular direct clue within the Psalm as to what situation aroused these words. I am the kind of person who wants to know what the Germans call the "sitz im leben", the situation in life, behind a scripture. If you can find the situation in life you will understand the emotions. If you can discover what was happening at the time these words were said, you will get to the real meaning and significance of what is expressed. Some of the Psalms are perfectly easy. That Psalm of confession "Have mercy upon me God according to your loving kindness, cleanse me." I can understand the meaning of that Psalm when I read the story of David and Bathsheba. When I see what the man had just done, breaking four commandments in one fell swoop on a momentary impulse of passion, I can understand that Psalm as a cry for cleansing, for forgiveness, to have the Holy Spirit given back to him; but when I read this Psalm I was so puzzled. What was the situation in which they went out weeping and came back laughing? What had happened? Now here I ran into difficulties even with the translation.

The very first phrase in the Psalm is ambiguous. It has two possible meanings. One is: "When the Lord brought us back to Jerusalem"; the other, "when the Lord made Jerusalem prosperous again". Here were two possible situations. One: the Lord brought them back from captivity; the other, the Lord brought them back to prosperity. I wrestled for days with which one of these it was. On my first reading "when the Lord turned our captivity" I assumed it referred to the day when they came back from exile in Babylon to Jerusalem, back home after seventy years. I thought that explained it. But then I read on and I thought: that cannot make sense of the harvest bit. What did they go out sowing when they went into exile in Babylon? They did not go out sowing. What kind of a harvest did they bring back? They didn't bring back any harvest.

Then I read the scholars and they all said: it doesn't refer to the exile but we don't know what it refers to. So then I tried the other tack and thought: they are talking about a harvest; let me take it quite literally. Because it is a good rule of Bible interpretation to take the words in the simplest possible sense unless there is an indication that they should not be. The simplest possible sense is that they were literally talking about sowing and harvesting.

So I thought: is the situation behind this that of a failed harvest? Then I read the Psalm and it said, "Lord, take us back to our land." I was back to the other one again. I hope I have conveyed to you some of the wrestling that a preacher has to do with a scripture before he gets up in the pulpit. I thought: which is it? Is it that he brought them back from captivity or brought them back to prosperity? Which is the situation?

Then a clue came to me through reading a novel featuring the failure of the potato harvest in southern Ireland. It was their staple diet – the potato. They had no other means of livelihood, and the poorer peasants living in the bogs of Ireland depended on the potato until that year when the blight struck and the potatoes went black and mushy, and it continued the next year and the year after. The result of the continued failure of the harvest meant that thousands upon thousands of Irishmen emigrated. They lost their harvest and their home in one tragic event. Suddenly the whole Psalm made sense. It did not refer to the exile, nor simply to a failure of the harvest, but the whole scene became quite clear. They had had year after year without rain. Here a little geographical knowledge of the Holy Land is so helpful. God sent them to live in the limestone, porous hills where they are absolutely dependent on rain from heaven. When the rain does not come, the land dries up and becomes barren. There is no harvest and they have no other source of food. Jerusalem, though it was a city, was dependent on the agriculture around it. It was not a trading city and was not on a trade route.

So the only thing they could do when they had a continued failure of the harvest was to go away from home, down from the hills to the plains where there was water from the rivers. That is why Abraham had gone down into Egypt; that is why Isaac went down into Egypt. Whenever the harvest up in the hills failed because the rain had not come and the land went barren, they went down into the valleys. They left their home to find work, money and food. Now that is the situation behind this Psalm.

Furthermore, I can see something more in the situation. I don't know what year it happened. I can place it in geography; I can't place it in history. Now let me go into the Psalm. With that in mind, remember that they have lost harvest and home. These are the two most needful and precious things – the food you eat and the place you live. To lose them is a sad experience.

I remember during the war when I was evacuated and I was terribly homesick for two years. Homesickness is one of the deepest pains of the human heart.

I don't know at what period of history in Israel it happened. I can't date it, but at some period the harvest failed so they left home in search of food and work. Now out of that situation was born Psalm 126. In it there is all the sorrow of losing and the joy of finding – a theme that comes throughout the Bible. Read Luke 15 – a woman losing a coin, a shepherd losing a sheep, a father losing two sons; the sorrow of losing and the joy of finding, the weeping and the laughter.

There are three notes struck in this Psalm. The first is a note of praise from the past. That is vv. 1–3. The second is a note of prayer in the present: vv. 4–5. But the third is a note of prophecy for the future: v. 6. Let us look at v.6 especially.

What is the first thing you should do when times are bad? What is the first thing you should do when you are in the sorrow of having lost what is precious and necessary to you? The first thing you should do is to remember that this has happened before and that the Lord dealt with it. The first thing to do is to praise God that when it happened before, he dealt with it. God has given us the sublime gift of memory with which we can recall his mighty deliverances of the past and that is why he gave you your memory. It is one of the lovely and delightful features of our memory that we can remember the happy things more easily than the unhappy. We can remember the good things better than we can remember the bad. We tend to bury deep within our subconscious that which we do not like to remember, that which hurt us, that which wounded us. But the good things we want to recall. So we look back on the old days as good even though, if we had the choice, none of us would go back and live in them. We nevertheless remember the "good old days" and it is right that we should. In this situation in which they have lost both home and harvest the first thing the man who wrote this Psalm did was to go back to a previous and parallel situation in which the same thing happened.

He recalled that the Lord got them out of it and that the sheer relief led to a spontaneous expression of joy. So that first phrase is deliberately ambiguous in the Hebrew. It covers both meanings of having lost home and harvest. When the Lord brought us back to Jerusalem; when the Lord brought prosperity back to Jerusalem – the double answer to the double need. At some time in the past within the memory of the man who wrote this Psalm, he could recall God having brought them out of that situation. So he says "when," not "if" – *when* the Lord did it.

You see, if you don't recall the blessings of the past and you are in a difficult situation in the present, you will say "If the Lord gets me out of this...." But if you use the divine gift of memory and go back over your life, you will say, "*When* the Lord...." He goes back in the first three verses to that remembrance of the deliverance that came. The Lord rescued us.... It seemed so unreal; it seemed like a dream. At this moment, try to recall some moment or some experience when the Lord got you out of trouble. He got you out of it in such a way that you had to pinch yourself to believe that it was real. When it was like a dream....

You might be recalling the day that the Lord first delivered you from sin and when you began to be saved. Do you remember that? Was it like a dream? People have told me that they were on cloud nine. Some have said it seemed so unreal. "I walked about and wondered why everybody didn't ask me about it. It was like a dream when the Lord rescued me." He may have rescued you from a pretty rough past and he delivered you. You would never even have dreamed that such life was possible. Recall that, praise the Lord for it.

Maybe by all natural and human reason you should be in your grave. But when the Lord delivered you, it was like a dream. Is this really happening? Is this really true? How we laughed, how we sang. It would be unnatural if you laughed and sang all the time. I have not yet met a saint who could honestly look me in the face and say, "Ever since I was converted I laughed and I sang" – unless they had been converted about three weeks earlier. Most of us would have to say, "I can recall when I laughed and when I sang." Then you got into that very difficult mess, that difficult situation. You thought there was no way through and it seemed a blank wall ahead and yet your Lord brought you through. People said to you, "What's happened to you?"

The reply: "God has done something for me."

I am looking forward to the day when God's people throughout this land, every church, is so full of laughing, singing people that others will have to say that the Lord did great things for them. When they see things happening among us which have no human explanation, when they have to acknowledge that our happiness is due to God, then what will happen will be spontaneous evangelism. We will not need to tell them God has done great things for us – they will see it. They will hear it as they did on the day of Pentecost. A great multitude came together. I used to think the Holy Spirit made the disciples move towards the people, but he didn't. If you read Acts 2, it was the people who moved to the disciples. They didn't move – well they did actually: they were sitting and they stood up. At least eleven of them stood up, the others sat down. But the people moved to them and they said, "What was happening? We hear them declaring in our tongue the mighty works of God." It was not a kind of forced evangelism. It was that God had done something so great for his people that the others came and said, "What is it? What's it all about? What has happened?" The first section of the Psalm finishes with a lovely act of remembrance; yes indeed, he did great things for us.

Has the Lord done one great thing for you in your lifetime? Indeed he has. How happy we were. But this Psalm was written in this situation when that no longer applied or it would never have been written. For now the same trouble has arisen again. Now they have lost their home and their harvest again. Verses 4–5 tell me that that was the double tragedy that had occurred because they asked that both may be restored.

The psalmist is praying now – he has moved from praise in the past to prayer in the present. Now here I want to underline a profound lesson. When you recall the blessings of the past, when you recall the happiness of the past, when you recall those moments when you were so happy because God did a great thing for you, I beg of you do not let that remembrance lead you into nostalgia. If there is one thing God is not interested in, it is nostalgia. He does not want you to live back there; he wants to deal with your present need now in order that you may rejoice again.

I have heard so many testimonies even from Christians who have been Christians for thirty years who still talk about the great things God did then, thirty years back. They are nostalgic about their first love, nostalgic about their honeymoon with Jesus, but God intends us to use the gift of the memory of the past blessings in order to pray for a repetition of them, in order to build up not nostalgia for the good old days, but expectancy for the good new days. Because God has not changed; he can do the same thing again.

There was a mother with a little boy and there was a terrible thunderstorm during the night and the mother thought the little boy would be frightened. She crept along to the bedroom door to hear if the little boy was awake and afraid and crying. She listened at the door and the little boy was sitting up in bed excitedly and at each clap of thunder he was saying, "Now another one God; now another one God." Finally there was a terrific burst of thunder right outside the bedroom. It seemed to reverberate through the house and the little boy said, "Stout fellow." Well, recall the great things but recall them in such a way that you turn the praise from the past into a prayer for the present – now another one God; do it again Lord. Deliver us again.

So you have the double prayer. The first part of the prayer (v. 4) is: take us back home, Lord. Then a vivid picture comes. Again, you really have to go to the Middle East. I once said to my church: if a millionaire came to me and said, "Here's a blank cheque to do something for your church members," I would take them all to Israel; because you would understand so much more of God's Word if you saw the place. Let me tell you what this prayer is saying: Take us back to our land just as the rain brings water back to dry riverbeds (or, as you probably know it more familiarly, streams in the desert or in the Negev). The Hebrew word is Negev, which means dry, arid. It is given to that whole area south of Beersheba in the Sinai Peninsula which is so barren, dry and dusty. But even there in the dry desert you will see riverbeds. It will astonish you to see them and you think in this dry, dusty land where there doesn't seem one drop of moisture: why are there riverbeds? There should be rivers in those riverbeds. There must have been rivers some time in the past. I recall travelling by coach along the road by the Dead Sea, and at one point the Dead Sea was on our right, filled with salt and looking very murky, and on our left were the absolutely barren hills of the Judean wilderness with only one little spot of green on them at the spring of En Gedi. Then there was a notice which said, "Danger Floods". I wanted to get a photograph of that but the bus has always been going too fast for that. When you look, there is a riverbed there in the Judean wilderness. I remember going to Petra and travelling on horseback through El Sheikh the narrow defile that leads into that magnificent ruined city. It is about ten or fifteen feet wide and maybe a hundred and fifty feet high. The whole city can be protected by two men with rocks to drop down the narrow gorge. We went through and the whole land was so barren and dry and yet the walls of the gorge were scoured smooth with water. When we reached the bottom, we saw the wreck of a large American taxi in which a party of nuns had been drowned just a week or two before.

What is the picture? It is of God sending rain and suddenly, within an hour or two, what is a completely barren desert becomes a place with rivers flowing. The flowers come and the desert can go green as soon as the water touches it.

Lord take us back to our land as suddenly an empty riverbed becomes a torrent. Take us back, Lord, as the rain brings rivers to the desert – like those riverbeds that are made for rivers fill up, your land is made for people. Take us back home to live there. It is empty, barren and dry, without people; that land needs its people.

Then comes the second part of the prayer — Lord, give us the harvest back. Let those who wept as they sowed their seed.... And: as they went out carrying their seed, gather the harvest with joy. I may be quite wrong in what I am going to tell you now, but I believe the Lord revealed to me the picture behind this of what was happening. I have explained they had continued failure of harvest so they had to leave home and go down to the plains. Well then, where did they go out sowing, and why did they weep? Indeed the second question was the one that teased my mind the most: why did they weep as they sowed?

The picture that came to me very clearly was that from

the places they had gone to, every year they sent up into the hills men with precious grain to scatter it on the hills to see if they could get a harvest up there again and go back home, and I got a picture of men going up. When you are starving or hungry, to take some of your grain and scatter it; not knowing whether you will get any harvest back is difficult. My sister-in-law and her husband were missionaries in Angola where there were troubles. Many of the Angolans had to flee into Congo but then they got back again. They had not enough food to live on but part of that precious food they sowed in the hope of getting a harvest. The tragedy was that just as that first harvest came, the troubles came again and they had to leave. If your family is hungry, to take some grain and scatter it on dry, dusty earth in the bare hope that you might just get some back is something very hard. I got this picture of these exiles sending men with grain to scatter it on the dry hills in the hope that there might be a harvest up there and they could go back home. Do you get the picture? Do you get the feel?

No wonder they wept as they took the grain from their children's mouths and went back up into those hills to try yet again, and scattered that grain on the dry, dusty ground with little hope of having much to take back to their families as a result. That is the picture. If only the rain would come this year. Lord, bring us back to our land as the rain brings back the rivers. Lord let those who sow with tears please let them have a harvest this year. That is the prayer.

We move to the final verse, which has been so misinterpreted and misunderstood. Let us try to get the truth of it now. I have given you the picture of people who lost their harvest so they also lost their home. But they praised God that when that happened before he brought them out of it with such joy that they laughed and sang and people said: "God must have done something great for these people." Oh how happy we were! But now comes the prayer, "Lord we're in the same situation again. Lord will you do it again? Will you get us back home?" Those men were standing up in the hills with a bit of our precious corn – please may they come back with a harvest, bringing their sheaves with them and laughing and singing. Do you get the picture?

Now comes the exciting moment in this Psalm, from praise in the past through prayer in the present we come to a note of prophecy in the future. The psalmist is saying that this year it is going to happen. They are going to come back with sheaves and we can go back home. Do you notice the change? Praise brought us back; prayer takes us back; prophecy will come back. Now do you see the pattern of Christian devotion here? Use your memory to go back into the past to remember your happiness when you praised God for the deliverances that he gave you. Then pray in the present: "Lord, do it again."

But I wonder if you can come with me into v. 6 for this year and move from prayer to promise and prophecy. We will come back with joy. Let me now say the thing, which may destroy this verse for you in your traditional understanding of it. I hope not. *The joy is not the result of the weeping, it is the result of the sowing*. I wonder if you understand what I mean. I have heard preachers use this text and I have read books that have used this text to say that if only we put more tears into our sowing we would get more reaping. The tears have nothing to do with it in one sense; the tears are incidental. They are real tears of disappointment or frustration. But it is not the result of the tears, it is the result of the fact that, in spite of the tears, people went up the mountain to sow.

There were tears of disappointment and frustration that year after year after year there had been no apparent result for their sowing. But they went on sowing the seed even though they wept while they did so and the harvest was not the result of the weeping but of the sowing. In the late 1970s I gave a word of encouragement to Christians in my church at that time – as individuals and as the body of Christ: we may have been through a barren period; we had never then in my lifetime had a proper harvest in this land. We had sown the seed but we had not had thirty-fold, sixty-fold, a hundred-fold. We had not even had two-fold. For all the Billy Graham crusades which had taken place, for all our evangelism, for all our church activity, there had not been a single year when we had converted more people than the Christians who had died. I don't call that a harvest, do you? Every major denomination in England had reported a decline for my entire lifetime. That is not harvesting. Many have given up sowing because of the frustration of it. Many ministers went into teaching and many ministers went out of the ministry because they were so discouraged, so disheartened. They sowed the seed faithfully and they went on. Many evangelists had given up; many Christian workers had lost heart. The morale among Christians had sunk so low that when a new push in evangelism was suggested, people would say, "Oh no, not another one."

Yes we had been through a barren time and retreated from areas that we occupied in this land. Let me name one or two. The trade union movement is one, which was once so full of Christians that they called the local branch meeting "the chapel". It met in chapels, but it is an area from which we retreated. There has been so little harvest in that area. We had retreated from the inner cities, which were perilously, dangerously low in Christian presence and influence. Politics is another area from which Christians retreated. We had "left the land" because the harvest had been so small.

What were we to do about the situation? The first thing is: recall the deliverances of God in the past on a national level. In the late 1970s I said that the last time God visited this country of England in great power was in 1859. (My audio talks on church history look at that period.)

Let us start where the psalmist started and say: "Lord you did it before; do it again. Lord, people laughed and sang; do it again. Lord, people stopped swearing in whole villages, in whole towns, in south Wales – Lord, do it again. Lord, the gin drinking of the eighteenth century was stopped; Lord, do it again. Lord, slavery was abolished in the British Empire as the result of your moving in people's hearts. Lord, do it again."

Go to the past for your inspiration. Go back in memory – not for nostalgia but to say that God is the same; he can do it and he will do it again. Lord bring us back home, bring us back to the land. Bring us back to that prosperity. Bring us back for harvest so that we begin to see thirty-fold and sixty-fold and a hundred-fold.

But now let me move from this prayer that I'm giving you and deliberately, consciously before God move into prophecy. Those who have kept on sowing the seed in spite of tearful disappointment and discouragement are going to come back singing with joy, bringing not a handful of corn but sheaves with them. I really do believe it. I believe we are going to live to see it in this land of ours. I have never seen a harvest in my lifetime. I have seen people converted, I have seen blessing, but I have seen a church that is only just keeping pace. In fact, it is not even keeping pace with the situation. I don't call that a harvest. I want to know the joy of real harvest.

I was in farming and I recall two occasions. One, when I was on a small farm in Northumberland. My friend Peter and I used to go out witnessing together. He was a lad who was wonderfully touched by God one night at a Young Farmer's Club service and I was a member of the Young Farmer's Club. We used to engage in agricultural activities. One night there was a club service. I remember I gave my testimony that night and Peter came to the Lord. It was spring, and a few months later I helped him in with his harvest and we got the harvest finished. We got a crowd of Christian youngsters all helping together in the harvest. It was a lovely time. We had a harvest festival service and the pulpit was the tractor. I sat on a tractor seat and I preached. We had the best harvest festival service I think I ever remembered. We were happy, and we laughed and sang around Peter's tractor. I think of another occasion on a farm in Northumberland when we had what we called a "Can Supper". It was a large farm of six hundred acres and we had finished the harvest and what we did on that farm every year (it goes back a long way) was to hold a supper to celebrate. We had cleared part of the barn and laid out tables with hams. We danced—all the old Northumbrian dances, with a Northumbrian fiddler; what fun we had, how we sang, how we laughed. I want to do that spiritually.

I want to share with you a vision that came to a simple man at a conference of ministers at Swanwick. This country vicar in a very ordinary voice, in a very ordinary manner with a strong country accent, in a matter-of-fact way, told us of his vision. He said,

> "I seem to be flying in an aircraft but flying very low over the fields. It was just like the country I know. The fields were all flat and they were all full of corn. As I looked, the colour was that lovely, slightly orangey colour, which means it is absolutely ripe – get it cut now. If you wait another week it is going to turn brown. The fields are all that colour. There are some little fields and there are some big fields. In every field I can see a tractor and a harvester. I'm flying so low that I can see every detail in every field. In hardly any of the fields is there any harvesting being

done. Yet there is a tractor and a harvester in every field. Why? Now, as I come lower, I can see why.

"In the first field the tractor driver is standing and looking at the harvester and he's looking into the machine and there in the machine is a lovely bird's nest. He is afraid to start the machine because of this bird's nest. It will be destroyed. How silly, it is harvest time so there are no eggs in the nest and there are no young birds there. It's just a nest. It is finished with but he is too afraid to destroy it. As I fly over the second field, the harvester is in pieces and all the pieces are laid out in the field and the driver is scratching his head because he doesn't know how to put them all together.

"In the third field I can see there is a little child with an injured arm and the tractor driver is bandaging up the child's arm and soothing the child. He is going on and on bandaging and soothing, bandaging and soothing. There's no harvesting being done because he's just soothing the injured child.

"In the fourth field the man is swinging his tractor trying to start it and I can see there is no petrol in the tank, there is no fuel there, and he is trying to start the tractor."

He just went on and shared this vision and then he sat down. What a vision. Do you know what that says to me? The fields are ripe unto harvest if we just realised it. What is the nest that you are afraid to disturb? What is it that you can't get together? What injured child is so occupying your attention that you cannot see the harvest waiting?

I had been a minister for many years, but I believed as never before that the field is white unto harvest and I was not the only one. I really do believe that God has been preparing this land. There has been so much seed sown; I believe the doors are opening to us, and they are going to go on opening quite unexpectedly.

Well I just want to tell you that even if you have wept, provided you have gone on sowing you will come back with sheaves of joy. So the singing and the dancing is not the result of the weeping. It is the result of going on sowing even when you weep to do so. It is the result of believing that seed has life in it. It is the result of believing that our duty is to go on doing our job, and our job is to go on sowing, and that God in his mercy will send the rain.

We plough the fields and scatter the good seed on the land, but it is fed and watered by God's almighty hand. Yes it has been frustrating, it has been disappointing and discouraging, but we have kept on sowing the seed. We have been going up into those hills carrying seed that we could have sat and eaten for ourselves and enjoyed. We have scattered it on apparently barren ground but we shall come singing with joy.

READ PSALM 133

Psalm 133 has only three verses that are so full of lovely truth. What a pleasure it is to read it: close relatives keeping together as real friends. Harmony spreads among them like the special oil falling from Aaron's head to his beard and falling from there to the collar of his robe. It spreads among them like the dew of great Mount Hermon, falling on the hills around the city of Zion. For in that setting the God who is always there has ordered that his family should be blessed with life that goes on forever.

What makes a songwriter write songs? I am afraid nowadays it has become a business and someone sits in a studio and analyses what will go over big and what touches a response and what is likely to get into the charts, But David the king was a songwriter and his songs were not written for a song contest, they were written to express his reactions to life. They were written as an emotional response to his circumstances. That is why I have yet to find myself in any mood for which I cannot find a Psalm which perfectly expresses how I feel to the Lord. I hope you have made the same discovery.

There are Psalms for those who are depressed and are sinking fast. Psalms 42 and 43 are a good example: "Why are you cast down, O my soul, and why are you disquieted within me?" It is interesting that when David wrote those Psalms he was not only low in spirits but he was low in body. He was down by the waters of En Gedi at the lowest point on the earth's surface. For David, his physical condition and his spiritual were so interlocked that when you get Psalms that are for the depressed and those who go down, you find he wrote them when he was down in the valley quite literally, physically as well as spiritually. But Psalm 133, which we are looking at now, is a Psalm for those who are rising.

It is called a song of ascent, which means here someone who is rising in body as well as in spirit, because it has come out of a real life situation, and I want to visualise the scene for you. He is looking at a group of people whose bodies and whose spirits are rising, so this is a song of going up or a song of ascent. It was written by David as he stood on the balcony of his palace and watched the people crowding up the main street, which went straight up past his palace and into the gate of the temple. It was one of those annual feasts when people had come from Dan to Beersheba, from one end of the country to the other, with their different dialects, with their different dress, and yet there they all were pressing up the street. David was inspired to write a song, the poetry and the music flowed out, and Psalm 133 is the result. So that was the scene and I am now going to take you through the Psalm.

I divide it into three parts. The first section, v. 1, I call "Showing Love". Every single word in the Word of God is important. I want to begin with the little word "behold". It means: there is something so unusual, even so rare, that you must look at it with me. I can almost hear David calling back into the palace, to his staff and his family, and saying, "Quick, come and look at that." It is something so unusual that it is worth seeing. Maybe you have said this about a beautiful sunset. You know, "Just come and look at this sunset." That is the feel of the word "behold". When it comes in scripture it means something worth your attention is coming. Something unusual is happening. Something rare is to be seen. Give it all your attention—behold. Now what is so unusual about what David is looking at – a crowd of people going up the street, heading up for the temple? Well there are two things that are highly unusual and quite rare in this world. The first is that there is something that is good and pleasant at the same time. That is unusual in our world especially when you are young if you can't get those two things together – and some older folk can't either. There are plenty of things in life that are pleasant but they are not good for you. There are plenty of things that are good for you that do not seem very pleasant. "Now eat up your vegetables they're good for you," and so we might associate something that is good for us with something we don't like. Then: "Now don't do that," and the forbidden becomes attractive. Many people too like to try the forbidden thing, because it seems pleasant; it gives pleasure.

It is very rare in this world for people to realise that what is good and what is pleasant belong together. Or to put it more starkly, it sometimes takes years of learning in the hard school of experience that holiness and happiness are one and the same thing. The difficulty is that sin offers so much pleasure that we are fooled. The Bible admits that, and acknowledges it openly, using the phrase "the pleasures of sin" but it adds a qualification "for a season". The difference is between those who take a short-term view and those who take a long-term view. In the short term view, that which is bad is pleasant. In the long-term view, only that which is good is pleasant. That is heaven itself where holiness and happiness will be perfectly blended and everything you enjoy will be good.

So David says: "Come and look at something that's good and pleasant. Come and look at people enjoying themselves, doing something good." Now that's a rare thing in this world. It is worth taking notice of. What is so different? What is David drawing attention to as the crowd surges past his balcony? Before I tell you, let us notice that those two words "good" and "pleasant" refer to different senses. "Behold how good" implies something that you see, something good to see as well as something good in itself. But the word "pleasant" is intriguing. The Hebrew word translated "pleasant" here means "harmonious to the ear". It is the word you would use of a choir in which everybody is in tune, or of an orchestra in which each instrument is perfectly in tune with the rest. In other words, it is harmonious to the ear and pleasant to hear. So David with both senses is saying: "Come quickly. There is something good to see and something very pleasant to hear." It gives you the clue as to what it is. In a word—harmony, and harmony among people is always good to see and pleasant to hear.

Isn't it lovely to hear a group singing together when you can see on their faces and know that all those people are not only in tune musically to the ear but in harmony to the eye and are together. This is God's great plan for his family, that they should be a choir, an orchestra, a family in which you can see the harmony and hear it. Not just hear it and not just see it, but see and hear it, which brings me then to the great and unusual and rare thing: "relatives are friends". In planning weddings most of us have two categories when we draw up lists. So we have a list for the reception – which relatives must we have and which friends shall we invite?

Happy are those whose relatives are friends – it is a rare and unusual thing. For the deepest rifts in our world are often rifts within the same family – people who are physically related not on speaking terms. When you read through the Bible up to this stage of 1,000 BC when David wrote this Psalm, the story is one long tale of brothers who could not keep together. It starts with the very first two brothers in history, Cain and Abel, and one murdered the other. From then on, the sad story is of brothers who cannot live together.

You turn the pages of the Bible and you come to Abraham and Lot. Abraham said to Lot: we are better living separately because we are not getting on together. It is a sad comment. Then there were Ishmael and Isaac, the two sons of Jacob. Look what happened to them. Ishmael bullied Isaac; the child of the flesh bullied the child of the spirit and there was no love between those two. That brotherly feud is responsible for the biggest rift in history today – the rift between Arab and Israeli.

The next generation is Jacob and Esau and look at the tension that came between those two brothers. In the next generation there were twelve brothers and the youngest of them dreamed dreams. His name was Joseph. What was the result? The other eleven hated him and sold him into slavery. This is the Bible story of brothers.

When Moses led the twelve tribes – who were therefore brothers because they were descended from the twelve brothers, when he led them out of Egypt – again and again he had to strive for unity. There were times when he had to sift them all, when he had to say to them all: I will stand over here and whoever is on the Lord's side let him come over and stand with me.

You find that all through the wilderness Moses was fighting for unity among brothers. Then when they entered into the Promised Land, twelve brotherly tribes, what happened? Read the book of Judges. The sad tale of the book of Judges – it comes in as a refrain again and again – every man did what was right in his own eyes for there was no king in Israel. The divided were defeated again and again.

When brothers are divided they can be defeated easily. When each does what is right in his own eyes they will be divided and defeated. So they said, "Let's have a king" and they got a king, Saul. But his reign was not a reign of peace and they finished up with an official king and an unofficial one. Saul was official and David was unofficial. But David, who wrote this Psalm within his own family, had had this strange experience. When Samuel came to look for a king to replace Saul, a better one, he came to the family of Jesse, and Jesse had seven sons. The older six stood there, handsome, tall, strong, and they were quite sure that Samuel would find one of them, but Samuel went through the lot and said, "No none of you. Are you sure you have no more sons Jesse?" Well he said, "There's the lad out looking after the sheep." "Bring him in."

Can you imagine what the other six brothers felt like? I am reading between the lines but David's closest friend on earth was none of his brothers but Jonathan, Saul's son. I think he was speaking from bitter experience here: how pleasant it is for brothers to dwell in unity. I believe his choice as king split his family and he lost his brothers. So right up to this very Psalm being written, the story of the Bible is brothers who could not get on. So David came to the throne, and when he came to the throne there was civil war. He was in hiding for a period of his early reign and there was strife and contention. David's longing for his nation was that he might live to see the day in his reign when the whole people of God stood united, together in harmony – that is what he was waiting for.

He fought for it, he prayed for it, he sang for it, he laboured for it, and, when Psalm 133 was written, he saw it. He saw at last a united nation. Brothers from both ends of the country, brothers from every tribe, and he looked from his balcony and saw the crowd on their feet saying: we are one, we are together; we are one family; we are heirs of the kingdom; we are joint heirs. As he watched from his balcony he too wanted to burst into song. I think he probably grabbed his guitar or some equivalent and said there is a song coming, quick. I want to put this into words and music. So he wrote this. Oh just look. Isn't that good to see? Isn't that pleasant to hear the song? Brothers staying together in unity and on their way to God.

Now that (v. 1) is the beginning of the Psalm and it is the theme. It was not a unity of dress; it was not a unity of dialect, it was not a unity of district; it was not any of the human kinds of unity. It was the unity of heart, mind, and will of a people who had a common purpose to worship the Lord.

Now he waxes very poetic, and because he is a poet he sees things in pictures and he paints pictures in words. He sees two extraordinary pictures in his mind and I puzzled for half a week as I thought about this Psalm. Why did he think about these two pictures to describe what he saw? I could not see the connection between Aaron's beard and that crowd and snowcapped Mount Hermon and that crowd. What is the connection?

I had to wrestle with this and say, "Lord, will your spirit of truth who caused this to be written tell me the connection?" I began to see they are quite different pictures. One comes from the ecclesiastical word – the anointing of a high priest. The other comes from the natural world, the grass of the dew. What is the connection? They are so different. What is the connection of either of them with the crowd that David was looking at? I just couldn't see it. For two days I didn't see the connection.

Then one thought began to come. Both of those pictures have liquid in them. Is there a clue there? Yes I think there must be. Then I thought: in both cases the liquid is falling. Is there a clue there? Yes I think there is. There is oil falling from his head to his beard to his collar and there is dew falling. Then I discovered in the Hebrew the word "falling" came in fact three times though it is disguised in the English. Now here are the people rising and yet he thinks of a liquid falling and I began to see.

Then I thought: let us be thoroughly realistic. What in fact did he see as he looked at the crowds? Then I realised, because I had seen this on a Palm Sunday afternoon: shining faces. Why shining? Well because it was hot and because they were happy. Hot, happy people perspire. That reminds me of two things – oil on Aaron's face and dew on the hills I saw as a shepherd. We are going to draw some profound lessons from this.

So let us look first at the oil on Aaron's head. Of course, David never saw Aaron anointed, but he saw every successor in his time anointed in the same way. It was a great ceremony. The new high priest, the successor of Aaron the first high priest, was clothed with magnificent robes, with a special breastplate, with jewellery, with headdress, but there was one very special point in the consecration. A point which still occurs in the coronation of every sovereign of this country and I remember vividly the point when Queen Elizabeth II went through this particular thing: the anointing or unction with oil. I went back to the book of Exodus to find out a little more about this oil because I knew it was special. In fact it says: "It is like the special oil that flowed from Aaron's head to his beard and then to the collar of his robe."

I found that they used to take five quarts of olive oil, which is comparatively tasteless and without scent. They used to add no less than four hundred and fifty ounces of solids. Spices like myrrh and cinnamon and sweet cane and a number of other things, and special perfumers used to blend this together. Then they would take this special perfumed oil and they would pour it on Aaron's head and the smell of it was beautiful, rich, sweet, and it covered his head and it dripped down his face and off his beard, onto his collar. You knew when the high priest was around, but why did they do it? I'll tell you why, so that he might smell sweet to God. God does not like bad smells. Time and again, God's sense of smell is mentioned in the Bible. Have you ever noticed that? Sin stinks to God, "It stinks in his nostrils," says the Word of God. God enjoys a good smell as well as you. If that sinful man Aaron were to come into the presence of God then he must come smelling sweet. So they anointed him with this lovely oil. David, as he looked at the crowd, saw this sea of shining faces with the drips going down from the head to the beard – why? Not just because they were hot but because they were happy to be together worshipping God. He saw in a flash: their harmony fits them to go into God's presence because God loves the smell of harmony.

Do you get the message? It was fitting them all to be priests. It was fitting them all to go to the house of the Lord. It was fitting them all to be a sweet smelling savour uno God. We are called in the New Testament to be a sweet smelling savour to God and we make a mistake if we think that is addressed to individual Christians – it is not; it is addressed to the fellowship, and it is said that the fellowship must be a sweet smelling savour. The "you" is plural, and what will make us smell sweet to God? The oil of harmony. That is what prepares us to be a kingdom of priests unto God.

Doesn't the picture come to life now? Then, as David began to sing, and sang on about the oil on Aaron's head and beard, he looked down again and his memory went back to the days when he had been a shepherd boy and he had to lie out watching the sheep all night. In the morning he often woke up with his clothes soaked with one of the great wonders of nature – early morning dew.

We don't value dew in this country because we don't use it much. We have plenty of water and plenty of rain. If we lived in Israel, we would value dew. For many it was the difference between life and death. Have you seen a dew pond? That is a great hollow in the middle of a field that has been hollowed out in porous soil and then lined with clay.

The dew comes down and filters down and fills up the dew pond. So there are places in this country where fresh springs are not available and the farmers use dewponds, but in Israel it is a matter of life and death. From about the fifteenth of April to the fifteenth of October there is no rain. The only source of moisture on those porous limestone hills is the heavy dew. They would not have been able to grow grapes in Israel but for the dew that swells the grapes and keeps the vines alive during those hot summer months.

Now there is a bit of a meteorological mystery here and I don't want to get too involved with this. He says the dew comes from Hermon to Zion, and strictly speaking that is not true. Studying the meteorology of the Middle East: in fact, the dew is brought from the Mediterranean from the west. As the day warms up, the air over the Mediterranean picks up moisture from the sea, and because there is normally in summer an anticyclone over Cyprus fairly steadily, the wind south of Cyprus sweeps into Israel in a kind of westerly direction and it brings its moisture with it. So it heats up the land fairly quickly during the day. At night, when it cools off, then the moisture that has been brought is precipitated very heavily. Did you know that in the northern area of the Negev there are 250 nights of dew per year? If that can be harnessed you can grow things there. So the dew descends on the hills around the city of Zion at night during the summer. Now it falls heaviest on Mount Hermon because the Mount Hermon air cools, because on the top of Mount Hermon even in summer there is snow. The air cooled by the snow drifts down the mountainside and meets the warm air that has come over the hills from the Mediterranean and the precipitation on Mount Hermon is very heavy indeed. So in the olden days they believed that the snow was being transferred down to the dew. In fact, it wasn't. It was the cold air from the snow meeting the warm moist air from the

Mediterranean that brought the heavy dew.

Now sometimes in the summer, the cold air at night veers around to the north and comes from Mount Hermon, south towards Zion, and when that happens they get a very heavy dew. It is understandable that they assumed it was the snow being brought from heaven. It was the cold air from Hermon meeting the moist air from the Mediterranean above Zion and precipitating heavy dew. But whether David got his meteorology exactly right or not does not matter. He knew that when the wind blew from Hermon, they got a lovely dew on the hills of Zion. He knew that this dew was life or death. He knew that green grass for his sheep was dependent on that dew through the summer.

As he looked at the dewy, shining face of the crowd going up to the temple, he said, "It's like the dew". Dew makes a barren, hard, dry ground green, soft, fruitful and fertile. As he looked at the harmony among the people of God he observed: first that makes them a sweet smell to God and enables them to go into God; second, it is like dew that will make them fruitful and fertile instead of hard and cold and rocky. Harmony does both things. Oil and water don't mix except in scripture. Oil fits them to go into God, and water fits them to go out and bear fruit, and David is so thrilled he has to sing.

We come then to the last part of v. 3. It is a logical conclusion from the dew. Why is it so good and so pleasant to see harmony? The answer is because then something can happen. More than that, then something will happen that cannot happen until there is that oil, and until there is that dew. David now says: "For there God has commanded the blessing." Where? In Zion? The scholars say that is what it means but I am not sure they have discovered the full meaning. For there – where? In Zion? Is God's blessing limited to one place, one location? To one hill called Zion?

No. David is not looking at the hill of Zion, he is not looking at the temple, he is looking at the people going up to the temple and he says: "there God has commanded the blessing." In other words, where there is harmony among brothers there God has ordered blessing. It is not just they may be blessed. They certainly will because it is one of his laws. As certain as the law of gravity caused the oil on Aaron's head and beard to flow down, and as certain as the law of nature and meteorology causes the dew to fall upon the hills, so certainly the law of God has commanded that where brethren dwell together in unity, the blessing will fall down. It is as sure as that.

I am certain that when all the believers in one town stand together in unity, God will pour the blessing down. Moses had to fight for that unity and David had to fight for that unity. Neither managed to bring all the people of God into that unity, but they got the unity and the blessing came. What will the blessing be? David said it will be the blessing of life that goes on forever – everlasting life.

Now people say: "Well, surely in Jesus we have everlasting life." Yes, we have, and we don't have to wait for it. We can have it now, but I do believe that many brethren are not enjoying everlasting life now because it is a life that is not only a life of quantity and existence that goes on forever. It is a life of quality, otherwise the thought of everlasting life would put me off, wouldn't it you?

If it is mere existence, going on forever, I can understand the astronomer Fred Hoyle who said, "I don't want to live forever." He said, "I would like to live for about three hundred years. I believe that in that time I could do all the things I wanted to do. But I would not like to live forever." I will tell you why he wouldn't. Do you notice the word in three hundred years I could do all the *things* I want to do. Those who live for things would not like to live forever.

But those who live for people, those who see that life is essentially relationships of love, want to live forever.

A couple who have fallen in love want that to last forever and ever. It is why they exchange a ring, a symbol of an everlasting love. They sing their songs about it; they want to love each other forever. Of course you do, when you love someone you don't want that to break up. If you are really in loving relationships you could go on forever, couldn't you? Time passes like that. There is no problem with time when you are in love and in harmony. It is when you are in discord that time drags and goes slowly and you wish it would get over with. But when you are in concord, time is nothing.

So he will bless you with a life that goes on forever. It is a life that will not only last forever but it is a life that is sent from above because no human being has the power to give you a life that will last forever. It must come down like the oil came down, like the dew came down. It is a gift from above where every good and perfect gift comes from. So David finishes the Psalm with this matchless blessing. In doing so, he has understood God's heart and God's heart is like this: when he sees discord and division among his children he wants to stop it. It was because of this that he introduced death to our world. But when God sees his children in harmony, he wants to keep that family forever.

Now that is why he introduced death and that is why he offered everlasting life, because he wants a family of brothers and sisters who will live together in harmony, and when they do so, then he can give them everlasting life. Then he wants to, he has ordered that that kind of family can have the kind of life that he says will last forever.

So I come to the conclusion and I want to apply it. The saddest thing I have to tell you is that the concord that fell upon Israel at that time, like other concords, passed rather quickly and disappeared. Within a year or two of writing this

Psalm David's own two sons Absalom and Amon, were at each other's throats and Absalom killed Amon. The Cain and Abel incident happened all over again. Towards the latter part of David's reign there was unrest, there were rebellions; there was civil war. When Solomon came to the throne he made the great mistake of thinking that the place is more important than the people. He erected the most magnificent temple for the house of God instead of the tent which God had been content with until then.

Though he built a beautiful building, the people in it were not in harmony. As soon as Solomon died there was civil war and the ten tribes in the north split from the two tribes in the south. They have never been together again in two and a half thousand years. So the tragic truth is that since David wrote this Psalm it has not been possible for it to be sung with truthfulness by his people. No wonder that since his day they longed for another king like David. They longed for a Messiah, they longed for a Christ.

They still long for the Son of David to come and restore the harmony, peace and prosperity, and the invincibility that came through that harmony which they had for that brief little spell while David was their king. It is a sad story and I want to tell you something that is even more tragic and more sad. The Son of David came, but it says of him: He came to his own place and his own people received him not, but as many as did receive him to them he gave the power to become the sons, the family of God. So the Son of David is creating a new family today. The Son of David is saying, "Oh how good and pleasant it is to see brothers dwelling, staying together, as real friends. So that relatives and friends are the same group."

The Son of David came and he started all over again with twelve men – such a varied bunch. He called them "brethren" and that word is unique in the New Testament to the followers of Jesus. It is not used in any other connection. "My brethren"; "... the least of these my brethren." He is not ashamed to call us brethren. He did not keep all twelve in a unity of brotherhood. On that last night of his life he knew that one of them was not with him and so he told him to go quickly.

With the eleven he prayed. What was the burden of his prayer to the Father? It was that when he had gone they would stay together – that they may be one. Not a visible unity of organisation but a unity of heart and mind and will, such as he had with the Father and the Father had with him.

On the day of Pentecost his prayer was answered because they were in one place – but that was not enough. They were with one accord in one place and there God had ordered the blessing and so it came. It came as fire and wind but the blessing came on people who were in one place with one accord with no barriers between them, no suspicions, no bitterness, no resentment, no criticism, no grumbling, just 120 people.

God can do more with 120 who are really united in one accord in one place than he can do with thousands who are not. So, there, God commanded the blessing. It happened to be the same city where David wrote this Psalm but I think that is beside the point. They were with one accord in one place and there God gave them the enjoyment of everlasting life. It simply deepened their unity so that they had all things in common and they continued steadfastly, loyally, regularly in the apostles' doctrine, and in the fellowship and in the breaking of bread and the prayers. If any had need, the others met the need. There was just one family. But isn't it interesting that in the New Testament the Holy Spirit is also likened to oil and water? Isn't that significant? Not just fire and wind, but oil and water.

So at Pentecost the Holy Spirit came. But even though

the first signs were fire and wind, Peter got up and said, "Don't you know that God has poured this out. It's falling, it's pouring out like a liquid on us." Isn't that an interesting phrase? Poured out upon all flesh.

The oil and the water was running down from the head to the beard to the collar and the face was covered with the dew of the Holy Spirit. Not just dew but living springs, and frankly you can do without the dew if you have the living springs.

There was not just plain oil but oil specially mixed with ingredients. When you read the book of Exodus, you find the ingredients that went into the oil used for Aaron, and how much they would have put in of the cinnamon and of myrrh and so on.

Is there any hint in the New Testament of the ingredients that have to be added to the oil of the Holy Spirit to anoint his people to be priests to God? I found twenty-four ingredients that the New Testament tells us to add to the oil of the Holy Spirit to make it a sweet smelling savour. Here they are:

1. Love one another.
2. Kindly affection to one another.
3. In honour, prefer one another.
4. Have oneness of mind.
5. Edify each other.
6. Receive each other.
7. Admonish one another.
8. Salute one another.
9. Care for one another.
10. Serve one another.
11. Bear one another's burdens.
12. Be forbearing to each other.
13. Be kind to each other.
14. Submit to each other.

15. Esteem others better than yourselves.
16. Forgive one another.
17. Abound in love to each other.
18. Comfort one another.
19. Consider one another.
20. Confess your faults to one another.
21. Pray for each other.
22. Be hospitable to each other.
23. Refrain from judging each other.
24. Restore one another when fallen.

Twenty-four ingredients. The Holy Spirit is there, the "oil" base of the perfume. These are the ingredients we are to add so that we may be anointed like Aaron to go in to God and to be a sweet-smelling family to him. Such harmony is a foretaste of heaven. It demonstrates that holiness and happiness really do belong together. It shows the world a pleasure that will not dry up, a pleasure that is not just for a season, but a pleasure which lasts forever because it is good. We are called therefore to maintain the spirit of unity in the bond of peace.

"Whoever is on the Lord's side," said Moses....

"Let him come to me."

Let us make a new beginning. Let us dwell together in unity. Then I believe people will say: "Behold; look at that." It is something that is good and pleasant at the same time – we have never seen that before, and relatives are friends. Look at that: behold how good it is to see, and how pleasant it is to hear, brothers who stay together in unity.

READ PSALMS 149–150

Bible religion has always been musical religion. Wherever the grace of the Lord has gone, singing has immediately followed. That is because music is so expressive of thoughts and emotions. So right in the middle of the Bible (and if ever you want to find the book of Psalms quickly, just halve your Bible and open it) you are right in the middle of the collection of songs. At the heart of God's revelation is this lovely collection of praise.

It begins with a solemn warning that there are two ways in life. There is a way that leads to life and a way that leads to death, and a choice must be made. Before you can sing any of the other songs in the book of Psalms, you have to decide whether you are going to walk in the way of the godly or the way of the wicked, and that is a choice that you must make. It is no use attending a service and joining in the singing and enjoying the song and the dance and the music without having made that choice. So there is a blessing pronounced at the beginning of the Psalms on those who have made the choice not to sit with the scornful, with the ungodly, with the wicked, but to be with God's people, to be planted by a river, and produce fruit.

Then from that choice onwards, throughout the book of Psalms, you have the whole gamut of the experience of a man or woman of God. You have the depths of despair — thank God for the honesty of God's Word. If you have never been depressed as a Christian, then you are a very rare bird, but I would like to meet you because all of us who have walked with God, I think, have known moments where we have had to say, "Why are you cast down, O my soul? What has gone wrong? Something needs putting right." Then there are heights of joy here, unimaginable to the world trying to find pleasure; and everything in between. But as we get to the close of the book of Psalms, you reach five which are solid praise—the "hallelujah psalms". Every one of them has that word running right through. The word "hallelujah" is the only word that is used by Christians the world over in exactly the same form. Even the name of Jesus is different in different languages, but you can go anywhere in the world and, wherever you are, just shout "Hallelujah" and the Christians will turn around immediately. It is the quickest way to find out who they are.

Why should we have five psalms like this at the end of the book of Psalms? In a double sense, praise is the end. What is the chief end of man? To glorify God – that is what you are for; that is why God made you. That is what it is all heading for; that is what life is all about – that we should be to the praise of his glory. He created us for that purpose; he redeemed us for that purpose. But also it is the end in another sense. There will come a day when your soul will never be cast down again. There will come a day when you will not have to pray for deliverance from your enemies. There will come a day when prayer will give way just to praise. Therefore, the book of Psalms pictures the whole Christian life from the first choice to walk the way of the godly, to the final moment of sheer praise when there is nothing else but praise.

Psalm 149 gives us instructions in praise, and the first comment is this: God can get tired of old songs. I mention this because there is that within us which loves to sing the familiar, and we love to sing the old songs. The first instruction here is: "Sing to the Lord a new song." Let him have a fresh time of worship from us. If you only stay with the old songs, then frankly, your spiritual life will grow stale and stagnant and you will just repeat the songs. You become nothing more than a spiritual parrot, mouthing the things.

There are those who create new music, new avenues of worship. If it is new to you, if it is fresh to you, then bear in mind that it is biblical to keep fresh. If God's mercies can be new every morning, than so ought our worship to be. We are to sing in our meetings because God loves to hear his children singing together, and doing this as a unit, praising our Maker and our King.

We have moved into something that many of us have not been used to until comparatively recently: that is, to praise him with the whole body. Why should it be thought a moral thing to use our vocal chords, our tongues, our mouth, our lips, and not to use the rest of the body? I just cannot understand the thinking that says: this bit is moral, but this bit is not. After all, we use our hands in worship, if only to hold the hymnbook up; we use our feet in worship, if only to hold our bodies up – so why not use the whole lot for worship?

Indeed, one of the new discoveries that the Holy Spirit is giving more and more people is that we are to present our bodies as a living sacrifice, holy and acceptable to him, which is our spiritual worship. One of the reasons that we have wrong impressions of worship is this: we ask the wrong question. We ask, "Did I enjoy it or not?" That is the wrong question in worship. I hope you will enjoy worship, but even if you don't, that is not the important thing. The important question is: "Did God enjoy the worship?" It is immediately after this verse on dance and instrumental worship that we are told that "The Lord takes delight in his people." That is the test of true worship: whether God has enjoyed it, not whether we have; and we meet to give God a blessing.

Now to many people, the rest of the Psalm is a shock. Suddenly, the cloud seems to obscure the sun and the atmosphere changes. Suddenly, we are into an extraordinary situation. Hints of it begin to appear. The Lord delights in his people. He gives victory to the humble. Now what does that have to do with singing and dancing? We move on through the Psalm. "Sing for joy on our couches" – well, that is fine. I think if that had been written today, it would have been singing in the bath. It means when you are really relaxed, when you are by yourself and at home. I suggest that there is something wrong if we sing the praise of God in the assembly of the faithful, but never sing it when we are by ourselves. The two belong together. If you only sing hymns and songs when you are in church, then you should examine your soul very carefully. Do you sing when you are driving along? Do you sing when you are washing up?

Billy Graham's wife, Ruth, put a notice above her kitchen sink: "Divine service is held here three times every day." She understood what the psalmist is saying. But, suddenly, we are through this now, and we are into battle. Vengeance on the people; let those who have a song in their throats have a two-edged sword in their hands. Now this is extraordinary.

Suddenly we are out of the jamboree and we are into a battle; out of the concert and into a conflict. Now why does David include this in the Psalm? Surely it was going to be a Psalm of worship, praise, singing and dancing – publicly and privately. Why suddenly into the battle? The answer is this: that the song in the throat and the sword in the hand are necessary to each other.

There are some Christians who love to sing, but don't bother to fight. There are some Christians who fight, but never sing, and the two go together. Remember the battle in the Old Testament where they put the singers in the frontline? That is a good place to put them, right in the frontline, not just because they will get the first brunt of the attack but because they are the best weapon – the weapon of praise.

Let me enlarge on this. There are those who sing but do not fight; who just want a long, glorified celebration, but do not want the discipline and the duty, and don't want the conflict to which we are called, who want to stay far behind the line, singing the battle songs, but not singing them in the battle. It is a temptation, when we are gathered together to sing and praise the Lord, to forget that we will need a sword in our hands and we have got a battle facing us. Indeed, I believe that the devil pays peculiar attention to those who sing, to the musicians, and that they are subject to particular temptation precisely because of this, and they need a sword in their hands. They need the sword of God's Word. You see, we have to transpose this Psalm now into New Testament teaching. Our weapons are not carnal, and the two-edged sword in our hand is the Word of God.

The Welsh revival disappeared for this very reason. I was talking to a dear old saint in Swansea, who was in the revival, and Wales had a revival in the last century where England has not had such a revival. Yet if you go to Wales today, where has it gone? I said to this old man, "Where has it gone? Why did it fizzle out?" He said, "Well, it finished up in song and there was not enough teaching of God's Word underneath the singing to undergird it and give the foundation to it." Well, that was one man's insight, but he was a very great saint with deep discernment. You will still hear them singing in Wales the songs of Zion. You will hear them singing at the sports matches, but they forgot the two-edged sword in the hand. The song in their throat was not enough. So let us sing and fight.

Then there are those who fight who have been doggedly loyal to the Lord over many years and have struggled through. Praise God for their determination; praise God for their loyalty, but they are not the sort that like to sing. Do you know what I mean? They are fighters; they are tough, and yet, how one would love them to see them break out in praise as well, because that will refresh them in the fight. So the psalmist puts these two things together – let a song be in your throat and a sword in your hand. Let us fight, and worship the Lord in beauty.

A Dr Monsell left us many songs, but the two that are best known are "Worship the Lord in the Beauty of Holiness" and "Fight the Good Fight", which tells me that he understood this Psalm and that he was not just going to set people worshipping in song in the beauty of holiness, but he wanted them to fight the good fight. So, praise the Lord, the glory for his faithful people is the glory of having fought and won, and then they can sing. I have noticed that singers who have had real battles to fight, and who have gained the victory in Christ, have a dimension to their singing that others do not have. They have been through the battle.

Finally, a few words about Psalm 150, the last Psalm of all. The battle is left behind now, and here is a little picture of the fact that in heaven the battle will be over. Altogether, thirteen times in six verses, the word "praise" comes. Hebrew poetry is based on couplets, on double thoughts. I think God is saying through this that what we need is so often balance between two complementary truths. You have one couplet here: "Praise the Lord" and "Praise God". We need to keep in balance Lord and God. "Lord" is the intimate term for the personal relationship; "God" is the impersonal term for the great Creator. We need to keep the intimacy and the reverence together. "Praise the Lord; praise God."

We need to balance together the local and the universal. "Praise God in his sanctuary." There is a particular local place where you praise, but don't think you are bound to that place. "Praise God in his firmament." Wherever you go in his firmament, you can praise God, the balance of the local and the universal. There is a balance here between praising

God for what he does – his mighty deeds – and what he is; his excellent greatness. We need to keep that in balance too.

But now, the whole orchestra comes in, and what a lovely variety of instruments. I believe that God doesn't like just one instrument. I expect that the reason why the organ has become so popular is because it can simulate so many instruments, but I believe God likes a variety of sound. So he has given people the ability to create through wind and stringed and percussion instruments different sounds, and he loves them. As I looked at all these instruments, I thought: how like God to want this variety.

When I look at people, I find the same variety. I find some people who are just a loud trumpet. God has blessed them with a noisy personality. Let us praise God for people who have been given a trumpet personality and temperament; but let us praise God we are not all like that. I know that some feel like little piccolos, just a tiny little sound, but God wants your praise too. He wants the variety.

Let us get over this idea that God prefers quiet music. I don't know where we got it from, but somehow people have got the idea that if music is nice and quiet, that is more worshipful. There are times when quiet music is worshipful, but God is not confined to quiet music. "Praise the Lord with cymbals" – and not just cymbals but loud, clashing ones. God wants every style of music, the quiet and the noisy. He wants every kind of instrument. He wants every kind of temperament all harmonised together in an orchestra to his praise.

Some years ago, it was my privilege to go up one of those three great peaks above Interlaken, in the Swiss Alps: the Eiger, the Mönch, and the Jungfrau. I went up the easy way, not straight up the face of the Eiger, but inside the train which winds for some miles through a tunnel inside the mountain. Higher and higher it goes, and it comes out at 13,000 feet.

Then, from the station, you climb up over the glacier; you really feel you are on top of the world. One lady in the group we were with said, "Look at the earth down there." Through a crack in the clouds we saw the valleys below, a wonderful sight. But just coming straight out of a train up there, you are a bit short of breath and oxygen. You are staggering up this glacier; you come to the top. There there is a plaque with the text: "Let everything that hath breath praise the Lord." So you stagger up to it, breathing deeply to try to get enough oxygen, and a few of us sang to the Lord: "Let everything that has breath praise the Lord".

You know, most of us think that God gave us breath primarily to breathe in. That is the important part for our bodies, because as we breathe in, vital oxygen from the air is being transferred to the bloodstream and to every organ of the body to make life possible. But God made us so that we breathe out as well as in. The breathing out is not just to expel carbon dioxide; breathing out enables us to communicate.

We have a built-in wind instrument here, and if we didn't breathe out we couldn't communicate; we couldn't talk, we couldn't sing. So breath was given that air might enter our bodies and help them and might leave our bodies and help our souls. We were given breath to praise. So let everything that has breath, let everything that breathes, use the breath not just for our own good, to keep our bodies going, but breathe the glory of God and breathe his praise. So praise the Lord. If you want to use your hands and feet, be free to do so. If you don't want to, then be free not to. That is real freedom, when you are free not to as well as to do so.

Printed in October 2021
by Rotomail Italia S.p.A., Vignate (MI) - Italy